T0295549

# Pension Funds and Sustainable Investment

# Pension Funds and Sustainable Investment

## Challenges and Opportunities

Edited by

P. Brett Hammond
Raimond Maurer
and
Olivia S. Mitchell

OXFORD
UNIVERSITY PRESS

OXFORD
UNIVERSITY PRESS

Great Clarendon Street, Oxford, OX2 6DP,
United Kingdom

Oxford University Press is a department of the University of Oxford.
It furthers the University's objective of excellence in research, scholarship,
and education by publishing worldwide. Oxford is a registered trade mark of
Oxford University Press in the UK and in certain other countries

Published in the United States of America by Oxford University Press
198 Madison Avenue, New York, NY 10016, United States of America

British Library Cataloguing in Publication Data
Data available

Library of Congress Control Number: 2022948850

ISBN 978–0–19–288919–5

DOI: 10.1093/oso/9780192889195.001.0001

Printed and bound in the UK by
Clays Ltd, Elcograf S.p.A.

Cover image: Tennessee Valley Authority

Links to third party websites are provided by Oxford in good faith and
for information only. Oxford disclaims any responsibility for the materials
contained in any third party website referenced in this work.

# Preface

There is a diversity of opinion about what should be done about climate change, who should pay to mitigate its worst effects, and what role institutional investors should play in the process. This volume offers viewpoints from a variety of countries, stakeholders, and regulators, on how and when environmental, social, and governance (ESG) criteria should, and should not, drive pension fund investments. Part of the controversy is due to the fact that measures and models of ESG risk are often founded on poor and inconsistent data. Additionally there are many kinds of risks facing us, including transition risk, or the degree to which a company is prepared for regulatory and market changes; physical risk, or the exposure of factories and other assets to floods and other climate change effects; disclosure risk, or how companies disclose risks to water and other resources that are necessary to their function but are not reflected on their balance sheet; liability risks due to potential lawsuits; and how firms disclose the risks of labor strife and customer or supply chain disruption.

In what follows, we offer research on these and related matters to better inform institutional investors, money managers, governments, international organizations, and pension plan participants to clarify what can and should be done. As such, the volume will be informative to researchers, plan sponsors, students, and policymakers seeking to enhance retirement plan offerings.

In preparing this book, many people and institutions played key roles. Brett Hammond and Raimond Maurer were very helpful in identifying many of the authors who provided us with invaluable insights in the chapters that follow. We remain deeply grateful to our Advisory Board and Members of the Pension Research Council for their intellectual and research support. Additional support was provided by the Pension Research Council, the Boettner Center for Pensions and Retirement Research, and the Ralph H. Blanchard Memorial Endowment at the Wharton School of the University of Pennsylvania. We also are pleased to continue our association with Oxford University Press, which publishes our series on global retirement security. The manuscript was expertly prepared by Natalie Gerich Brabson and Sarah Kate Sanders.

Our work at the Pension Research Council and the Boettner Center for Pensions and Retirement Security of the Wharton School of the University of Pennsylvania has focused on aspects of pensions and retirement well-being for almost 70 years. This volume contributes to our ongoing goal to generate useful research on, and engage debate around, policy for retirement security.

Olivia S. Mitchell
Executive Director, Pension Research Council
Director, Boettner Center for Pensions and Retirement Research
The Wharton School, University of Pennsylvania

# Contents

# List of Figures

# List of Tables

# Notes on Contributors

**Rob M.M.J. Bauer** is Professor of Finance and holder of the Elverding Chair on Sustainable Business, Culture, and Corporate Regulation at the Maastricht University School of Business and Economics in The Netherlands. He is also Co-Founder and Director of the European Centre for Corporate Engagement at Maastricht University and Executive Director of the International Centre for Pension Management in Toronto. He cofounded GRESB, a real estate sustainability benchmarking company, and co-chairs the Global Research Alliance on Sustainable Finance and Investment. Bauer holds a Ph.D. from Maastricht University School of Business and Economics.

**Nathan Fabian** is the Chair of the European Platform on Sustainable Finance, a public and private sector expert panel set up to develop sustainable finance policies and tools in Europe, including the EU Taxonomy. Fabian is also Chief Responsible Investment Officer at the United Nations-supported Principles for Responsible Investment (PRI). Previously he served as CEO of the Investor Group on Climate Change Australia/New Zealand; head of ESG Research at Regnan, a provider of ESG research and engagement services; and Corporate Governance Policy Advisor in the Australian Parliament. He is also a founding Partner of Full Corp Partners, a financial services and IT start-up company advisory firm. Fabian earned his M.A. in International Relations from the University of New South Wales and his BBus from the University of Newcastle (Australia). He is also a Vincent Fairfax Fellow in ethics and leadership.

**Christopher C. Geczy** is Academic Director of the Jacobs Levy Equity Management Center for Quantitative Financial Research at the Wharton School, where he is also Academic Director of the Wharton Wealth Management Initiative at Wharton Executive Education. He earned the Best Elective Course Teaching Award in the Wharton Executive MBA Program and the Wharton Teaching Excellence Award, and he created Wharton's first survey course in sustainable/ESG investing. He received his B.A. in economics from the University of Pennsylvania and his Ph.D. in finance and econometrics from the Graduate School of Business at the University of Chicago.

**John B. Guerard Jr.** is a member of the McKinley Capital Management Scientific Advisory Board, and he teaches as a Zoom Affiliate Faculty member in the Computational Financial and Risk Management Program at the University of Washington, in Seattle. Previously he served as Director of

Quantitative Research at McKinley Capital Management, and he taught at the McIntire School of Commerce, the University of Virginia, Lehigh University, New York University, Rutgers, and the University of Pennsylvania. While serving as Director of Quantitative Research at Vantage Global Advisors (formerly MPT Associates), he was awarded the first Moskowitz Prize for research in socially responsible investing. He earned his A.B. in Economics from Duke University and Ph.D. in Finance from the University of Texas, Austin.

**Anita Margrethe Halvorssen** is the Director of Global Legal Solutions, LLC. Previously, she served as Adjunct Professor at University of Denver and Legal Counsel at the Norwegian Ministry of Climate and Environment; she has also consulted for the World Health Organization. She has researched and published on the Norwegian Government Pension Fund Global (formerly known as the Norwegian Oil Fund). Halvorssen is a member of the International Law Association committee on International Law and Sea Level Rise. She earned her Master's (LL.M.) and Doctor of The Science of Law (J.S.D.) from Columbia University, and her first law degree was from the University of Oslo, Norway.

**P. Brett Hammond** is a research leader at the American Funds of the Capital Group; he is also Executive Vice President of the Q Group and member of the Pension Research Council's Advisory Board. Previously he directed research teams at MSCI, and he served as chief investment strategist at TIAA-CREF while working on the creation of target-date funds, inflation-linked bonds, and individual financial advice. He also served on the senior management team at The National Academies, responsible for behavioral and social sciences studies; he also taught at The Wharton School. His research focuses on investing, institutional and individual asset allocation, pensions, higher education, and public policy. He received his bachelor's degree in economics and political science from the University of California at Santa Cruz, and a Ph.D. from the Massachusetts Institute of Technology. He is currently Editor-in-Chief of the peer-reviewed *Journal of Retirement.*

**Mikael Homanen** is a Senior Specialist, Research at Principles for Responsible Investment (PRI), where he leads the development of internal academic research and ESG data integration projects. He is also an Honorary Research Fellow at the Business School (formerly Cass) in London. He was previously a Bradley Fellow at the University of Chicago Booth School of Business, a visiting scholar at the Wharton School, University of Pennsylvania, and visited Singapore Management University. He has also consulted with the World Bank's Development Economics Research Group, Finance and Private Sector Research team. He received his BSc and MSc from Tilburg University and his Ph.D. from City, University of London.

**Stéphanie Lachance** is Managing Director, Responsible Investment at the Public Sector Pension Investment Board (PSP Investments) where she leads the Responsible Investment group, which plays a key role in the organization's investment strategy to ensure that environmental, social, and governance factors are incorporated in investment decisions and across all asset classes. Her interests include corporate governance, responsible investment, securities law, and regulations; prior to joining PSP Investments, she advised public issuers, stock exchanges, and securities regulators. She serves on the boards of the Food Banks of Quebec and the Canadian Coalition for Good Governance, and she is a member of the Investment Fund Review Committee of the Corporation de services du Barreau du Québec. She holds a Law Degree (LL.B.) from the Université de Montréal and is a member of the Quebec Bar; she also holds the Institute of Corporate Directors Director designation.

**Linda-Eling Lee** is Global Head of Research for MSCI's ESG Research Group, where she oversees all ESG- and climate-related content and methodology. She has been named a Top 100 Women in Finance by Barron's, and she was twice voted #1 Individual Making the Most Positive Overall Contribution to Sustainable Investment/Corporate Governance by Extel/IRRI. She received her A.B. from Harvard, M.St. from Oxford, and Ph.D. in Organizational Behavior from Harvard University.

**Raimond Maurer** is Professor of Investment, Portfolio Management, and Pension Finance at the Finance Department of the Goethe University Frankfurt. His research focuses on asset management, lifetime portfolio choice, real estate, and pension finance. Previously he was in residence at the Wharton School as Visiting Professor, and he serves as Advisory Board member of the Pension Research Council. His other professional activities include serving on the Union Real Estate Investment Group, the Society of Actuaries, and the Association of Certified International Investment Analysts. He recently completed a Deanship at the Faculty of Economics and Business of the Goethe University, where he currently serves on the Faculty Senate. His habilitation and dissertation were awarded by Mannheim University, and he also was awarded an honorary doctorate from the State University of Finance and Economics of St. Petersburg.

**Olivia S. Mitchell** is the International Foundation of Employee Benefit Plans Professor, and Professor of Insurance/Risk Management and Business Economics/Policy; Executive Director of the Pension Research Council; and Director of the Boettner Center on Pensions and Retirement Research; all at The Wharton School of the University of Pennsylvania. Concurrently Dr. Mitchell serves as a Research Associate at the NBER; Independent Director on the Wells Fargo Fund Boards; Co-Investigator for the Health and Retirement Study at the University of Michigan; and Executive Board Member for the Michigan Retirement Research Center. She also serves on the Academic Advisory Council for the Consumer Finance Institute at the Philadelphia Federal Reserve; the Advisory Committee of the HEC Montreal Retirement and Savings Institute; and the UNSW Centre for Pensions and Superannuation. She earned her B.A. in Economics from Harvard University, and her M.S. and Ph.D. degrees in Economics from the University of Wisconsin-Madison.

**Luba Nikulina** is Global Head of Research at Willis Towers Watson, where her team includes more than 100 investment professionals responsible for economic and capital markets research, evaluating asset management firms, coming up with investment recommendations, and creating new investment solutions. Previously, she led the private markets team and then the manager research team at WTW. Nikulina is a non-executive director of the Investor Forum, a not-for-profit organization seeking to position stewardship at the heart of investment decision-making. She holds an MBA degree from London Business School, a M.S. in Finance from the Finance Academy in Russia, and a B.A. in Linguistics from the Linguistic University in Belarus. She has also completed the Financial Times Non-Executive Director Programme and attended the Advanced Management Program at Harvard Business School.

**Amy O'Brien** is Global Head of Responsible Investing (RI) at Nuveen, where she leads a team responsible for creating a holistic RI vision and unified framework across Nuveen and TIAA, regarding the firm's overall RI philosophy as well as guidelines for incorporating RI disciplines in investment decisions and new product development. Her interests include environmental, social, and governance matters, as well as impact investing initiatives. She has served on the Boards of the Social Investment Forum, the Investor Responsibility Research Center Institute for Corporate Responsibility, and the Steering Committee of the Global Initiative for Sustainability Ratings. She has been identified by Barron's as one of the most influential people in ESG investing. She earned her B.S. in Biology from Boston College and her M.S. in Environmental Management and Policy from Rensselaer Polytechnic Institute.

**Nikolaj Pedersen** is a Senior Researcher in the Sustainable Markets department at Principles for Responsible Investment (PRI). His research focuses on retirement systems and responsible investment activities. He previously held roles in the Signatory Relations team, servicing institutional investors mainly in Europe, North America, and the Middle East. He earned his master's degree in International Studies from Aarhus University and he holds IMC and CAIA qualifications.

**Zacharias Sautner** is Professor of Finance at the Frankfurt School of Finance & Management where he teaches corporate finance, valuation, and corporate governance. He previously taught at the University of Amsterdam and was a research fellow at the Saïd Business School of the University of Oxford. His research is in the area of empirical corporate finance and focuses on ESG, climate finance, and corporate governance. He earned his Ph.D. in Finance from the University of Mannheim, and he also studied at the University of York and the University of Cooperative Education Stuttgart.

**Morgan Slebos** is the Director of Sustainable Markets at the United Nations-supported Principles for Responsible Investment (PRI), where he leads the sustainable financial system program, aimed at addressing barriers in market structure, investment practice, and policy and regulation that prevent financial markets from functioning sustainably. He has extensive experience in economics, policy and sustainable finance, including previous roles at the Institute and Faculty of Actuaries, the Association of British Insurers and the New Zealand Treasury. He earned his M.A. in Political Studies and BCom in International Trade from the University of Auckland.

**Paul M.A. Smeets** is Professor of Philanthropy and Sustainable Finance at Maastricht University, where he investigates what motivates individuals to behave pro-socially through donations and sustainable investments. His research and teaching also inquires how to maximize the positive impact of philanthropy and sustainable finance for enhancing well-being in society. He has also advised the European Commission, the Dutch ministry of finance, the ministry of social affairs and the ministry of defense. He received his Ph.D. in Finance, his M.S. in International Studies, and a BSc in International Economic studies, all from Maastricht University.

**Laura T. Starks** is the Charles E. and Sarah M. Seay Regents Chair in Finance at the McCombs School of Business, University of Texas at Austin. Her research focuses on ESG issues, including climate finance and board diversity, as well as molecular genetics and financial decisions. She is also a Research Associate of the NBER, Senior Fellow of ABFER, and Research Member of the ECGI; she also serves on the board of directors of the TIAA-CREF Mutual Funds and CREF Retirement Annuities; and she is President-Elect of the American Finance Association. Previously, she served as President of the Financial Management Association, the Society of Financial Studies, and the Western Finance Association; and she served on the Investment Advisory Committee for the Employees Retirement System of Texas, the Board of Governors of the Investment Company Institute, and the Governing Council of the Independent Directors Council as well as on Councils for the Norwegian Government Pension Fund. She earned her

Ph.D. and B.A. at the University of Texas at Austin, and her MBA from the University of Texas at San Antonio.

**Judith C. Stroehle** is a Senior Researcher at the Saïd Business School of Oxford, where her research focuses on the role of finance, measurement, and reporting for the implementation of purposeful business. She leads the Oxford Rethinking Performance Initiative and co-established the Oxford Impact Roundtable for sustainability reporting and accounting. Previously, she worked as an international business developer in the German online start-up scene and as a data strategy analyst and consultant for international channel marketing. She frequently works with non-profits, companies, and asset managers on their non-financial strategies, reporting, and measurement practices. She earned her Ph.D. Europaeus in Economics and Sociology at the University of Milan in collaboration with the International Labour Office, and her B.A. and M.A. from the University of Bamberg.

# Chapter 1

# Sustainable Investment in Retirement Funds

## Introduction

*Olivia S. Mitchell, P. Brett Hammond, and Raimond Maurer*

Since its green shoots first emerged around 50 years ago, acceptance of environmental, social, and governance (ESG) considerations in institutional investing—especially in pension funds—has evolved with distinct shifts in investor preferences. This Pension Research Council volume traces these shifts and their implications, leading up to the present day. Our volume notes that investors have diverse reasons for devoting attention to ESG criteria when deciding where to invest their money. Some have had religious motives, such as Quakers who focus on values; this approach can offer some risk mitigation. Yet models that look at whether divestment actually changes behaviors of companies show that that rarely occurs. So, it is not always screening and divestment that bring about the changes that investors seek. Accordingly, this book offers a selection of distinct viewpoints from a variety of countries, on whether, how, and when ESG criteria should, and should not, drive pension fund investments.

## The Long View

Economists tend to agree that ESG concerns may logically arise where there are market failures, often of the externalities type. Such externalities generally arise because a firm will impose costs or benefits on third parties on individuals or society, other than the consumer or producer, and these occur when the externalities are not properly priced. For instance, an oil refinery producing pollution that poisons the local population or the surrounding countryside creates a gap between the price that consumers pay for the refined oil, and the gain or loss to those injured by the pollution.

Economics offers two general types of solutions for such problems: either the government can alter the costs and benefits of such production, or the government can change the fiduciary rules under which the producer operates. In the case of pension investments, while a pension fund might wish

Olivia S. Mitchell, P. Brett Hammond, and Raimond Maurer, *Sustainable Investment in Retirement Funds*. In: *Pension Funds and Sustainable Investment*. Edited by P. Brett Hammond, Raimond Maurer, and Olivia S. Mitchell, Oxford University Press.

to invest in fossil fuel firms, it might not wish to impose the social losses on society. It is this tension that often drives debate over the pros and cons of ESG investment.

In Chapter 2, P. Brett Hammond and Amy O'Brien (2023) point out that ESG principles have been shaped by numerous social movements, governments, and regulators, independent advocacy and service organizations, and asset owners and asset managers, notably pension funds. Their work outlines the origins of ESG to the pre-modern era, from the post-Industrial Revolution late nineteenth century to about 1970. That period was characterized by concentrated ownership of public companies in the US and elsewhere, the transformation of work and consumption, and little to no activism by small shareholders or pension funds on social or environmental issues.

Governance concerns, however, were prominent in the pre-modern era. They included policies to limit monopolies and ownership of companies by banks and families, antitrust regulation, the emergence of uniform accounting, reporting, and disclosure rules, and the advent of a two-tiered board structure where supervisory boards retain control and management boards execute company strategies. Other features of the pre-modern era included regulation of working conditions and hours, food quality, and the beginnings of an environmental movement.

The modern era for ESG began around 1970, yet governance policies and practices varied across countries, as did social and environmental concerns, note the authors. For instance, in the US, company management was dominant, whereas family and/or bank control persisted in some European countries, and cross-holdings and bank influence were common in Japan. On social issues, the US and the UK saw debates over employment practices and the declining influence of unions. The US was ahead of others in tackling environmental challenges, with the birth of the US Environmental Protection Agency coinciding with the dawn of ESG's modern era.

Early on, the debate was over whether institutional investors should have separate portfolios for E, S, and G, versus a single common portfolio for all three; over time, there has been a growing recognition that true integration will likely work better. Hammond and O'Brien point to clear evidence of 'convergence,' which refers to a shift in thinking about environmental, social, and governance concerns such that they are now treated jointly. 'Integration' refers to the notion that investors need not consider E, S, and G factors separately from other decisions they make regarding their portfolios. For instance, some firms may currently underperform on ESG measures yet are likely to get better in the future. In addition, investors with well-integrated portfolios will need to balance and consider multiple dimensions of assets at once. Moreover, it is possible that higher ESG returns have arisen in certain sectors due to government support for ESG investments, as in the case of government subsidies for solar and wind power. Accordingly, the regulatory environment must be kept very much in mind when predicting the future of ESG performance.

## Roles of the United Nations and Universal Owners

Notable among the substantial shifts in the ESG evolutionary process were the first wave of government mandates and governance attributes, bringing an early focus on environmental and social issues, and catalyzing actions by the United Nations. In 2006, the UN helped frame the Principles of Responsible Investing, integrating a global network of investors (UNPRI). In 2016, it articulated its Sustainable Development Goals, which continue to inform much of ESG investment approaches. These were in addition to the UN's climate change conferences, goading signatory countries to implement laws to combat greenhouse gas emissions. As Hammond and O'Brien note, the UN has been extremely influential in the development of ESG principles. For instance, UNPRI adopted the theme of building a bridge between financial risk and real-world outcomes for 2021–2024.

These moves advanced awareness of ESG among corporations and regulators, but important shifts in ESG investing occurred only after institutions with substantial asset pools, such as pension funds, and other universal owners exerted their influence. A 'universal owner' is defined as a pension fund or a large institutional investor, such as BlackRock, which invests long-term in widely diversified holdings throughout the global economy. Universal owners must deal with, or are incentivized to deal with, externalities such as the environmental and social effects of the companies in which they invest. Moreover, governance systems can help those companies address their externalities. As of 2020, US pension funds managed US$6.2 trillion of total assets incorporating ESG principles.

In addition to the rise of the concept of universal ownership over the last few decades, drivers of ESG investing include economic transformation going back to the Industrial Revolution, the increased focus on stakeholder interests, and improved data and analytics that help capture the outcomes.

## How ESG Developed Globally

ESG investing has developed differently across countries and much depends on national asset ownership patterns and legal frameworks. Pension funds' and other institutions' interests and approaches have evolved over time. A brief summary of developments is as follows:

> **1970s:** The concept of 'ESG as a principle' took hold as investors aligned around key social concerns such as apartheid in South Africa and the Vietnam

War. As well, pioneering institutions emerged in this decade, such as the Interfaith Center on Corporate Responsibility (ICCR), which broke new ground with shareholder advocacy among faith-based institutions to press companies on ESG issues.

**1980s:** This decade saw the articulation of 'ESG as a product,' with the formation of dedicated industry networks such as The Forum for Sustainable and Responsible Investment (US SIF) and increased emphasis on corporate governance and the environment.

**1990s:** The idea of 'responsible investing as a product' took shape in this decade, with the development of social indices to track ESG and Socially Responsible Investing (SRI) funds.

**2000s:** In this decade, 'ESG as a process' took hold, with investor convergence on climate issues and the formation of global investor networks such as the UNPRI and the Global Impact Investing Network (GIIN).

**2010s:** The concept of 'ESG as an outcome' gained ground as responsible investing approaches expanded across asset classes, and ESG data and reporting practices saw refinements. The adoption in 2016 of the UN's 17 Sustainable Development Goals was another key catalyst. In December of 2019, the European Commission adopted a series of policy measures (called the 'green deal') in an effort to stipulate a green (climate neutral) transition of the European economy by 2050. These measures included various regulatory interventions imposed on the financial sector, aiming to reallocate capital from 'dirty' to 'green' activities. The core of the regulatory interventions is transparency, so investors can more readily identify green financial instruments. Following Steuer and Tröger (2021), they can be categorized into (1) *disclosure requirements* for raw data on climate impact (e.g. carbon emissions) by issuers of debt and equity instruments, and (2) unified *green quality labels* (taxonomies) of large-asset portfolios managed by institutional investors (such as mutual funds, insurance companies, pension funds) on behalf of third parties.

**2020s:** This decade saw the evolution of 'ESG as a system,' with many institutional investors going 'all ESG.' This grew out of an increased sense of urgency worldwide on climate issues. Companies that indulged in 'greenwashing' or faking environmental friendliness in their products also began receiving increased scrutiny.

In the process, countries where institutional owners such as pensions have played a dominant role include the US, the UK, Canada, and the Netherlands. A close second in terms of influence on ESG investing are those with relatively less institutional ownership, such as France, Germany, Japan, and Sweden. That influence has been less in countries where the public sector is the dominant asset owner, such as China and Hong Kong. Institutional ownership is also relatively lighter in Malaysia, Russia, and Saudi Arabia. A combination of private corporations and strategic individuals dominates asset ownership in other nations including Argentina, Brazil, Chile, India, Indonesia, Pakistan, and Turkey. Private ownership is particularly strong in Mexico.

## ESG to What End?

Amidst the trend toward convergence and integration, a fundamental debate has centered on the question of 'ESG to what end?' Some argue that it enhances investment performance; others that it adds alpha potential; and still others argue that it can mitigate portfolio risk. In fact, this ongoing debate is helping to clarify who gets to decide about ESG investing, particularly when it comes to ESG performance and the role of the regulatory regimes. In the case of pension funds, ESG has been viewed through the business case lens, even when it is more difficult to make a business case for it. As a result, some institutional investors have struggled to find the proper balance between social responsibility and the fiduciary duty to act to maximize return on behalf of their participants (Tapiria 2021).

Moreover, institutional investors such as pension funds face the central question of 'values versus value' in virtually every investment decision they make. That is because they have a fiduciary responsibility to protect the financial interests of their members, who depend on them to secure their retirement nest eggs. Therefore, all investment decisions must clear the test of financial prudence, including environmental and social factors, in guiding those decisions.

Recent pivotal moves by some of the world's largest pension funds to advance the case of ESG investing are discussed in Chapter 3 by Stéphanie Lachance and Judith Stroehle (2023). For instance, in March 2020, the California State Teachers' Retirement System (CalSTRS), the Japanese Government Pension Investment Fund (GPIF), and the largest UK pension fund—the Universities Superannuation Scheme (USS)—publicly pledged that they would integrate ESG factors into their investment decisions. Six months later, a similar pledge was made by the CEOs of the eight largest Canadian pension funds—the so-called 'Maple 8.' A related move came in December of 2020 from the New York State Common Retirement Fund, when it set 2040 as its goal to transition its portfolio to net zero greenhouse gas emissions.

A related point regarding how to measure the inputs and impacts of ESG is taken up in Chapter 4 by Linda-Eling Lee's (2023) research. Unfortunately, there remains a widespread lack of understanding about, and confidence in, how ESG concepts are measured, when such concepts are material, and how to work with ESG data in the investment process when the available data are very different from traditional financial data. In the pension context, Lee notes that data quality issues remain a challenge, along with problems that arise when comparing ratings and capturing different ESG objectives. Nevertheless, as more investors examine the track records and as the track records capture more funds, investors will become better able to analyze what is and is not performing well. Nevertheless, there remains concern about why the ESG data often disagree, and why ratings differ so much, one from the other. There has also been a sea-change in how the data are used, rotating away from a reliance on third-party ratings, toward firms reaching out for raw data and building their own models and assumptions. Moreover, Lee argues that ESG investments are likely to outperform in all sorts of market cycles and environments due to their long-term horizons. She also points out that, analytically, it is possible to conduct attribution analysis on ESG funds.

Making this a more complex task is recent work by Berg et al. (2019), who caution that the average correlation of scores from different ESG raters varies from 40 percent to 70 percent; this can create complications in constructing a portfolio. This ongoing research seeks to quantify the noise and clean it up by underweighting the 'noisier' ratings agencies and overweighting the agencies with less noise.

## Finding a Balance

Drawing on existing literature, several interviews, and an in-depth study of PSP Investment, Lachance and Stroehle demonstrate the role of historical, organizational, and contextual factors, and identify five pension fund characteristics that have an important impact on the funds' ability to integrate ESG. These include the historical origins of funds and the extent of embedded regulatory authority; their mandate and legal structure; the importance of corporate governance and leadership at the funds; their investment strategies and asset mix; and the funds' ability to engage in collaborative and advocacy activities.

In addition, pension funds must follow national regulation guiding the mandates and legal structures covering retirement plans. In particular, these mandates and legal structures form the basis for the corporate governance standards advocated by pension funds, as well as the freedom to decide whether and how to implement environmental, social, and governance considerations. Pension funds therefore determine their investment strategies and asset mixes that can include ESG principles through engagement and stewardship. Collaboration and advocacy are the tools they use, by taking public stands around environmental and social issues, and by working with other funds, as in collaborative engagements such as the Climate Action 100+. Launched in 2017, Climate Action 100+ is now backed by more than 545 investors with over US$52 trillion in assets under management, including 145 North American investors.

There are also factors enabling and inhibiting ESG investments in pensions, reflecting the practical and real-life challenges that pension funds face. For instance, the ESG climate in the UK and Canada has been judged as more favorable than in the US, particularly because the Employee Retirement Income Security Act (ERISA) requires pension fiduciaries to act in the participants' best interests. Nevertheless, and particularly in Europe, 'success' in the ESG arena has recently expanded to engaging with companies, rather than simply buying and selling companies with good ESG track records. As a result, there is currently far more ongoing activism in the EU, where investors are focused on changing outcomes beyond the financial ones.

Additional challenges to ESG investments include differences of opinion and lack of information in processes and methods not traditionally reported under Generally Accepted Accounting Principles (GAAP). Under traditional moral, ethical, or other screening bases, investors searching for utility would tend to sell investments that do not meet their criteria. But once they eliminate an asset, they must replace it with another. In Chapter 5, Chris Geczy and John Guerard (2023) note that this is complicated in the US by the need to satisfy fiduciary responsibilities despite a lack of clear and consistent guidance from the US Department of Labor and other regulatory authorities.

The authors examine various methodologies, attitudes, and understandings about what ESG is and when it could enhance pension investment performance. Their empirical analysis shows that firms with high environmental scores do provide excess returns over those with low scores unconditionally, but also conditional on expected return from additional models including a variety of factor controls. Accordingly, they conclude that pension trustees, consultants, and money managers should combine information from both expected return models and ESG criteria as these could enhance their equity portfolio construction efforts. Alternatively, if fiduciaries focus on risk and return considerations alone when selecting investments, the authors suggest that incorporating non-GAAP information via earnings, price momentum, and ESG characteristics, along with a collection of weighted value measures, may collectively and individually add value rather than impose a constraint on the investment universe. Nevertheless, they have no firm conclusions, as yet, regarding whether portfolios formed from only high scoring ESG firms maximize Sharpe ratios.

Further analysis of the impact of ESG for pension investments in Chapter 6 by Zacharias Sautner and Laura Starks (2023) notes that pension plans' long horizons render them particularly vulnerable to many long-lived ESG risks. The authors warn that the potential consequences of being underfunded, especially in the case of defined-benefit pensions, leave the funds particularly vulnerable to ESG-related downside risks. ESG-induced risks include reputational risk, when a firm has poor environmental practices; human capital-related risks, such as how firms treat their workers;

litigation risk, such as due to pollution or wildfires; regulatory risk, including government-required disclosures; corruption risk; and climate risk, including physical risk, technological risk, and the risk of stranded assets, among others. Their chapter underscores the need to develop processes to identify, measure, and manage those risks more carefully, if pension funds are to remain sustainable. Their analysis demonstrates that, in many cases, investors prefer to deploy risk management and engagement strategies, rather than divestment, to address the climate risk in their portfolios. A recent quantitative analysis of ESG divestitures by Berk and van Binsbergen (2022: 1) similarly concludes that 'socially conscious investors should invest and exercise their rights of control to change corporate policy.'

The need to engage with multiple stakeholders, along with the growing need to examine investment impacts and systems-level engagement, are altering how global pension funds behave, according to Luba Nikulina (2023) in Chapter 7. She proposes that the key is culture, looking beyond immediate returns and focusing on long-term impact universal ownership: by this, she means that when pension participants own a slice of the system, they must be responsible to the system. Of course, this will require a transformation in the way pension funds are managed, with strengthened governance and system-wide collaboration. Moreover, Nikulina noted that individual pension funds, particularly of the defined-benefit variety, face different opportunities and constraints, yet as institutional investors, they tend to have very long time horizons. They are expected to deliver returns over many decades, and perhaps over an infinite horizon. Accordingly, their required returns need to encourage engagement with systemic risks and challenges beyond specific considerations of their own current portfolios.

At the same time, Nikulina cautions that science still needs to determine the cost of not investing over a longer horizon, and how dynamics—including a changing legal framework—may be factored in. Ultimately, she concludes that pension funds will become more engaged in the ESG arena, but investment organizations will first need to strengthen their governance structures, do a better job measuring inputs and outputs, and institute system-wide collaboration and innovation.

## How ESG Is Changing Pension Governance, Engagement, and Reporting

In Chapter 8, a topic of keen interest to Rob Bauer and Paul M.A. Smeets (2023) is what drives the sustainable investment agenda and whether beneficiaries of pension plans should have a voice in their pension plan's investment choices. Noting the difference between the US approach to this—leaning toward hard law and sometimes-conflicting DOL regulations—and the European approach—more driven by social norms, they suggest that the answer depends on a fund's legal and societal contexts, benchmarking pressure, and fund-specific factors such as the fund's size and the board's composition. While beneficiaries generally are not part of the debate over sustainable investments, the chapter reviews the experiences of a large Dutch pension plan that did so, and summarizes the lessons learned.

In particular, the authors discuss how this occurred at Pensioenfonds Detailhandel (PD), the Dutch defined-benefit pension fund for retail sector employees. A majority of participants voted in favor of extending and intensifying the voting and engagement program and approved the sustainable development goals proposed by the board. Importantly, the majority support for sustainable investments was not undermined by the 2019 COVID-19 pandemic. Additionally, Bauer and Smeets argue that a better understanding of the beliefs and preferences of the clients of financial services can help bring back confidence in the financial sector and enhance customer loyalty.

While many agree that participants deserve a voice in their pension fund investments, no one yet knows whether a simple majority rule is the right approach. Moreover, given financial illiteracy, many participants may not understand the tradeoffs, and individual investor goals may be mutually exclusive. Of course, when two investments have the same financial return, but one has positive ESG externalities, the evaluation process can be easier; even so, however, people may disagree on how to compare nonfinancial attributes. A related point is that one might think of investing in two different types of technologies, each of which would improve environmental outcomes. For instance, one might wish to hold fossil fuels in her portfolio while the other would not, in the hopes of engaging the potentially polluting firms. Ultimately it might be unclear whether and when to walk away from the first technology.

A comparative study in Chapter 9 by Nathan Fabian, Mikael Homanen, Nikolaj Pedersen, and Morgan Slebos (2023) focuses on policy frameworks and important structural variables relative to private retirement systems in Australia, the UK, and the US. The authors believe that investment organizations, as either corporations or custodians of long-term value, do have international and national social obligations and commitments to social outcomes, under both human rights laws and employment regulations. For organizations within these systems, enumerated by OECD guidelines for multinational enterprises, the view is that there is a clear regime or framework indicating financial institutions' responsibilities.

By analyzing reports, interviewing experts, and using data from the Principles of Responsible Investment, as well as national pension and retirement authorities, the research identifies three key structural challenges to national retirement systems. These include market fragmentation, which tends to undermine the responsible investment support and activities among retirement plans; the increasing importance of fund managers and investment consultants, along with their limited sustainable investment incentives; and the growth and lack of a sustainability emphasis in personal pension systems. At present, they argue that retirement plans are less likely to consider responsible investment practices, while commercial service providers lack incentives to deviate from the 'norm.'

The authors also suggest that policymakers should consider fund consolidation in private sector retirement systems, along with whether service-provider incentives could be better aligned with sustainability incentives. For instance, policymakers could boost transparency in these markets, helping generate better-informed policies, while providing beneficiaries with information relevant to their savings choices. It remains an open question as to whether beneficiary sustainability interests are truly being met and serviced. For instance, regarding the lack of ESG investment options in defined-contribution (DC) personal pension plans, consideration of climate change could be made mandatory in view of evidence that investments may be affected by changes in market pricing, regulations, technology, and customer preferences over the medium term and over the life of most DC funds. Yet it is more difficult to do so if no agent in the financial value chain is ultimately responsible for the long-term interests of the beneficiary or client.

In Chapter 10, Anita Margrethe Halvorssen (2023) addresses the issue of ESG and alternative asset investing in the context of Norway's Sovereign Wealth Fund, giving as an example the Fund's 50 percent stake recently taken in Danish energy firm Ørsted's offshore windfarm in the Netherlands. Although the Fund is not involved in managing the real estate, she suggests that ESG integration is a necessity, considering the frequency of global extreme weather events. She believes that ESG disclosure will eventually be required in financial statements and, as that occurs, investors will become increasingly active rather than reactive. As a result, selecting the right investments will probably be somewhat easier than altering non-ESG firms' behavior in the future.

## Looking Ahead

While some people may still believe that the ESG concept remains limited to the old concept of 'socially responsible investing,' this volume clearly shows that ESG-related thinking and investment have evolved to focus on several new components. Included among these are multiple risks, including transition risk, or the degree to which a company is prepared for regulatory and market changes; physical risk, or the exposure of factories and other assets to floods and other climate change effects; disclosure risk, or how companies disclose risks to water and other resources that are necessary to their function but are not reflected on their balance sheet; liability risks due to potential lawsuits; and how they disclose the risks of labor strife and customer or supply chain disruption. Some investment managers, consultants, and pension fund trustees may be wary of ESG investing due to a lack of consistent guidance from regulatory agencies, but in many nations, institutional investors are increasingly moving ahead in a very thoughtful way.

This volume also discusses a range of challenges facing the ESG movement, particularly in the context of pension funds. Data with which investors can learn about such risks are not yet commonly available across firms, sectors, or nations. Perhaps eventually there may be a single global standard, though stakeholders could still differ in their views of its applicability and the weights placed on each key element. For instance, the Sustainability Accounting Standards Board (SASB) criteria focus on materiality, while the Global Reporting Initiative (GRI) takes a much broader purview. Further movement in the ESG direction is likely to wait until US pension fiduciaries receive more guidance from their investment advisers and investment managers; in turn, the latter will await clearer guidance from the US Department of Labor and settled case law. In the Australian and New Zealand DC pension systems, institutional investors have devoted increasing attention to, and active engagement in, pushing an energy transition from fossil fuels (Klijn 2020).

Moreover, models of ESG performance differ from one consultant or provider to another and, sometimes, firms that advertise themselves as ESG-friendly or 'carbon free' are actually priced identically to those that do not (Larcker and Watts 2020). An additional challenge to pension funds contemplating ESG assets is that large institutional investors may have difficulty getting into new ESG products. This is because they tend not to be able to invest in allotments of under US$100 million, while many ESG opportunities are small, early-stage opportunities. Relatedly, many institutional investors are often prohibited from owning over half of any given firm's investment, nor can the allocation exceed 10 percent of the pension fund's assets. Some hedge funds and private equity are working to make this more feasible, using fund-to-fund models dedicated to getting money to smaller managers and companies. Consultants are also finding ways for large institutions to allocate assets to smaller opportunities and smaller investors. Nevertheless, the 'silver bullet' has not yet been found.

A final consideration is that there remains controversy about what to do about climate change, and who should pay to mitigate its worst effects. The Stern Report (2007: xii) on the economics of climate change argued that 'the scientific evidence that climate change is a serious and urgent issue is now compelling,' and that the study, along with many others, helped drive international efforts to pursue the goal of keeping global temperatures from rising. But while the 2021 UN Climate Change Conference brought together almost 200 nations, who negotiated the Glasgow Climate Pact, several important nations, including the US, India, and China, refused to sign the agreement. Moreover, the conflict in Eastern Europe has confirmed the challenge of reducing nations' reliance on fossil fuels, along with the controversy over whether nuclear and natural gas should be labeled as 'green' (Abnett 2022). Consequently, the debate remains far from settled.

Further research on these and related matters is a top priority for institutional investors, money managers, governments, and international organizations to strive to clarify what can and should be done. In particular, little is known as yet about the ways in which pension funds develop and document their ESG policy and practice, how they determine their fiduciary responsibilities regarding ESG, how they comply with their reporting requirements, how they report their ESG practices and results to stakeholders, and when they can and should use divestment versus engagement, relative to investment opportunities. Much remains to be done.

## References

Abnett, L. (2022). 'Lawmaker Group Asks EU to Withdraw Green Investment Label for Gas,' *Reuters*. https://www.yahoo.com/now/lawmaker-group-asks-eu-withdraw-111059059.html?guccounter=1&guce_referrer=aHR0cHM6Ly93d3cu YmluuZy5jb20v&guce_referrer_sig=AQAAACTXejW_fMibnnDpVwu5bNOvZ19Q 7lpsIbSpclsG7RARNrEmTSHIQme2gBcGhbp4sWMH92fs2wsmFKcymboQ5qw GlYaNRlVmnJZ4sBgKETdMS_qY8c0528ov-v8RwPrZ61fSUdb-WqTGahWR59C_ gYgn_NPHNYVDkhMARhLWVN3I

Bauer, R. and P.M.A. Smeets (2023). 'Eliciting Pension Beneficiaries' Sustainability Preferences: Why and How?' In P.B. Hammond, R. Maurer, and O.S. Mitchell, eds., *Pension Funds and Sustainable Investment: Challenges and Opportunities*. Oxford: Oxford University Press, pp. 173–198.

Berg, F., J. Kolbel, and R. Rigobon. (2019). 'Aggregate Confusion: The Divergence of ESG Ratings,' SSRN Working Paper. https://papers.ssrn.com/sol3/papers. cfm?abstract_id=3438533.

Berk, J.B. and J.H. van Binsbergen. (2022). 'The Impact of Impact Investing,' Law & Economics Center at George Mason University Scalia Law School Research Paper Series, 22-008.

Fabian, N., M. Homanen, N. Pedersen, and M. Slebos (2023). 'Private Retirement Systems and Sustainability: Insights from Australia, the UK, and the US.' In P.B. Hammond, R. Maurer, and O.S. Mitchell, eds., *Pension Funds and Sustainable Investment: Challenges and Opportunities*. Oxford: Oxford University Press, pp. 199–219.

Geczy, C.C. and J.B. Guerard, Jr. (2023). 'ESG and Expected Returns on Equities: The Case of Environmental Ratings.' In P.B. Hammond, R. Maurer, and

O.S. Mitchell, eds., *Pension Funds and Sustainable Investment: Challenges and Opportunities.* Oxford: Oxford University Press, pp. 105–136.

Halvorssen, A.M. (2023). 'How the Norwegian SWF Balances Ethics, ESG Risks, and Returns.' In P.B. Hammond, R. Maurer, and O.S. Mitchell, eds., *Pension Funds and Sustainable Investment: Challenges and Opportunities.* Oxford: Oxford University Press, pp. 220–234.

Hammond, P.B. and A. O'Brien (2023). 'Pensions and ESG: An Institutional and Historical Perspective.' In P.B. Hammond, R. Maurer, and O.S. Mitchell, eds., *Pension Funds and Sustainable Investment: Challenges and Opportunities.* Oxford: Oxford University Press, pp. 17–57.

Klijn, W. (2020). 'A Guide to ESG in Australasia,' Investment Innovation Institute (i3-invest.com).

Lachance, S. and J. Stroehle (2023). 'The Origins of ESG in Pensions: Strategies and Outcomes.' In P.B. Hammond, R. Maurer, and O.S. Mitchell, eds., *Pension Funds and Sustainable Investment: Challenges and Opportunities.* Oxford: Oxford University Press, pp. 58–81.

Larcker, D.F. and E. Watts. (2020). 'Where's the Greenium?' *Journal of Accounting and Economics,* 69(2): np. https://www.sciencedirect.com/journal/journal-of-accounting-and-economics/vol/69/issue/2.

Lee, L.-E. (2023). 'ESG Investing: Financial Materiality and Social Objectives.' In P.B. Hammond, R. Maurer, and O.S. Mitchell, eds., *Pension Funds and Sustainable Investment: Challenges and Opportunities.* Oxford: Oxford University Press, pp. 82–101.

Nikulina, L. (2023). 'Global Pensions and ESG: Is There a Better Way?' In P.B. Hammond, R. Maurer, and O.S. Mitchell, eds., *Pension Funds and Sustainable Investment: Challenges and Opportunities.* Oxford: Oxford University Press, pp. 157–169.

Sautner, Z. and L. Starks (2023). 'ESG and Downside Risks: Implications for Pension Funds.' In P.B. Hammond, R. Maurer, and O.S. Mitchell, eds., *Pension Funds and Sustainable Investment: Challenges and Opportunities.* Oxford: Oxford University Press, pp. 137–156.

Stern, N. (2007). *The Economics of Climate Change: The Stern Review.* Cambridge: Cambridge University Press.

Steuer, S. and T.H. Tröger (2021). 'The Role of Disclosure in Green Finance,' SAFE Working Paper No. 320. https://papers.ssrn.com/sol3/papers.cfm?abstract_id=3908617.

Tapiria, H. (2021). 'The World May Be Better Off without ESG Investing,' *Stanford Social Innovation Review,* July 14. https://ssir.org/articles/entry/the_world_may_be_better_off_without_esg_investing.

# Part I

# Defining and Measuring Sustainable Objectives and Outcomes

# Chapter 2

# Pensions and ESG

An Institutional and Historical Perspective

*P. Brett Hammond and Amy O'Brien*

Whether labeled sustainable, responsible, or ESG investing, sustainable investing is growing into its moment, with pensions and other institutional investors playing important roles. Although once quite separate, environmental, social, and governance (ESG) concerns are converging, as pensions and other investors increasingly treat these strands as three parts of a whole. In addition, sustainability considerations are also being increasingly integrated into institutions' overall investment processes.

In our view, convergence and integration are becoming irreversible trends, as pensions and institutional investors around the world expand their sustainable investing capabilities or require their managers to do so. Several suggestive indicators include the following:

- In 2006, 63 asset owners, managers, and service providers around the world, representing about US$6.5 trillion, signed on to the UN's first Principles of Responsible Investment (PRI). In 2021, the UN PRI had over 4,000 signatories, of which over 300 are asset owners or managers representing about US$100 trillion (UN PRI 2021a).
- In 1995, US institutions managed about US$2 billion using a variety of E, S, and G criteria, whereas by 2020, ESG AUM (assets under management) in the US had grown to over US$17 trillion, a compound annual growth rate of about 14 percent (US SIF 2020).
- Japan's Government Pension Investment Fund (GPIF), with over US$1.5 trillion AUM, is now requiring its fund managers to integrate environmental and social concerns into security selection (GPIF 2020).
- The European Union has been engaged in a multiyear program to increase ESG disclosure by public companies, and to require institutional investors to incorporate sustainable investing principles and practices into their investment programs (EC 2018b).

P. Brett Hammond and Amy O'Brien, *Pensions and ESG*. In: *Pension Funds and Sustainable Investment*. Edited by P. Brett Hammond, Raimond Maurer, and Olivia S. Mitchell, Oxford University Press. © P. Brett Hammond and Amy O'Brien (2023). DOI: 10.1093/oso/9780192889195.003.0002

- Australian superannuation schemes are increasingly supporting ESG shareholder proposals and emphasizing their commitment to sustainable investing in response to regulatory and participant pressure in response to the debate about fossil fuel investing and several corporate fiascos (Roddan 2021).
- In the US, CalPERS, the California public employee-defined benefit plan, has long been a leader in ESG convergence and integration; and TIAA, an early innovator among defined-contribution plans, with separate social choice funds and a strong governance program, is considering how to bring sustainable investing criteria to bear on its entire investment portfolio.
- Among global asset managers, BlackRock announced in 2020 that it is in the process of reorienting its entire US$7 billion plus investment portfolio to incorporate sustainable investment criteria, while Capital Group has integrated ESG-based securities analysis into its investments. Many other asset managers either preceded those actions or are following suit (Williamson 2020).

## Four Forces Driving Convergence and Integration

In this section, we identify four forces behind these trends toward convergence and integration in sustainable investing.

### Economic transformation, movements, and organizations

Social movements and government programs intended to ameliorate the worst of the effects of industrialization are well-known and long recognized. In the last few decades, reemergence of wealth and income inequality, increasing industrial concentration and globalization, identification of climate change, and other environmental and social effects have stimulated regional and global movements and independent organizations to advocate and pressure government regulators and companies into addressing the negative consequences.

### Information and analysis

Better data and research on environmental and social issues, including increased disclosure by companies, have enabled governments, independent organizations, and shareholders to understand the case for companies to act on ESG considerations. This has also enabled the creation of multiple measurement systems for evaluating companies according to ESG criteria.

## Institutional ownership

Pension and mutual fund ownership of public securities grew several-fold over the last few decades, so that by 2020, pensions accounted for over 60 percent of the US$20 trillion in assets among the world's top 100 asset owners (Hall et al. 2020). Sovereign wealth funds accounted for most of the rest. Recognizing the growing size of institutional holdings, pension participants, mutual fund investors, and governments began increasingly to pressure those institutions to engage with the companies they own.

## Stakeholder, rather than simply shareholder orientation

While the legitimacy of a stakeholder view of corporate responsibility varies by country and region, wider acceptance of a broad definition of stakeholders to include all of those affected by company actions has been growing. This is true both in the US, where, by the late twentieth century, a narrow shareholder view dominated, and in Europe, where employees in many EU countries have long been recognized as legitimate stakeholders.

These forces have contributed to a more comprehensive approach by institutions to ESG investing across the developed world and, in turn, to changes in the way many companies behave and report. Yet complete convergence and full integration into the investment process by pensions and other investors remains incomplete, given numerous environmental, social, and governance considerations.

# Current ESG Challenges for Pensions

If the trend toward convergence and integration is to continue, it will depend on several challenges that are actively being addressed and debated.

## Goals and objectives

There has been a sea change regarding two basic issues: pensions' fiduciary responsibility with respect to sustainability versus investment returns, and companies' responsibility to shareholders versus broader stakeholders. However, neither issue has, as yet, been fully resolved.

## Analytics

As other chapters in this volume illustrate, there is far from universal agreement on how to define environmental, social, and governance factors. This is important both for what companies disclose regarding their activities along ESG dimensions, as well as practices for and impacts on investment analysis of companies. A variety of disclosure standards and measurement systems has been developed over the past several decades, yet there remains disagreement on what factors to consider, how to define those factors precisely, and what weight should be given to each factor.

## The investment toolbox

Investors are developing their own preferred mix of ESG investment tools or approaches, including negative screening to exclude certain companies, industries, or countries; positive screening to include companies, or both. Additionally, many pension managers seek to identify best-in-class investing within industries; impact investing to further specific ESG goals; engagement and voting on ESG matters; and integration of ESG factors into the securities analysis and portfolio construction process. The fastest growing of all approaches is ESG integration into the investment process (EC 2020e).

## Global standards and practices

Pensions and other institutions operate within regional and global systems, which include a variety of other powerful public and non-government organizations regulating or advocating sustainability policies and practices, all of which can vary across countries and regions.

Although the trends toward ESG convergence and integration are unmistakable, pensions and other institutions cannot simply adopt universal goals and standards, common valuation metrics, and off-the-shelf engagement programs. For example, even with general agreement on reducing carbon emissions, institutions must still determine by how much and by when which companies can or will contribute to reductions, and which companies will do so efficiently. In other words, investors must identify and prioritize their ESG objectives, define specific metrics, and apply them to security selection, while simultaneously creating and managing sustainability programs.

This chapter traces the evolution of ESG investing as it has evolved into a more, but not completely integrated, framework. We begin by laying out a conceptual framework based on the concept of the 'universal owner,' whom we define as a long-term global investor in a position to benefit from evaluating and acting on ESG principles through improvements in corporate governance, and by reducing harmful externalities. We then document the development of practical approaches to achieving sustainability that, today, consist of a formidable set of tools with which to evaluate companies and influence their behavior. We also examine the critical public policy issues affecting sustainable investing, for example how definitions of fiduciary duty differ with respect to sustainable investing, and how these in turn affect pensions in different countries and regions. We also illustrate how frameworks, definitions, tools, and public policies have begun to converge. We conclude by considering sustainable investing challenges that pensions and other institutional investors will face in the years ahead.

## A Conceptual Framework

While ESG, sustainable, responsible, and impact investing each have somewhat different connotations, they all reflect the United Nations Principles for Responsible Investment (UN PRI) 'strategy and practice to incorporate environmental, social and governance factors in investment decisions and active ownership' (UN PRI 2020, 2021a, 2021b). While the UN PRI goes on to list six specific principles, the seeming simplicity of this basic definition, which treats environmental, social, and governance as three parts of a whole, raises important questions, such as: how are the three parts of ESG related? What exactly are the factors that need to be incorporated? Who is responsible for investment decisions? And to whom is the investment decision maker responsible?

### Universal owner

Environmental, social, and governance objectives have not always been treated as an integrated whole. Today, what brings them closer together is the concept of the 'universal owner,' a pension or another institution that, by intention or requirement, invests long-term in widely diversified holdings throughout the global economy (Urwin 2011), and that can speak with a unified voice (Clark and Hebb 2004). These institutions must manage total market exposure, for example, by recognizing that environmental and social costs are unavoidable since they affect the portfolio through insurance premiums, taxes, inflated input prices, unrest, and instability, which in turn can generate costs reducing returns for some investments. Examples include environmental degradation, poverty, pandemics, and many others. Looming over all of this, poor company governance can lead to short-termism, insufficient attention to pertinent environmental and social issues, and suboptimal decisions that reduce long-term performance. As we will see, universal owners have played a major role in patterns and policies for sustainable investing today, acting both individually and in consortia, including with the UN PRI and independent as well as industry groups.

Besides universal owners, other stakeholders may also have an interest in sustainable and responsible corporate practices. The most influential of these are governments, which, even more than universal owners, have a long-term stewardship interest in the effects of corporate actions on society. They also control a variety of tools such as legislation and regulation, to direct and affect corporate behavior. While governments and universal owners cannot afford to avoid sustainability issues, individual shareholders may also see an interest, although their influence will be less than that of governments and universal owners. Finally, corporations can assess their own stances and take action to either embrace or avoid sustainability and responsibility (Urwin 2019).

## Externalities and agency

To better understand the interests of these actors in ESG investing, it is helpful to turn to two well-known but fundamental economic concepts: externalities and agency theory. Simply put, an economic externality is a cost or benefit that accrues to third parties: society, organizations, or individuals that did not directly agree to take it on. The externality may also affect how firms (and their shareholders) produce it, but a significant portion of the cost or benefit still attends to third parties. For instance, a plant's stationary source air pollution could result in higher health insurance costs and reduced productivity among its workers, thus affecting profits; nevertheless, substantial impacts are likely to be felt by many others through air particulates or climate change. Conversely, a plant that scrubs its emissions will benefit many others who do not pay directly for the costs of doing so. More generally, an externality occurs when a product or service's market equilibrium price does not reflect the true costs or benefits of that product or service for society as a whole. From society's perspective, then, because resources are suboptimally allocated, the externality cannot pass the Pareto optimality test and results in a market failure.

While it may be in society's interests to reduce or eliminate externalities, the dilemma is that when the cost of doing so is borne by one or more firms, they are unlikely to be able to fully capture related positive benefits (e.g., cleaner air and climate stability). A firm might still spend the money, hoping that ESG-minded customers and investors will reward it by their willingness either to pay higher prices for the firm's goods and services or to purchase its securities. For example, customers of the US clothing manufacturer, Patagonia, are willing to pay more for its highly publicized environmentally friendly cotton-based clothing. In other cases, however, a firm acting alone is unlikely to reap a return on its actions.

A different approach could be for a group of competitors to all agree on reducing specific negative externalities. Even if they cannot capture all of the positive effects, they may incur similar extra costs, so that their relative competitive positions can remain the same. In these cases, trade associations or standard-setting groups can play a central role.

Yet a different approach is for third parties to step in and pressure firms to act. These may include regulators charged with stewardship over public goods, consumers able to direct their purchasing dollars (e.g., boycotts), or pensions and other investors who can pressure company managements using a variety of tools—carrots and sticks—at shareholders' disposal. This is where agency theory comes into play. A conflict or moral hazard arises between a principal—the shareholder, and the agent—company management, when the two parties have different interests and asymmetric information; that is, management knows more about the business than do the shareholders (Berle and Means 1967). In such an instance, shareholders cannot directly ensure that management is always acting in their best interests, particularly when activities that benefit the principal are costly to the agent, and/or where what the agent does is costly for the principal to observe. In these cases, there may be suboptimal outcomes—agency costs—that reduce societal welfare. The agency problem can get worse when company management acts on behalf of multiple principals or shareholders, some of whom may not want to share in the cost of monitoring and enforcing certain company policies and practices, or who may not agree on what those policies and practices should be.

Agency problems affect pensions and other institutional universal owners. Among other things, institutional shareholders may be reluctant to act because they receive a fraction of the benefits resulting from stewardship activities, while having to handle all the costs.

It might seem that the problems of externalities and agency theory are closely related, and that responsible investing efforts should easily recognize the connection. Those using the externality lens, as well as those using the agency lens, can both favor incentives such as shareholder and customer preferences, or regulation to internalize certain negative externalities. More likely, a narrower view of agency that focuses on shareholders interested primarily in short-term profits to the exclusion of externalities, will conflict with a broader conception that includes a wider set of stakeholders interested in addressing externalities. For example, efforts to align manager and shareholder interests to produce policies that ignore or amplify negative externalities (e.g., reducing costs by moving jobs to countries that allow sweatshop labor) can be aligned on the profit question, albeit not in ways that always produce sustainable, responsible outcomes.

### Stakeholders versus shareholders

As a US example of this issue, the California Public Employee Pension System (CalPERS) defines corporate governance as 'the relationship among various participants in determining the direction and performance of corporations. The Primary participants are: shareholders; company management … and the board of directors' (quoted in McRitchie 2020: 1). By contrast, Milton Friedman laid out the case for a definition of corporate governance confined almost entirely to a firm's owners' return on investment:

> In a free-enterprise, private-property system, a corporate executive is an
> employee of the owners of the business. He has direct responsibility to his
> employers. That responsibility is to conduct the business in accordance with
> their desires, which generally will be to make as much money as possible while
> conforming to their basic rules of the society, both those embodied in law and
> those embodied in ethical custom.
>
> (Friedman 1970: section SM: 17)

To Friedman, corporate governance must be evaluated by how it trans-
mits and enforces actions that maximize monetary returns to shareholders,
tempered only by the need to conform to the basic rules of society.

There is, however, an alternative and more expansive definition hinted
at in the CalPERS formulation, one exemplified by the Johnson & Johnson
Company's Credo, penned by Robert Wood Johnson in 1943, recognizing
that the company's activities touch employees, customers, and communities,
as well as shareholders (J&J Credo 1943). In other words, according to this
definition, the J&J Credo makes clear that the company creates externalities which must be acknowledged and managed. Accordingly, governance
should be evaluated by how it serves the needs of all of these entities, not
merely by returns to stockholders. This position also allows for a consideration of externalities, that is, effects on stakeholders that do not accrue
exclusively to shareholders or management.

This tension between a shareholder versus a stakeholder conception
of corporate governance is present wherever limited liability corporations
exist, but it has had a different flavor across countries and regions in terms
of the roles, responsibilities, and influence of company management, shareholders, stakeholders, and governments. The varying perspective continues
to challenge pensions, other institutions, and other shareholders in efforts
to improve corporate governance around the globe.

Recognizing that a focus on externalities and the narrower view of governance can conflict, it is also possible to separate externality and agency
issues. For example, stakeholders primarily interested in improving societal and environmental outcomes might choose to focus on mechanisms
such as regulation or proxy votes that work toward those ends without
directly addressing agency issues. Alternatively, those interested in better
aligning shareholder and management incentives—perhaps in search of
higher profits—might focus on governance policies, such as board independence and firm takeover policies, to the exclusion of concerns about
externalities.

In this vein, a comprehensive way to define the challenge for proponents
of responsible investing requires an effort to gain agreement regarding a
broader definition of principals in the agency problem. In the process,
stakeholders affected by a company's externalities will be included and then

their interests aligned with management, shareholders, and stakeholders, so they agree on policies to reduce negative externalities and capture positive externalities. This challenge is a formidable one, and even if the key players could agree on a broader definition of whose interests a company should serve, there is no universal agreement on how to weight those interests, that is, how to prioritize externalities and how to address them.

Such challenges have shaped the evolution of ESG investing, and they remain very much alive today. In the next section, we will see that the modern origins of responsible investing were grounded in this dilemma and essentially led to separate tracks for efforts to improve environmental, social, and governance outcomes. For pensions and some other institutional investors, improving governance, that is, programs and policies to better align management with shareholder interests, emerged early on in what might be called the modern era of sustainable investing. As it did so, better governance proponents did not at first recognize the relevance of environmental and social concerns to their project. What brought the three tracks closer together was the recognition of a broader, more encompassing longer-term focused definition of shareholder interests that includes negative and positive externalities.

## Strands and Spheres: 'Pre-Modern' to 'Modern'

Here we are primarily interested in understanding the place of pensions and other institutions in modern ESG investing, but this requires us to recognize the developments that brought both pensions and ESG to where they are today. We refer specifically to three observations about what we might call the 'pre-modern' era (roughly prior to the 1980s), as opposed to the 'modern' era of ESG policies. First was the absence of pensions in sustainable investing until the late twentieth century, largely because funded pensions were small compared to other institutional and most individual investors. Thereafter, with rapid asset and participant growth, pensions began to recognize their emerging status as universal investors with an interest in long-term issues of sustainability. Second, due to government policies, sustainable investing evolved quite differently across countries and regions. As governments, pension plans, and others began to recognize that ESG raises issues that are global in nature, policies and practices that varied between countries began to be reexamined. Third, there was initially very little attention devoted to the environment (E) strand of ESG, later followed by attempts to treat G separately from S and E. With a growing recognition that agency and externality issues are highly intertwined, policymakers, pensions, and other investors began to bring the E, S, and G strands together.

In effect, the transition from the pre-modern to the modern ESG era is one of evolution and convergence.

## The pre-modern era

Some observers group countries with respect to ESG investing exclusively by each nation's type of corporate legal system. Yet while legal systems differ, two simple but powerful drivers of the evolution of sustainability practices in the private sector have been patterns of stock market ownership, and government involvement in social reform and corporate regulation across countries and regions.

Prior to the turn of the twentieth century, early social reforms benefiting employees and then consumers began to emerge in developed countries, but they were often the result of pressure from workers, voters, and advocacy groups with little investor involvement. (See this chapter's Appendix for details on premodern ESG developments in selected countries.)

What investor interest there was centered on what we now call corporate governance, as corporate control in industrial economies was concentrated in three ways: in monopolistic or oligopolistic industries; control by wealthy families; and financial institutions. For example, in some countries, families used pyramidal ownership structures[1] and/or banks used special share classes and proxy voting to give them effective control. This began to change, but not always in the direction of greater protections for other shareholders and with differences among countries, notably in the role of government control. The US, for example, used antitrust policy and regulation to virtually eliminate family and financial institution control of public companies by the 1940s, but policy still tended to favor the interests of company management over those of shareholders. By contrast, in most European countries, family and financial institution control was tolerated for far longer. In addition, in the name of worker and consumer protection, and to preserve declining industries after World War II, some European governments took direct ownership of companies in certain industries and/or exerted a stronger role in capital allocation. We also note that environmental issues took a back seat to governance and social concerns, or were often non-existent, until the 1960s and 70s.

At the dawn of the modern era of ESG investing, the landscape looked as depicted in Table 2.1. Here we see that several of the tools and approaches used to promote good corporate governance in the modern era were already in use but not widespread, including the 2-tier board structure, a degree of uniform accounting and disclosure, limits on institutional and family ownership, anti-monopoly enforcement, and formal recognition of stakeholders. Other approaches, such as shareholder initiatives, prohibition

TABLE 2.1  ESG investing landscape at the dawn of the 'modern' era

| | | US | UK | Netherlands | Germany | France | Italy | Sweden | Japan |
|---|---|---|---|---|---|---|---|---|---|
| Corporate Governance | | | | | | | | | |
| | 2-Tier Board Structure (+ worker participation) | | | X | X | X | | | |
| | Limit institutional ownership | X | X | | | | | | |
| | Separate commercial & investment banking | X | | | | | | | |
| Policies and Tools | Government owner-ship/direction of certain industries | | | | | X | X | | |
| | Formal/legal recognition of stakeholders | | | X | X | | | | |
| | Strong anti-monopoly enforcement | X | X | | | | | | |
| | Higher degree of uniform accounting, reporting & disclosure rules | X | X | | X | | | | |
| | Small shareholder activism | | | | | | | | |
| Continuing Issues | High degree of manager control/low degree of shareholder control | X | X | X | | | | | X |
| | Relatively higher use of voting caps, multiple share classes, etc. | | | X | | | | X | |

*Continued*

TABLE 2.1 *Continued*

|  | US | UK | Netherlands | Germany | France | Italy | Sweden | Japan |
|---|---|---|---|---|---|---|---|---|
| Interlocking directorates |  |  | X |  |  |  |  | X |
| Family or bank control common* |  |  |  | X | X | X | X |  |
| Takeover defenses | X |  | X |  |  |  |  |  |
| **Social & Environmental** Environmental regulation and activism | H | L | L | L | L | L | L | L |
| Consumer and worker protections | M | M | H | H | H | H | H | H |
| Family and individual protections** | L | M | H | H | H | H | H | M |
| Union activism: negotiation, lobbying | L | M | H | H | H | H | H | L |
| **Pensions** Growth of funded pension assets (DB and DC) | H | H | H | L | L | L | H | H |
| Social & environmental investments | L | L |  |  |  |  |  |  |

*Note:* * Family control often exercised through pyramid ownership structures; bank control often exercised by proxy voting or direct ownership; ** Health insurance, child support, other family support.

*Source:* Morck (2005); Authors' calculations.

of interlocking directorates, independent board members, etc., were scarce or missing.

There was a long history of employee and consumer protections regarding social and environmental issues in many countries, but the impetus rarely came from shareholders. Rather, most often it arose from union activism and other interest groups leading to government regulation and/or ownership of industry. For example, the US government created a wave of regulatory agencies at the start of the twentieth century. Pensions were not in a position to exercise much influence in those days, since in many countries they were either unfunded public entities or, as in the UK and the US, they were funded but had not yet accumulated substantial financial clout.

## The modern era

What we call the modern era of ESG investing began in the late 1970s and early 1980s, marked by the rise of pension ownership, the retreat of direct government ownership of companies, and separate movements to promote corporate governance and environmental reforms. For example, in 1969, the US Environmental Protection Agency was created, exemplifying a new era of government regulation in response to environmental activism; this was later followed by similar programs in other countries.

The establishment of funded pensions earlier in the twentieth century, particularly in the US, the UK, the Netherlands, and later in Australia, meant that by the 1980s these had become substantial asset owners, along with sovereign wealth funds. In addition, a small number of asset managers joined asset owners in controlling a growing percentage of public company shares. While these trends were far from identical across industrial countries, and the assets under management appear small from today's vantage point, the largest institutions could even then be considered universal owners who had no choice but to purchase shares in most public companies in search of capital appreciation and income for their beneficiaries.

The result of these shifts in stock ownership patterns can be observed in Figure 2.1. Institutional investors, which include pensions, other asset owners, and asset managers who work, in part, for asset owners, now own over 70 percent of outstanding shares in the US, with similar percentages in the Netherlands, the UK, and Canada. By contrast, institutional investors own less than 40 percent of public shares in other European countries, about one-third in Japan, and less than 10 percent in China. Corporate cross holdings, which are high in Asia, are quite low in Europe and the US. In addition, in countries such as Norway and Japan, government agencies directly invested pension savings in the stock market, while in others such as China, governments took direct ownership of companies. (The figure does

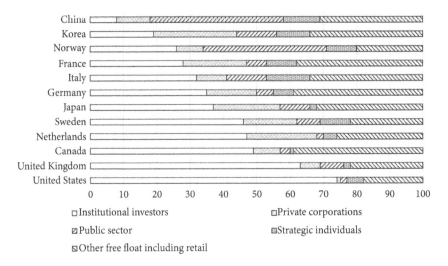

**Figure 2.1** Total stock market holdings by investor categories across countries, 2017

*Note*: Distribution of total holdings by investor category in each market for the universe of 10,000 largest listed companies. Both domestic and foreign holdings by category are aggregated in USD as a percentage of total market cap in each market. Assignment of assets to categories follows each country's classifications. For example, Norway's public sector assets include those held by the Government Pension Fund of Norway. Canada's public pension fund assets are classified as institutional holdings.

*Source*: De La Cruz et al. (2019), based on OECD Capital Markets Data Set, Thompson Reuters and Bloomberg.

not reflect the legacy and continuation of pyramidal ownership and share class structures in Asia and Europe.)

Given these patterns, it is not surprising that interest in ESG investing issues emerged among pension plan managers. This occurred slowly, evolving with different patterns across institutions, countries, and the three strands of sustainability: environmental, social, and governance.

## Governance
### Pensions

Several leading US pensions, such as TIAA, CalPERS, and other institutional investors, were instrumental in the corporate government movement of the 1980s and 1990s. In addition to their growing asset bases, these institutions were operating with the legacy of pre-WWII reforms that favored company management over other stakeholders, a rising stock market, and an accompanying wave of mergers. For example, management-controlled boards, limited disclosure, opaque shareholder initiative processes, and other measures all enabled managers to operate with little scrutiny. Although there was a dearth of concrete evidence available, institutional investors began to respond to the view that it was in their interest to propose and/or support policies that would shift the balance of power toward shareholders and away from management.

No two pensions (or other institutional investors) pioneered identical approaches to corporate governance programs. For example, CalPERS tended to employ public statements aimed at changing corporate behavior, while TIAA more often used direct and relatively more private communications with company management. Nevertheless, these and other programs largely shared four elements: a legal orientation; similar, though not identical, reform proposals; cross-fertilization with investment managers; and separation from environmental and social concerns. Conceptually, corporate governance reform was, for the most part, viewed through a legal rather than a financial or economic lens, meaning that problems and solutions were more likely to be evaluated by whether they conformed to a set of preferred principles such as a definition of board independence, or a process such as a streamlined shareholder initiative process. Economic impacts, such as increased shareholder returns, were mostly ignored, or they were assumed to follow from the implementation of corporate governance initiatives. Organizationally, new corporate governance units were, for the most part, housed in the legal departments of institutional investors. For pensions as well as corporate governance service providers, these units were led by experts with a legal background.

In keeping with this focus on principles and process, many pension managers could agree on the need for assistance. TIAA, CalPERS, Cal-STRS (California State Teachers' Retirement System), and others were co-founders of the Institutional Investor Responsibility Center (IRRC) in 1972, which sought to aid investors in understanding corporate governance issues. Along with international pensions, these entities were also among the founders of the Council of Institutional Investors (CII), which assisted with proxy voting, regulatory advocacy, and other activities (see Table 2.2). These and other research, service, and advocacy programs helped pensions and other institutional investors further the following policies: greater independence of board members, separate audit and compensation committees, changes in executive compensation, removal of poison pill provisions, support for the shareholder initiative process, regular proxy voting, and various forms of engagement.

In terms of cross-fertilization, although corporate governance programs were not generally housed in investment departments, organizations that directly managed corporate governance staff could learn from investment analysts and managers knowledgeable about the management, governance

TABLE 2.2  ESG in the 1970s

| 'ESG as a principle' | Key Institutional Developments |
|---|---|
| • Investors align around key social concerns (e.g., South Africa, Vietnam War, poverty)<br>• Forerunning ESG research, and shareholder advocacy, and community development institutions are founded | • Council on Economic Priorities/CEP (1969)<br>• Pax World Fund (1971)<br>• Dreyfus Third Century Fund (1972)<br>• Interfaith Center for Corporate Responsibility/ICCR (1972)<br>• Investor Responsibility Research Center/IRRC (1972) became IRRC Institute after 2005 sale of IRRC to ISS<br>• South Shore Bank/Shorebank (1973)<br>• National Federation of Community Development Credit Unions (1974)<br>• Calvert Social Investment (1976) |

*Source*: Authors' calculations.

structure, and processes of the companies they covered. This, in turn, enabled them to recommend companies that might benefit from certain reforms. Likewise, investment analysts and managers could incorporate into their investment decisions information about initiatives being proposed by corporate governance staff (see Table 2.3).

Moving ahead in time, but still prior to the 2010s, corporate governance programs rarely considered environmental or social issues to be part of their universe. Their legal orientation may have made it difficult to incorporate these relatively more outcome-oriented issues. Also, some activists considered corporate governance reform to be fundamental, while other issues were often seen as derivative. In other words, establishing good governance practices was intended to lead companies to evaluate and treat all externalities properly.

## Corporate governance organizations

One cannot understand the emergence of activism among large institutional investors such as TIAA and CalPERS without noting the crucial role played by independent corporate governance service organizations. In the US, investors and companies for many years had been able to turn to business groups such as the Chamber of Commerce, the Business Roundtable, and, for fund companies, the Investment Company Institute, for informed views on corporate structure and process. In turn, these often-supported company management over shareholders.

TABLE 2.3 ESG in the 1980s and 1990s

| 'ESG as a product' | Key Institutional Developments |
|---|---|
| • Dedicated industry networks are formed in the USA (Ceres, US SIF) <br> • Triggered by corporate takeovers and environmental disasters—Exxon Valdez spill, Bhopal India (Union Carbide) chemical leak—investors increase their focus on corporate governance and the environment <br> • First social indices launched and universe of Socially Responsible Investing (SRI) funds expands <br> • Advanced business case for sustainability and reporting (Global Reporting Initiative—GRI) <br> • DOL issues guidance that plan fiduciaries are permitted to consider social benefits | • CalPRS, CalSTRS <br> • US Social Investment Forum/US SIF (1984) <br> • Franklin Research & Development (1982) <br> • later renamed Trillium in 1999 <br> • Grameen Bank (1983) <br> • Self-Help Credit Union (1984) <br> • Working Assets founded (1985) <br> • Social Venture Network (1987) <br> • CERES & the Valdez Principles (1989) <br> • initially a project of the US SIF <br> • TIAA Social Choice Account (1990) |

*Source*: Authors' calculations.

Beginning in the 1970s, new service organizations were established that played various advisory and advocacy roles oriented to institutional investor interests. The IRRC sought to provide independent, impartial research on proxy voting, corporate governance, and corporate social responsibility issues (Weinberg Center 2021).[2] Another independent organization, the National Association of Corporate Directors (NACD), was established in 1977 to train and set standards for board directors (see Table 2.4).

In 1985, during a period of heightened corporate mergers, the Council of Institutional Investors began an effort to pool resources in exercising shareholder oversight through proxy voting, shareowner resolutions, pressure on regulators, discussions with companies, and litigation. Membership today includes 140 US public, union, and corporate employee benefit plans, endowments, and foundations, with combined assets under management of approximately US$4 trillion. Associate members include non-US asset owners with more than US$4 trillion, and US and non-US asset managers with over US$35 trillion in AUM (CII 2021). Around the same time, the Institutional Shareholders Services (ISS) group began to advise institutional shareholders (including mutual and hedge funds) on proxy voting and, when requested, to vote their shares. The firm later acquired the IRRC and was in turn sold to MSCI. In Europe, the European Corporate Governance Network (ECGN) was established in 1995 to focus on company ownership and control issues. In 2002, this network was transformed into the more permanent European Corporate Governance Institute (ECGI), which brings

TABLE 2.4 Major corporate governance research, service, and advocacy organizations

| Organization | | Est. | Primary Focus | Non-Profit? | Membership/Support | Notes |
|---|---|---|---|---|---|---|
| **Investor Responsibility Research Center** | IRRC | 1972 | Research, Proxy Voting | Yes | Subscription | 2005 sale to ISS funded the U Delaware Weinberg Center's IRRCi |
| **National Assn of Corporate Directors** | NACD | 1977 | Board member practices and education | Yes | Corporate directors | |
| **Council of Institutional Investors** | CII | 1985 | Proxy voting, shareholder resolutions, regulatory advocacy, engagement, litigation | Yes | US and non-US pensions, endowments/foundations, asset managers | |
| **Institutional Shareholders Services** | ISS | 1985 | Proxy voting | No | Fee for advisory service | Acquired by MSCI |
| **International Corporate Governance Network** | ICGN | 1995 | Governance and stewardship standards and practices | Yes | Pensions, asset managers, public companies, advisory services | Primarily North America and Europe |
| **Weinberg Center for Corporate Governance** | | 2000 | Discussion forum, teaching, research | Yes | Law firms, asset managers, companies | |
| **European Corporate Governance Institute** | ECGI | 2002 | Discussion forum, research | Yes | Academics, legislators, practitioners | Grew out of ECGN |

| | | | | | |
|---|---|---|---|---|---|
| **Harvard Law School Program on Corporate Governance** | 2003 | Research, teaching | Yes | Law firms, companies | |
| **Harvard Law School Forum on Corporate Governance** | 2006 | Discussion forum | Yes | Law firms, companies | |
| **Ira Millstein Center for Global Markets and Corporate Ownership** | 2012 | Teaching, research, discussion forum | Yes | Law firms, companies | Columbia U law school |
| **Arthur and Toni Rembe Rock Center for Corporate Governance** | 2006 | Teaching, research, discussion forum | Yes | Law firms, companies | Stanford U Law and Business Schools |

*Source*: Authors' compilations from https://www.weinberg.udel.edu/; https://www.weinberg.udel.edu/; https://www.nacdonline.org/; https://www.cii.org/about; https://www.issgovernance.com/; https://www.icgn.org/; https://www.weinberg.udel.edu/; https://pcg.law.harvard.edu/; https://corpgov.law.harvard.edu/; https://law.stanford.edu/arthur-and-toni-rembe-rock-center-for-corporate-governance/; https://millstein.law.columbia.edu/; https://law.stanford.edu/arthur-and-toni-rembe-rock-center-for-corporate-governance/.

together academics, legislators, and practitioners, and sponsors and disseminates research. On the international front, the International Corporate Governance Network (ICGN), started in 1995, was created to promote dialogue and education regarding governance and stewardship practices. Its members, drawn from over 45 countries primarily in North America and Europe, include pensions, asset managers, public companies, and advisory firms (ICGN 2021).

Institutional investors differed in how they used these corporate governance resources. Some relied on organizations such as ISS to research and form positions, as well as to vote their shares. Many mutual fund companies, by contrast, refrained from active or intense participation in corporate governance issues and shareholder voting. Others relied on external research by the IRRC, CII, and other organizations, after which they developed their own corporate governance positions and programs.

While the world of corporate governance only gradually started to recognize its connections with environmental and social issues in the late 1980s, these two strands of sustainable investing also began to develop in the modern era.

## Environmental and Social Issues

As with governance, investor concerns for social and environmental topics evolved over time into what is now often treated under the banner of socially responsible investing (or SRI). A stakeholder orientation provides the foundation for social and environmental investing, on the basis that companies' activities affect not only shareholder returns, but also communities, employees, customers, and the environment, implying that these latter interests should also have a voice in company activities. At first, environmental and social initiatives focused on three approaches: shareholder activism, community investing, and guideline investing. Of the three, social investing emphasized shareholder activism and community investing, while environmental investing emphasized both shareholder activism and guideline investing. Nevertheless, as time went on, all three strategies became important for both environmental and social concerns.

### Shareholder activism

For pension plans required to act as fiduciaries, an initial avenue for shareholders to gain clout was to exert influence on companies identified as 'doing harm' with their products, or where they were doing business (e.g., South Africa). This took the form of informal and formal engagement with companies, including communications, and, in some cases, formal shareholder initiatives. In the US and in other countries, a recurring theme was the role of government vis-à-vis stakeholders and companies. Governments can spend to improve social and environmental conditions, and they can also direct companies to do so as well. Accordingly, stakeholders could pressure government, public, and private pensions and other asset owners to push companies to act, in turn. In that vein, SEC rules regarding shareholders' standing and shifting guidance on what constituted fiduciary duty, all helped to shape pension activism.[3]

Apartheid in South Africa was also an early defining social issue. In 1977, the Sullivan Principles became a voluntary code of conduct for companies operating in that country. In this spirit, in 1978, TIAA issued its own statement on companies doing business in South Africa, and in 1983 it fully divested from these assets. Other investors followed suit. Additional instances of global activism included, in the 1980s, actions against Procter & Gamble and Philip Morris for their involvement in El Salvador in the 1980s, and, beginning in the 1990s, wages, working conditions, and child labor in companies with factories that operated outside the US.

These initiatives fueled a formal corporate social responsibility (CSR) movement that helped alter companies' expectations regarding their responsibility to internalize the effects (externalities) of their supply chains. The CSR movement resulted in greater demand by direct investors and other stakeholders for improved reporting, including both S and E. For example, CERES (the Coalition for Environmentally Responsible Economies), established as a response to the Exxon Valdez oil spill disaster of 1989, took a more comprehensive view of sustainability reporting. In turn, this led to the Global Reporting Initiative (GRI) program in 1997 (with Tellus Institute and the UN Environment Programme). The GRI would eventually become an independent organization in 2001, with headquarters in Amsterdam (GRI 2021). Beginning with the Valdez disaster, state pensions such as New York, CalPERS, and CalSTRS became increasingly active in designing and supporting these organizations.

During the 1990s, US pensions began to recognize the need to apply additional lenses to their portfolios, mainly through proxy voting and engaging with companies of concern. They also felt growing pressure from participants and other constituencies to use more E and S information to exclude portfolio holdings. To that end, pensions began to develop their ability to create and manage ESG portfolios.

## Guideline investing

This approach began in the 1970s by fund managers Calvert, Dreyfus, and Pax World, and it was used by investors to exclude tobacco, alcohol, weapons, and other products or activities poorly aligned with ethical or faith values. Later, guideline investing expanded to impose systematic negative screening, positive screening, and best-within-a-sector (best-in-class) security selection. Pensions as well as asset managers were active in these developments, including TIAA, CalPERS, CalSTRS, and others.

As the approach evolved, tension emerged between those using segregated funds versus applying ESG criteria to security selection and portfolio construction. For example, TIAA, which created the TIAA-CREF Social Choice Account as one among many investment options for participants in 1990, faced continuing participant pressure to eliminate tobacco and other products from all funds, not just the Social Choice Account. Moreover, among institutional investors, there was also no general agreement on how to select securities. The question that managers then faced was whether they should select companies in which to invest on an absolute basis, or instead to select the best companies within an industry or sector.

A related problem was that, while there might be agreement on certain issues such as tobacco, there was far less agreement on what exactly constituted ESG objectives. Part of this conundrum was due to the lack of data and analysis to provide a foundation for investment decisions. For example, in 1986 when the US Environmental Protection Agency required the first toxic release reports, that system focused on facilities rather than companies, making it difficult for investors to use the information for portfolio selection. In many cases, the early research providers serving institutional investors did not make raw data available, but, rather, they interpreted ratings and assessments. In retrospect, this may have harmed the cause more than it helped, because institutions first needed to unlock 'black box' methodologies, and later to determine how the information should inform investment decisions. In turn, this led to initiatives such as the GRI, set up to develop better reporting and measurement systems, along with efforts to define and reach agreement among investors and others on ESG objectives. While the establishment of the Intergovernmental Panel on Climate Change (IPCC) in 1988 was not primarily investor-driven, its periodic assessment reports did help shape investor understanding of how company and industry actions affected climate degradation and the resulting investment risk.

*Community investing* or economically targeted investment (ETI) was the precursor to today's impact investing, developed to generate particular social outcomes alongside financial return. This strategy was based on the belief that 'the plight of the homelessness and joblessness cannot be "fixed" through conventional Wall Street investments,' but instead required involvement by credit unions, foundations, community-based revolving funds, worker cooperatives, and other entities (Domini et al. 1992: 3). Another impetus was provided by the federal Community Reinvestment Act of 1977, which required the Federal Reserve and other federal banking regulators to 'encourage' financial institutions to help meet the credit needs of the communities in which they did business, including with loans and direct investments. Organizations such as the Local Initiatives Support Corporation (LISC) were formed to work with financial institutions to channel funds into local projects; pensions and other institutional investors were also encouraged to participate.

Nevertheless, for pensions, challenges to community investing included the need to develop appropriate investment vehicles, gain scale, develop return expectations, and, for ERISA plans, shift Department of Labor (DOL) guidance on fiduciary duty regarding what constituted responsible lending practices. Alliances with Shorebank and other community banks, as well as the Local Initiatives Support Corporation, and the launch of Impact Community Capital (1998) founded by TIAA and seven other insurance companies, all provided solutions, particularly for low-income housing initiatives. In addition, activism played a role, as shareholders pressured banks on practices that harmed vulnerable customers via predatory lending and redlining practices.

Pension and other institutional involvement in community investing took a more global turn in the 1990s and 2000s, with attention to microfinance and the broader concept of financial inclusion. The term 'impact investing' was first coined in 2007, and it gained traction through the launch and fieldwork of the Global Impact Investing Network which included foundations and pensions in different countries. The initial focus was on private equity, with a concern for specific goals and outcomes that depended, for credibility, on advances in ESG-related measurement. Impact investing has more recently gained traction in other classes.

## Bringing the Three Strands Together

The years around the turn of the twentieth century also saw growing acceptance among pensions, other investors, and activists that environmental, social, and governance issues are intertwined and mutually reinforcing. On the one hand, investors, regulators, and independent organizations increasingly recognized that progress on corporate environmental and social concerns would only be successful if they were supported by governance reforms. On the other hand, they also saw that the next steps in corporate governance reform would likely lead to a discussion of environmental and social reforms. To illustrate these trends, several earlier events were arguably treated contemporaneously as primarily social (South Africa divestment) or environmental problems (the Union Carbide plant in Bhopal and the Exxon Valdez disasters) that did not involve the central concerns of corporate governance. Looking back on those events, we can now see that corporate decision-making and governance were not only intertwined with these issues, but that changes in one were needed to produce improvements in the others.

Leading the way to integration of ESG was a movement to coordinate E and S activities across different countries and regions (see Table 2.5). Principal among these was the consortium of global pensions and other institutional investors that, in 2005, pressured the United Nations to sponsor a 20-person group from 12 countries to develop an ESG framework for the investment industry. The result, first issued in 2006, firmly linked E, S, and G together as follows: 'As institutional investors, we have a duty to act in the best long-term interests of our beneficiaries. In this fiduciary role, we believe that environmental, social, and corporate governance issues can affect the performance of investment portfolios (to varying degrees across companies, sectors, regions, asset classes, and through time). We also recognize that applying these principles may better align investors with broader objectives of society' (UN PRI 2021b: 1) (see Table 2.6).

TABLE 2.5 ESG in the 2000s

| 'ESG as a process' | Key Institutional Developments |
|---|---|
| • Investors coordinate on climate reporting issues<br>• New global investor networks begin to unite investor approaches from different regions<br>• In 2008, the US DOL narrows 1994 guidance: fiduciaries should only rarely consider non-economic factors when picking investment options for retirement plans | • Carbon Disclosure Project/CDP (2000)<br>• UN Global Compact (2000)<br>• UN Principles for Responsible Investment (2006)<br>• Global Impact Investing Network/GIIN (2009) |

*Source*: Authors' calculations.

TABLE 2.6 UN Principles of Responsible Investment

1. We will incorporate ESG issues into *investment analysis* and decision-making processes.
2. We will be active owners and incorporate ESG issues into our ownership policies and practices.
3. We will seek appropriate disclosure on ESG issues by the entities in which we invest.
4. We will promote acceptance and implementation of the Principles within the investment industry.
5. We will work together to enhance our effectiveness in implementing the Principles.
6. We will each report on our activities and progress toward implementing the Principles.

*Source*: UN PRI (2021b).

In addition, a UN-affiliated organization, Principles for Responsible Investment, was established to put the framework into practice, and it continues to lead integration efforts at a global level. Initially, PRI reporting requirements for its signatories were not seen as stringent. Nevertheless, backed by the principles and their own participants, global pensions, and other institutional asset owners could and did increase pressure on investment managers to incorporate ESG considerations into portfolio decisions. In 2011, the UN PRI increased the specificity of reporting requirements, further encouraging ESG progress.

While visible and far-reaching, the UN PRI was far from the only group making initiatives in this period. The EU established a unit with the European Commission's Directorate-General for Economic and Financial Affairs to launch a series of studies, consultations, and directives moving in the direction of requiring institutional investors to consider ESG in the investment process. In the US, while integration of ESG was far from universal, two trends were evident. One was that CalPERS, CalSTRS, and TIAA-CREF began to connect their corporate governance units residing in legal departments more closely with their investment professionals. The second was to more closely connect staff tasked with environmental and social research, analysis, and investments, with the staff responsible for non-ESG-oriented investment decisions. In other words, these organizations took the first steps to integrate ESG with 'regular' investing.[4]

The trend toward integration, which began in the late 1990s and 2000s, accelerated in the 2010s (see Table 2.7). Within pensions (again, particularly TIAA-CREF, CalPERS, CalSTRS, and other independent pensions) and other institutional investors, the movement to fully integrate ESG analysis into investment decisions reached fruition. Near the end of the decade, for example, TIAA (as it was then called) announced that ESG factors would be considered in all funds and portfolios across all asset classes (TIAA 2021).

At the international level, the Paris Agreement of 2015 was a watershed. One of a series of conventions and projects that originated with the *United Nations Framework Convention on Climate Change* (UN 1992), the Paris Agreement was signed by 195 countries and the EU (though not the US). It set out a definition of climate change and goals for limiting global warming and called for action to achieve goals by government and non-government actors (UN 2015). It has helped galvanize investors and companies to focus attention on sustainable investing and corporate challenges with respect to climate change, including but not limited to production processes, new products, and discussions of stranded assets.

At the regional level, in the EU the European Commission (EC) continued to stage a series of consensus-building consultations and to issue ESG-related rules. Following from reports issued by the Financial Stability Board and the Basel Committee on Banking Standards, the EC began to

TABLE 2.7  ESG in the 2010s

| 'ESG as an outcome' | Key Institutional Developments |
|---|---|
| • ESG investing expands across asset classes<br>• Expansion of ESG data and reporting to better quantify ESG factors<br>• Greater focus on 'intentional' outcomes and impact measurement<br>• In 2015, DOL reversed its 2008 guidance, which 'unduly discouraged fiduciaries from considering [economically targeted investments] and ESG factors.'<br>• Heightened investor urgency around climate change as COP 21 establishes the Paris Agreement, aiming to limit global warming<br>• EU issues a series of sustainable investing guidelines and regulations | • UK Stewardship Code launched (2010)<br>• Global Initiative for Sustainability Ratings/GISR (2011)<br>• Sustainability Accounting Standards Board (2011)<br>• Investment Leaders Group/ILG (2013)<br>• Japan Stewardship Code launched (2014)<br>• Taskforce on Climate Related Financial Disclosure/TCFD (2015)<br>• UN Sustainable Development Goals/SDGs (2015/2016)<br>• Investor Stewardship Group/ISG (2017)<br>• Impact Management Project (2017)<br>• International Finance Corporation (IFC)<br>• Operating Principles for Impact Mgt (2019)<br>• 'Green Deal' disclosure requirements and quality labels (2019) |

*Source*: Authors' calculations.

focus on 'prudential measures' that would integrate ESG risk factors into investments and financial firm solvency (Ingman 2020). It also developed corporate 'conduct' legislation, for example the *Non-Financial Reporting Directive*, which required larger EU corporations, starting in 2017, to disclose data on their firm's impact on ESG and vice versa (EC 2014). Other examples include EC's *Action Plan: Financing Sustainable Growth* (EC 2018b), which clarified institutional investors' and asset managers' duties, incorporated sustainability into the suitability assessment of financial instruments, and increased transparency of sustainability benchmarks. Similarly, *The European Green Deal* (EC 2019b) and *The Proposal for a European Climate Law* (EC nd) were intended, among other objectives, to reorient capital flows toward sustainable investment in order to achieve sustainable and inclusive growth; limit global warming; manage financial risks stemming from climate change, environmental degradation, and social issues; and foster transparency and long-termism in financial and economic activity. The European Commission also examined and made recommendations for government investments, including pensions (EC 2018a, 2018b).

In addition to these initiatives, there was a near-explosion of similar developments by independent, industry, and quasi-governmental organizations to construct ESG frameworks, guidelines, and standards (see Figure 2.2). Of

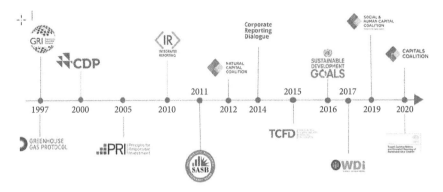

**Figure 2.2** Evolution of international ESG frameworks, guidelines, and standards, 1997–2020

*Source*: EC (2020a).

the 12 such initiatives in the figure, nine appeared between 2010 and 2020. It should be noted that while these initiatives reflected growing interest in ESG investing and integration of ESG, many of them were produced independently from the others and so contributed to confusion regarding just what investors should consider to be ESG and how to implement it. In that vein, in this period a number of private data and analytics providers began or continued major projects to identify, define, and measure ESG factors pertinent to investment risk and return and sell the results to investors, with an increasing emphasis on integrating these factors into organized ratings systems (see also Lee 2023). In addition, a number of firms launched or added formal securities indexes that could be used by investors interested in forming integrated ESG portfolios.

Several other indicators give us a picture of ESG growth and integration in this period. In particular, the left panel of Figure 2.3 shows the change in US shareholder support for formal environmental and social proxy proposals, compared to governance and compensation proposals. In 2010, over 60 percent of governance and compensation proposals, but only 12 percent of environmental and social proposals, received more than 30 percent of the total votes cast. By 2018, environmental and social proposals received over 35 percent of the votes cast. The right panel of Figure 2.3 also shows the change in support for environmental and social proxy proposals. Median support rose from about 10 percent in 2010 to just under 25 percent in 2018. The right panel also documents the increase of UN PRI institutional signatories from about 60 in 2010 to over 400 in 2018.

The trend toward integration and systematizing ESG is continuing in the 2020s. ESG data and reporting continue to deepen, with a greater focus

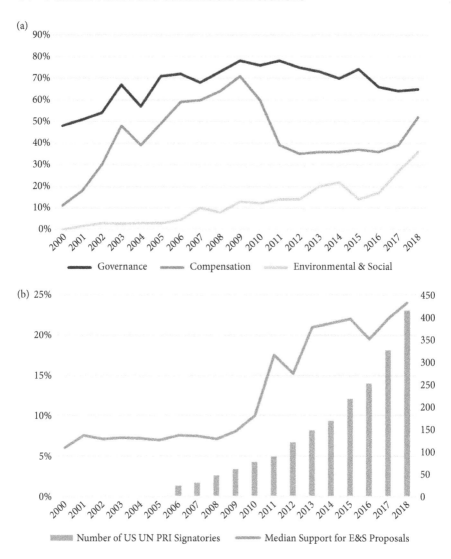

**Figure 2.3** Environmental and social issues join the mainstream among shareholders

*Source*: Papadopoulos (2019), p. 7 (fig. 3A) and p. 3 (fig. 3B).

on intentional outcomes and impact measurement. For example, in 2021, the US DOL announced that it intended to return to an earlier view of the prudent investment rule followed by pensions and other fiduciaries. Specifically, fiduciaries are now asked to consider all factors that affect investors'

TABLE 2.8  ESG in the 2020s

| 'ESG as a system' | Key Institutional Developments |
|---|---|
| • Expansion of ESG data and reporting to better quantify ESG factors<br>• Greater focus on 'intentional' outcomes and impact measurement<br>• COVID-19 and racial equity issues spur renewed emphasis on 'S'<br>• Increased scrutiny and global regulation to combat 'greenwashing' | • Capital Group, TIAA, Blackrock, and other asset managers go 'all ESG' (2020)<br>• US DOL rules that fiduciaries may only consider financial factors in investing (2020)<br>• US DOL announces it will not enforce the rule (2021)<br>• EU announces its plan for company ESG reporting and investor compliance (2021) |

*Source*: Authors' calculations.

portfolios and financial risks, including ESG factors (US DOL 2021) (see Table 2.8).

In the European Union, the EC has launched a project substantiating 'green claims,' with the intention of reducing 'greenwashing' by companies who are trying to appear to be improving their ESG scores but avoiding substantive reforms (EC 2020d). Additional EC initiatives have showcased a willingness to allow ESG a central role within the legislative process, including a circular economy action plan (EC 2020a), the food system (EC 2020c), climate (EC 2020f), and additional disclosures (EC 2019a). Most recently, the EC presented its new Sustainable Finance Package, intended to help improve the flow of money toward sustainable activities across the European Union, including proposals for new corporate sustainability reporting and revisions to previous rules for sustainability reporting and assessments (EC 2020b, 2021). Finally, pensions and other institutional investors have continued to boost commitments to ESG investing. For instance, the Capital Group (2021), TIAA, (Segal 2021), BlackRock (Williamson 2020), and other asset managers have announced plans to go 'all-ESG' and achieve future carbon neutrality in their investments.

## Looking Ahead: Challenges for Pensions

Four forces are leading to the convergence of E, S, and G for pension managers, along with the integration of sustainable considerations into asset owners' and asset managers' investment processes: economic transformation and accompanying social movements; the emergence of universal owners; stakeholders and small shareholders; and improved information and analysis. Despite these trends, convergence and integration will remain incomplete for several reasons that highlight challenges and directions for pensions and other institutions.

## Goals and objectives

As we have seen, pension sponsors and their asset managers have increasingly recognized their roles as representing participants in universal ownership of public companies. There is less agreement on specific goals and objectives, often summarized as fiduciary responsibility. One remaining question regards the extent to which *sustainability conflicts with returns*; that is, how does sustainability conform to regulations requiring pensions to invest prudently on behalf of participants? Reflecting continuing confusion on this issue, the late 2020 US Department of Labor requirement that pensions must focus on returns and, by implication, that ESG considerations reduced returns, was rescinded by a new Administration in early 2021. We believe that it is likely that the US will eventually follow the European view that sustainability can affect investment risk, and that proper fiduciary responsibility must balance sustainability risks with return.

Even with such a resolution, other questions remain, including, for example, the time dimension, or how much one should be willing to *sacrifice short-term return to achieve long-term benefits*. For example, an institutional investor may believe that a company with good short-term profit potential is undervalued, but that its long-term prospects are less attractive because of the nature of its business (e.g., tobacco or fossil fuels). Which is the better strategy: to avoid the company altogether, or own the company in the short run and determine when to sell it?

A third issue has to do with *participant heterogeneity*. Pensions and other financial institutions act for all participants and shareholders, but they need not all agree across all issues. One participant's negative, such as owning alcohol distributors or military suppliers, may be another's positive, and these differences may reflect both assessments of negative and positive externalities, as well as emotional positions. In either case, they pose challenges for investment institutions in setting responsive policies. One interim approach is to focus on ESG issues that gain wide approval among participants and shareholders, such as we saw in South Africa divestiture, and currently in long-term policies to reduce exposure to fossil fuels.

A fourth issue is other *organizational constraints*, including regulatory and other stakeholder concerns, affecting pension and institutional ownership. One such example is the series of EU regulations issued over the past decade under the sustainability banner. On the stakeholder side, unions, advocacy groups, and others using ownership stakes, shareholder meetings, and other mechanisms to pressure asset owners and managers are likely to continue encouraging investment institutions to focus on their preferred goals and objectives. Yet constraints can also work in the other direction. For instance, in Japan, while the Government Pension Investment Fund has established environment-oriented investment programs and criteria, it has not done the same with respect to governance and social issues to date. We speculate that this may be connected to the interests and views of some of the largest domestic public companies.

## Analytical tools

There is far from universal agreement on how to evaluate environmental, social, and governance factors important to company disclosure practices, performance standards, and investment evaluation. For disclosure, governments such as the EU and independent organizations such as the Sustainability Accounting Standards Board (SASB) are calling for more and better standardized company disclosure. Others, such as the International Organization of Securities Commissions (IOSCO), focus on performance standards to determine which activities can be considered more versus less sustainable (Eccles 2021a). In addition, we note that a wide variety of metrics have been developed over the past several decades, and these do not always agree on what factors to consider, how to define those factors precisely, and what weight should be given to each factor (e.g., Lee 2023). On the one hand, a lack of agreement provides opportunities for one investor with superior resources and skill to do a better job of securities analysis. On the other hand, analytical heterogeneity can limit or provide conflicting signals to companies as to what is expected of them regarding sustainable practices. Moreover, the design and choice of a measurement system reflects the sponsor's sustainability goals and objectives, which, as we have seen, vary by institution. One can imagine that information users—institutional owners, government overseers, activists, and others—will eventually be able to agree on disclosure standards. Nevertheless, the largest universal owners will likely continue to refer to one or more widely available ESG measurement approaches, as well as their own proprietary metrics, for identifying and incorporating ESG considerations in securities analysis and portfolio construction.

## Institutional shareholder initiatives

There is also general agreement on the benefits of, and necessity for, universal owners to give voice to sustainability improvements in the companies they own. Nevertheless, there is less agreement on how to do so, and how interventionist to be, ranging from proxy voting, private communications, and initiating shareholder resolutions, to public campaigns, lobbying, and lawsuits. TIAA and other institutions have pioneered programs that operate on all these levels, and more universal owners may use these models as templates for their own engagement activities.

## Global standards and practices

As we have seen, pensions and other financial institutions must operate within systems that include a variety of other powerful government and non-government actors. Regional and national regulators, both public (e.g., EU or US DOL) and private (e.g., SASB, FASB), are encouraging and/or requiring a consistent approach to accounting and disclosure, along with other practices that promise to affect sustainable behavior, both by companies and pensions. Other quasi-government (e.g., UN PRI) and non-governmental organizations will also, no doubt, continue to be active in promoting sustainability. And policies, practices, and levels of activism still vary across countries and regions. While international treaties and organizational initiatives such as the UN PRI have made substantial contributions to increased consistency, policies and practices are unlikely to completely converge without additional international-level enforcement, either through peer pressure or actual regulation. Also, an open question remains as to who will be the final arbiter of international standards, practices, and behavior. Some have argued that investors should not be the final arbiter of corporate behavior (Eccles 2021b).

## Implications for Pensions

In sum, while we can see movement toward convergence and integration among pensions and other institutional investors, there are forces or reasons why these developments are not yet, nor may not soon be, complete. We close with an assessment of the outstanding questions.

### Does further ESG progress require all investors to be on the same page?

While pension investing is increasingly global, pension plans serve participants in specific countries, and in some cases, occupations or industrial sectors. This diversity of beneficiaries is likely to mean that specific ESG objectives and motivations will continue to vary. For example, while most appreciate the implications of global climate change, even there, impacts, concerns, and programs differ across regions and populations. Accordingly, complete convergence may be impossible or undesirable.

Similarly, integration of ESG considerations into all investments may be a goal for some investors, but not for others. The TIAA experience, for example, suggests that some participants would like 100 percent of their investments to be driven by ESG criteria, while others favor less weight on ESG criteria. Progress can be achieved in a world with many actors—governments, pensions, other institutional investors, advocacy groups, etc.—and many tools for advancing ESG. In fact, such a world can encourage innovation and adaptation, if not always complete coordination.

## Who will make decisions?

As noted above, full national and international convergence is unlikely regarding ESG disclosure, what data should be evaluated and how, and how to integrate this information into investment and engagement decisions. Pensions operate in a multilayered system where multiple public actors at the international, national, and local levels can claim authority over ESG policies affecting investments. Furthermore, pension participants, other shareholders, and other stakeholders in both the nonprofit and profit arenas can also claim an interest in investment decisions, as we saw in the latter half of the twentieth century. For instance, one could imagine that as pension assets continue to grow, particularly in China, the rest of Asia, and Latin America, those players will increasingly express their views and take action.

## Who 'owns' the big picture?

There is no global ESG regulator, though many entities including governments and independent agencies all have a voice; they also cooperate as well as compete to set the ESG framework and guide action. This includes international pension consortia and even the very largest asset managers (e.g., BlackRock). To date it is unclear whether an effective global ESG ecosystem is necessary for the continued evolution of the investment industry, and if it is, who can direct such an ecosystem?

## What is the next unifying issue after climate change?

In the modern ESG era, climate change has been the topic that has generated the most interest and agreement among asset owners, managers, and other investors. Given that addressing climate change requires committing resources to analysis, as well as large and sustained public and private action, it will continue to be the most visible ESG issue for the foreseeable future.

Nevertheless, other ESG issues may also be candidates for unifying action, including what is now called economic equality (or inequality). Discussion of the equality issue goes back to the nineteenth century with concerns about workers, families, and consumers, along with regulation and social programs to address these problems. Interest in economic equality has waxed and waned over the decades, but it has now reemerged with proposals to improve working conditions, raise children out of poverty, and reduce the nearly unprecedented gap between the rich and the poor populations. Increasing economic equality is not exclusively a challenge for government and nonprofit organizations, since companies also play a role through wages and benefits, working conditions, supply chain design, and environmental and investment policies. For this reason, one can imagine that proposals and programs to address inequality engage companies in the future.

In any case, while these challenges remain, pensions and other asset owners can benefit from knowledge and experience gained from the evolution of ESG, deeper analytical and organizational resources, a more robust set of tools and initiatives, support (and constraints) from government and non-governmental organizations, and considerably more agreement among investors on goals and objectives. We anticipate that pensions will need to draw on these resources to address ESG concerns, both existing and emerging.

# Appendix

## 'Pre-Modern' Era in Selected Countries

### United States

The Progressive and Depression Eras' reaction to concentrated wealth and the negative externalities of industrialization did not just result in new government social, economic, and health protections for consumers, small businesses, and employees, such as strong regulatory agencies and support for strong unions and emergence of pensions. Later, government acted to require companies to provide pensions and to pay for publicly managed unemployment insurance. Notably, this period also produced protections for small shareholders, including major anti-monopoly policies, and court decisions that largely eliminated family pyramidal ownership structures, separated commercial from investment banking and limited the ability of banks, insurance companies, pensions, and mutual funds to take a controlling interest in other companies (Becht and DeLong 2005). It did not, however, solve the agency problem, as hired managers directed company activities, with oversight by a board whose members were effectively chosen by management and approved through votes by dispersed shareholders. By the latter half of the twentieth century, most public companies featured a relatively high degree of managerial control and a relatively low degree of shareholder influence.

### Germany

Worker and shareholder protections, as well as social programs, began in the late nineteenth century in Germany, with Bismarckian legislation establishing the first health insurance, publicly sponsored pensions and unemployment insurance, and union protections. These developments helped reduce negative externalities borne by workers and their families, and they enabled workers to band together to negotiate with corporate management. Nevertheless, as in the UK, France, and other countries, these initiatives were not driven by investor actions, but rather by workers themselves pressuring government and, through unions, companies (Fohlin 2005).

In contrast, investors were more influential in German corporate governance, as Germany mandated a form of uniform accounting and reporting rules and a dual corporate board structure that prohibited overlapping members, features that exist today. However, German banks could still collect and vote proxies of shareholders of companies underwritten by those banks, and companies themselves issued additional share classes favoring family control. Consequently, the larger banks and prominent families controlled an increasing percentage of the German stock market. Notably and perhaps remarkably, in 1938 a Nazi law was the first in the world to explicitly assign corporate responsibility to all stakeholders, not just shareholders. However, family owners responded by shifting away from special share classes to a pyramidal ownership structure (Fohlin 2005). Today, while diminished, German corporate governance continues to reflect bank and family control of companies.

## United Kingdom

In the UK, early social programs were also the result of worker pressure on government and, again through unions, on corporations, after the voting franchise was expanded several times in the nineteenth century. The original UK corporate structure was through grants of monopoly from the central government. In the late nineteenth century, not long after the first shareholder protections in Germany, UK legislation requiring greater company disclosure and making company directors liable for prospectus statements were both thought to have influenced a decline in family ownership of firms while supporting shareholder rights (Franks et al. 2005). Importantly, in the name of employee and consumer protection, government ownership of prominent industries advanced during WWII and then reversed in the 1980s, with the Thatcher government's emphasis on shareholder rather than governmental control. By the late twentieth century, UK corporate governance came to resemble more closely the US version, with strong management, a somewhat weaker board, dispersed ownership, and regulatory oversight.

## France

With a long history of financial market crises, France relied relatively little on banks and the stock market as it industrialized. Instead, both France and Italy followed the pattern in Germany and the UK, where investors were not instrumental in demanding social reforms. Firms tended to finance new investment largely out of earnings, thus favoring family control, which was further encouraged through inheritance laws as well as close government connections with family members. Like the UK, following WWII the French government took a controlling interest of major industries, such as transport, energy, and others, in order to promote employee and consumer interests. It also established a dual board structure with worker representation on the supervisory board. As in the UK, the French government later divested some of its industrial holdings, but maintains some of the strongest worker protections of any industrial country (Murphy 2005).

## Italy

Italy's major banks collapsed in the early 1930s, after which the central government assumed ownership and separated investment from commercial banking. Similar to the UK and France, after WWII the government owned and directed investment in capital intensive industries, propped up failing firms and used industrial policy to support development in southern Italy. It also supported the rise of family-controlled firms through the provision of capital and a lack of regulatory objections. Many family firms remained privately owned, while publicly traded companies were family-owned pyramids. By the 1990s, rising debt loads and poor performance among government-owned firms forced a round of privatization and more dispersed shareholding, giving rise to demands for better shareholder protections (Aganin and Volpin 2005).

## The Netherlands

The Netherlands has the oldest stock market in the world, but by the nineteenth century its development lagged due to a hangover from a series of bubbles and crises and a French-influenced aversion to bank financing. As in France, family-owned firms predominated, with financing from retained earnings. In the twentieth century, the use of public shares and long-term bank loans grew as family dominance gave way to management control. Although Dutch firms are required to have a two-tier board structure, shareholders had little say in board membership. Moreover, interlocking directorates, super- and preference-voting shares, income trusts, and other measures reinforced management control. While workers were not as influential in the Netherlands as in Germany, they did have a voice, both in corporate policies and through government worker protections. For example, industry-based funded pensions proliferated after WWII (CEPS 1995).

## Japan

After emerging from self-imposed isolation from the international economic system in the late nineteenth century, Japan's government worked to catch up by funding the development of major firms, which were then consolidated into large family-controlled conglomerates. In the 1930s, the military took effective control of these firms, but after WWII, the US wrested control away from government and families to create widespread ownership. However, in response to takeover fears, Japan's large public firms developed the system of persistent interlocking cross corporate holdings. Social benefit programs began for the military at the turn of the century, and over the years expanded to other employment sectors, so that by the 1970s health insurance was universal and retirement was supported by a combination of public and private insurance. Unions were not a strong force in this period.

## Notes

1. A pyramid ownership structure separates rights to a firm's cash flows from voting rights. In this case, a family uses a firm where it has controlling interest to set up one or more firms controlled by the first company, but with dispersed stock ownership as well. The first firm can capture a large percentage of the new firms' revenues but leave any losses at the level of the new firms. In this way the family can access the entire amount of the retained earnings of the first company, which can include the captured firms' revenues.
2. In 2005, the IRRC was sold to Institutional Shareholder Services and the IRRC Institute, a research center now housed at the University of Delaware, was created with the proceeds.
3. In particular, see SEC 17 CFR 240.14a-8 rule governing shareholder proposals. An explanation can be found from the Legal Information Institute (2021).
4. Based on authors' interviews with current and former staff of CalPRS, CalSTRS, and TIAA-CREF.

# References

Aganin, A. and P. Volpin (2005). 'A History of Corporate Ownership in Italy.' In R.K. Morck, ed., *A History of Corporate Governance around the World: Family Business Groups to Professional Managers*. Cambridge: NBER, pp. 325–366. https://www.nber.org/books-and-chapters/history-corporate-governance-around-world-family-business-groups-professional-managers/history-corporate-ownership-italy.

Becht, M. and B. DeLong (2005). 'Why Has There Been So Little Block Holding in the US?' In R.K. Morck, ed., *A History of Corporate Governance around the World: Family Business Groups to Professional Managers*. Cambridge: NBER, pp. 613–666. https://www.nber.org/system/files/chapters/c10278/c10278.pdf.

Berle, A.A. and G.C. Means (1967). *The Modern Corporation and Private Property*, 2nd edn. New York: Harcourt, Brace and World.

Capital Group (2021). *Our ESG Approach*. Los Angeles, CA: Capital Group. https://www.capitalgroup.com/institutional/about-us/esg/esg-approach.html.

CEPS 1995. *Corporate Governance in Europe*. Brussels: Centre for European Policy Studies. https://ecgi.global/download/file/fid/9359.

CII (2021). About CII. Washington, DC: Council of Institutional Investors. https://www.cii.org/about.

Clark, G.L. and T.M. Hebb (2004). 'Pension Fund Corporate Engagement: The Fifth Stage of Capitalism,' *Relations Industrielles/Industrial Relations*, 59(1): 142–169. https://ssrn.com/abstract=1661280.

Domini, A., P. Kinder, and S. Lydenberg (1992). *Social Investment Almanac*. New York: Henry Holt & Co.

EC (2014). Non-Financial Reporting Directive, 2014/95/EU. Brussels: European Commission. https://eur-lex.europa.eu/legal-content/EN/TXT/PDF/?uri=CELEX:32014L0095&from=EN.

EC (2018a). Study on State Asset Management in the EU, B-1049. Brussels: European Commission. https://ec.europa.eu/info/sites/info/files/economy-finance/dg_ecfin_am_final_report_pillar_1_eu28_summary_report.pdf.

EC (2018b). Action Plan: Financing Sustainable Growth. Brussels: European Commission. https://eur-lex.europa.eu/legal-content/EN/TXT/PDF/?uri=CELEX:52018DC0097&from=EN.

EC (2019a). Regulation on Sustainability-Related Disclosures, 2019/2088. Brussels: European Commission. https://eur-lex.europa.eu/legal-content/EN/TXT/PDF/?uri=CELEX:32019R2088&from=EN.

EC (2019b). The European Green Deal, COM(2019) 640 final. Brussels: European Commission. https://eur-lex.europa.eu/resource.html?uri=cellar:b828d165-1c22-11ea-8c1f-01aa75ed71a1.0002.02/DOC_1&format=PDF.

EC (2020a). *A New Circular Economy Action Plan for a Cleaner and More Competitive Europe*. COM(2020) 98 final. Brussels: European Commission.

EC (2020b). Study on Sustainability Ratings, Data and Research. Directorate-General for Financial Stability, Financial Services and Capital Markets Union. Brussels: European Commission. https://op.europa.eu/en/publication-detail/-/publication/d7d85036-509c-11eb-b59f-01aa75ed71a1/language-en/format-PDF/source-183474104.

EC (2020c). Farm to Fork Strategy. Brussels: European Commission. https://ec.europa.eu/food/horizontal-topics/farm-fork-strategy_en.

EC (2020d). Initiative on Substantiating Green Claims: Stakeholder Workshops. Brussels: European Commission. https://ec.europa.eu/environment/eussd/smgp/initiative_on_green_claims.htm.

EC (2020e). REGULATION OF THE EUROPEAN PARLIAMENT AND OF THE COUNCIL on establishing the framework for achieving climate neutrality and amending Regulation (EU) 2018/1999 (European Climate Law). COM(2020) 563 final. Brussels: European Commission. https://eur-lex.europa.eu/legal-content/EN/TXT/PDF/?uri=CELEX:52020PC0563&from=EN.

EC (2020f). European Climate Pact. Brussels: European Commission https://ec.europa.eu/clima/policies/eu-climate-action/pact_en.

EC (2021). Summary Report of the Stakeholder Consultation on the Renewed Sustainable Finance Strategy. Brussels: European Commission. https://ec.europa.eu/info/sites/default/files/business_economy_euro/banking_and_finance/documents/2020-sustainable-finance-strategy-summary-of-responses_en.pdf.

EC (nd). *European Climate Law*. Brussels: European Commission. https://ec.europa.eu/clima/policies/eu-climate-action/law_en.

Eccles, R. (2021a). 'The U.S. Struggle Over Climate-Change Disclosure Is Coming to a (Hopefully Successful) Head,' *Forbes*, February 28. https://www.forbes.com/sites/bobeccles/2021/02/28/the-us-struggle-over-climate-change-disclosure-is-coming-to-a-hopefully-successful-head/.

Eccles, R. (2021b). 'The International Sustainability Standards Board as an Intellectual Rorschach Test,' *Forbes*, July 13. https://www.forbes.com/sites/bobeccles/2021/07/13/the-international-sustainability-standards-board-as-an-ideological-rorschach-test/?sh=56cc04e63a6e.

Fohlin, C. (2005). 'The History of Corporate Ownership and Control in Germany.' In R.K. Morck, ed., *A History of Corporate Governance around the World: Family Business Groups to Professional Managers*. Cambridge: NBER, pp. 223–282. https://www.nber.org/books-and-chapters/history-corporate-governance-around-world-family-business-groups-professional-managers/history-corporate-ownership-and-control-germany.

Franks, J., C. Mayer, and S. Rossi (2005). 'Spending Less Time with the Family: Decline of Family Ownership in the U.K.' In R.K. Morck, ed., *A History of Corporate Governance around the World: Family Business Groups to Professional Managers*. Cambridge: NBER, pp. 581–612. https://www.nber.org/books-and-chapters/history-corporate-governance-around-world-family-business-groups-professional-managers/spending-less-time-family-decline-family-ownership-united-kingdom.

Friedman, M.A. (1970). 'The Social Responsibility of Business Is to Increase Its Profits,' *The New York Times*, September 13. https://www.nytimes.com/1970/09/13/archives/a-friedman-doctrine-the-social-responsibility-of-business-is-to.html.

GPIF (2020). *Stewardship Activities Report 2019–2020*. March. Tokyo: Government Pension Investment Fund.

GRI (2021). *Our Mission and History*. Amsterdam, The Netherlands: Global Reporting Initiative. https://www.globalreporting.org/about-gri/mission-history/

Hall, M., T. Hodgson, R. Urwin, and L. Yin (2020). *Top 100 Asset Owners: The Most Influential Capital on the Planet,* November. Arlington, VA: Thinking Ahead Institute, Willis Towers Watson.

ICGN (International Corporate Governance Network) (2021). About. London: ICGN. https://www.icgn.org/about.

Ingman, B.C. (2020). 'ESG Regulation: Where to Start,' *FACTSET,* April 29. https://insight.factset.com/esg-regulation-where-to-start.

J&J Credo (1943). *Johnson & Johnson.* https://www.jnj.com/credo/.

Lee, L.E. (2023). 'ESG Investing: Financial Materiality and Social Objectives.' In P.B. Hammond, R. Maurer, and O.S. Mitchell, eds., *Pension Funds and Sustainable Investment: Challenges and Opportunities.* Oxford: Oxford University Press, pp. 82–101.

Legal Information Institute (2021). 17 CFR 240.14a.-8 Shareholder Proposals, Cornell Law School. https://www.law.cornell.edu/cfr/text/17/240.14a-8.

McRitchie, J. (2020). *Corporate Governance Defined: Not So Easy.* Corporate Governance, December, CorpGov.net. https://www.corpgov.net/library/corporate-governance-defined/.

Morck, R.K., ed. (2005). *A History of Corporate Governance around the World: Family Business Groups to Professional Managers.* Cambridge, MA: NBER. https://www.nbcr.org/system/files/chapters/c10267/c10267.pdf.

Murphy, A. (2005). 'Corporate Governance in France: The Importance of History.' In R.K. Morck, ed., *A History of Corporate Governance around the World: Family Business Groups to Professional Managers.* Cambridge, MA: NBER, pp. 182–222. https://www.nber.org/books-and-chapters/history-corporate-governance-around-world-family-business-groups-professional-managers/corporate-ownership-france-importance-history.

Roddan, M. (2021) 'Industry Super drives increase in ESG Support,' Financial Review, September 7. https://www.afr.com/companies/financial-services/industry-super-drives-increase-in-esg-support-20210906-p58p50.

Segal, M. (2021). 'TIAA Set Net Zero Emission Commitment for $280 Billion Investment Account,' ESG Today, May 12. https://www.esgtoday.com/tiaa-set-net-zero-emissions-commitment-for-280-billion-investment-account/.

TIAA (2021). *Responsible Investing.* New York: TIAA. https://www.tiaa.org/public/about-tiaa/how-we-help/how-we-invest/responsible-investing.

UN (1992). United Nations Framework Convention on Climate Change. New York: UN. https://unfccc.int/resource/docs/convkp/conveng.pdf.

UN (2015). Paris Agreement. New York: UN. https://unfccc.int/files/meetings/paris_nov_2015/application/pdf/paris_agreement_english_.pdf.

UN PRI (United Nations Principles for Responsible Investment) (2020). *Enhance Our Global Footprint. In the PRI Annual Report 2020.* London: UN PRI. https://www.unpri.org/annual-report-2020/how-we-work/building-our-effectiveness/enhance-our-global-footprint.

UN PRI. (2021a). What is Responsible Invesment? United Nations Principles for Responsible Investment. London: UN PRI. https://www.unpri.org/an-introduction-to-responsible-investment/what-is-responsible-investment/4780.article.

UN PRI. (2021b). What are the Principles for Responsible Investment? London: UN PRI. https://www.unpri.org/pri/what-are-the-principles-for-responsible-investment.

Urwin, R. (2011). 'Pension Funds as Universal Owners: Opportunity Beckons and Leadership Calls,' *Rotman International Journal of Pension Management*, 4(1): 26–34.

Urwin, R. (2019). *The 4-3-2-1 Pin Code for a More Sustainable Economy.* Arlington, VA: Thinking Ahead Institute, Willis Towers Watson.

US DOL. (2021). 'US Department of Labor Statement on Enforcement of Its Final Rules on ESG Investments and Proxy Voting by Employee Benefit Plans,' March 10. Washington, DC: US DOL. https://www.dol.gov/sites/dolgov/files/ebsa/laws-and-regulations/laws/erisa/statement-on-enforcement-of-final-rules-on-esg-investments-and-proxy-voting.pdf.

US SIF (Sustainable Investing Forum) (2020). Report on US Sustainable and Impact Investing Trends. November 16. Washington, DC: US SIF. https://www.ussif.org/trends.

Weinberg Center. (2021). 'The Weinberg Center and the IRRC Institute,' John L. Weinberg Center for Corporate Governance, University of Delaware. https://www.weinberg.udel.edu/irrci/about.

Williamson, C. (2020). 'BlackRock Is All in on Firmwide Sustainability,' *Pensions & Investments*, January 27. https://www.pionline.com/esg/blackrock-all-firmwide-sustainability.

# Chapter 3

# The Origins of ESG in Pensions

Strategies and Outcomes

*Stéphanie Lachance and Judith C. Stroehle*

On November 23, 2020, the CEOs of the eight largest Canadian pension funds—the so-called 'Maple 8'—made a public pledge about their commitment to 'creating more sustainable and inclusive growth by integrating environmental, social and governance (ESG) factors into our strategies and investment decisions.' Arguing that this was not only the correct thing to do, they also stated that this 'is an integral part of our duty to contributors and beneficiaries [which] will unlock opportunities [. . . and] deliver long-term risk-adjusted returns' (PSP Investments 2020a: 1). A similar open letter was issued only six months earlier, in March 2020, by the then-leaders of three of the world's largest pension funds: the California State Teachers' Retirement System (CalSTRS), the Japanese Government Pension Investment Fund (GPIF), and the largest UK pension fund, the Universities Superannuation Scheme (USS). Here, the three giants outlined that 'if we were to focus purely on the short-term returns, we would be ignoring potentially catastrophic systemic risks to our portfolio,' and underlined how 'asset managers that only focus on short-term, explicitly financial measures, and ignore longer-term sustainability-related risks and opportunities are not attractive partners for us' (GPIF 2020: 1).

These statements tell us that pension funds can have many good reasons to embrace a sustainability lens in their investment practice, and that they are increasingly—and publicly—willing to do so. A main driver of the move to embrace ESG in pensions is the inherent need for long-term managers of corporate risks and opportunities to live up to their responsibilities as intergenerational stewards of capital. Nevertheless, the particular structure of pension funds creates both advantages and disadvantages for the adoption of sustainable finance practices and the integration of ESG. While asset owners are often hailed as the ultimate enablers of a sustainable transition on the financial market,[1] in many instances, pension funds do not live up to this expectation. In particular, pension managers must consider how

Stéphanie Lachance and Judith C. Stroehle, *The Origins of ESG in Pensions*. In: *Pension Funds and Sustainable Investment*. Edited by P. Brett Hammond, Raimond Maurer, and Olivia S. Mitchell, Oxford University Press. © Stéphanie Lachance and Judith C. Stroehle (2023). DOI: 10.1093/oso/9780192889195.003.0003 to include ESG, given their primary mandate and fiduciary duty to secure long-term financial returns for their beneficiaries. Accordingly, pension managers seeking to integrate ESG must operate within a web of pension regulation, the legal interpretation of fiduciary duty, and the organizational characteristics of pensions.

To analyze these institutional and organizational enablers and inhibiters of ESG integration in pension funds, we employ the notion of 'social origins' (Eccles and Stroehle 2018; Eccles et al. 2019) in our review of the historical and structural characteristics of the pension sector. Social origins are defined as a combination of the historical and organizational origins of actors that condition the social construction and use of often-vague concepts, such as ESG, within them. In our analysis, we mostly focus on large public and private sector pension funds. By drawing on existing literature and primary interview data, we seek to identify the characteristics and capabilities of these funds that help or impede them in contributing to a larger sustainability agenda within their mandate. To do so, we focus on three levels of analysis: *the institutional level*, which discusses historical and regulatory policy embedded within the interpretation of fiduciary duty; *the organizational level*, which reviews how investment mandates are translated into policies, governance structures, and collaborations; and *the portfolio level*, which reviews investment strategies and asset allocation, relationships with asset managers, and pension funds' stewardship activities. While drawing on the larger literature about sustainability in pension funds, we focus our review on the pension systems in Canada, the US, and the UK. An in-depth case study of the Canadian Public Sector Pension Investment Board ('PSP Investments' or 'PSP') supplements this structural comparison with more detailed and practical insights.

Ultimately, our question is: what is it that makes these funds so well-positioned to drive a wider integration of ESG, and why is this potential only partly being realized to date? Accordingly, our research seeks to draw attention to both the potential that pension funds have in disseminating good practice in the wider investment community, and the inhibiting factors relevant to this system.

## Pensions in the Twenty-First Century

A growing body of literature discusses how and why ESG is a potentially important source of information for the investment decisions made by pension funds. Much of this debate frames ESG as a tool that helps address the growing risks that have arisen globally, such as climate change and income inequality, alongside the realization that sustainability-related systems-level challenges can and will have a material impact on market financial stability. The integration of ESG factors in investment decision-making is then meant to hedge against this risk, while at the same time being potentially able to identify companies with a higher growth and performance potential (Bender et al. 2018).

To verify this, studies have reviewed the use of ESG in pensions' asset allocation strategies (Hawley and Lukomnik 2018; Alda 2019), their fiduciary duty and responsibility toward beneficiaries (Hoepner et al. 2011; Ambachtsheer and Bauer 2013; Bird and Gray 2013), their different schemes (Hoepner et al. 2011), and their investment horizons (Ambachtsheer 2014; Kecskés et al. 2020). Since many pension funds manage their assets, at least in part, externally, there is also a growing interest in how ESG features in pension funds' mandates to their asset managers (ICGN 2012). Furthermore, the relationship between pensions and sustainability is also considered in broader debates such as the universal ownership thesis (Monks and Minow 2004; Urwin 2011; Quigley 2019a, 2019b), moral relativism (Eabrasu 2018), collective action (Woods 2011; Gond and Piani 2013), the politicization of investors (Clark and Monk 2011) and in debates around the tragedy of the commons (Kiernan 2007).

In parallel to the increasing importance of ESG, two important structural developments have influenced the pension industry. Firstly, the size of pension funds has grown significantly since the 1990s, correspondingly expanding the influence these funds have on the larger economy (Johnson and De Graaf 2009). Secondly, many funds are transitioning from defined-benefit (DB) to defined-contribution (DC) plans (Fabian et al. 2023). Both developments have important implications for a potential integration of ESG.

## The size of pension funds

According to a study of the Thinking Ahead Institute in 2020,[2] the value of assets under management in the pension funds of the 22 major retirement countries were on average equivalent to 62 percent of the GDP of their home countries. In Canada, the UK, and the US, these numbers are even higher, with 90.5 percent, 108.7 percent and 85.8 percent respectively in 2019,[3] highlighting just how important pension saving is in these markets. Globally, pension funds are worth just over US$50 trillion. In terms of equity holdings, pension funds in the US held shares representing approximately 21 percent of the US equity market and 11 percent of global equities. Canadian and UK pension funds held shares equivalent to approximately 19 percent and 8 percent, respectively, of their national equity markets value.[4]

Due to their size, pension funds have an important and expanding influence on the capital markets (Johnson and de Graaf 2009), and are often described as the archetype of universal ownership. This is particularly true for large public sector funds (Fabian et al. 2023). Universal owners are commonly defined as large diversified institutional investors who have a long-term investment horizon (Quigley 2019a). In the ESG debate, the notion postulates that these institutions must take into account externalities, both across their (usually global) geographical portfolios, and in accordance with intergenerational equity (Urwin 2011). In line with this, Clark and Monk note that pension funds, 'by reason of their size, hold such significant stakes in the market for traded securities that portfolio diversification is not an adequate means of risk management' (2010: 1731). Academics have therefore suggested that pensions take a systems-level approach in investing (Hawley and Lukomnik 2018), to use their size for influence through active (even activist) stewardship of companies (Quigley 2019b), and to make use of their collective power in lobbying for change, both through the investment chain and at the policy level (Gond and Piani 2013).

## Transition from DB to DC

Over the last 30 years, a large majority of pension funds has shifted away from the traditional DB model, which provided benefits based on workers' salaries and lengths of service, toward DC plans, where contributions are made to investment accounts and funds are paid as benefits upon retirement (Fabian et al. 2023; Thurley and McInnes 2021). While this shift has been more marked in the private, compared to the public, sector, the trend is likely inexorable. This leads to concerns around the possibility of integrating ESG into retirement systems, as most DC plans do not offer a sustainability fund. In the US, for example, only 2.8 percent of 401(k) plans in the US offered an ESG fund on their menus as of 2018 (Plan Sponsor Council of America 2018). This is likely due to concerns about fiduciary duty and conflicting regulatory policy, both of which led to confusion about the legality of pension products incorporating ESG (Fabian et al. 2023). Since, in practice, most plan participants tend to stick with the fund into which they are defaulted when they join a plan, the creation of an ESG default option could be a useful place to start (The Pensions Regulator 2021). To date, however, ESG default options are largely non-existent in DC plans.

## ESG Strategies and Outcomes in Pension Funds

When reviewing ESG strategies and outcomes, one needs to keep in mind that the ESG concept and the underlying data are used in different ways. For instance, many believe that the inclusion of ESG in investment decisions is critical for pension funds' long-term risk management and financial sustainability, yet there is no unique pathway by which this can be accomplished.

For instance, plans may distinguish between risk-focused use of ESG, financial value-seeking ESG strategies, strategies based on normative principles, and those seeking positive social impact (Eccles and Stroehle 2018; Giese et al. 2019). Many investors will use a combination of these approaches; for instance, some could exclude morally sensitive sectors while simultaneously electing a long-term value-seeking strategy through ESG integration. Figure 3.1 provides an overview of the range of choices that investors may confront when seeking to include ESG in their investment decision-making.

Because these strategies have fundamentally different motivations, their logic can be contradictory. For example, exclusion is under heavy debate, because it has been proven to have financial downsides (Atta-Darkua et al. 2020); at the same time, there is no real proof for its effectiveness in pushing firms to act in a more sustainable manner (Kölbel et al. 2020). ESG integration, on the other hand, seeks a financial upside—an objective that can be complemented with a simultaneous exclusion strategy. Due to this, there is an increasing call to embrace stewardship and engagement, instead of exclusion as a strategy. Engagement is argued to be a more effective tool for creating behavioral changes in companies, therefore inducing both a positive impact on the world and creating a financial upside (Blitz and Swinkels 2020; Broccardo et al. 2020).

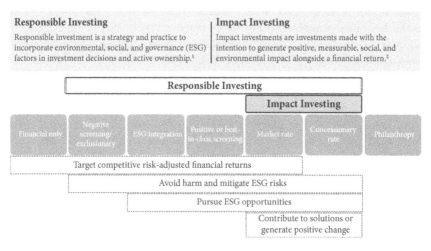

**Figure 3.1** The spectrum of choices for investors

*Source*: Authors' elaboration of Information and classification based on (1) UN PRI (2021a), and (2) GIIN (2021).

## Pension Origins and Key Characteristics for ESG Integration

Based on our literature review, numerous expert interviews we conducted (see this chapter's Appendix), and case studies, we next discuss pension fund characteristics which appear to be particularly important for the adoption of ESG practices. The three levels on which we focus are the *institutional, organizational,* and *portfolio* levels. Figure 3.2 summarizes the elements discussed.

### The institutional level

This level sets the legal boundaries to a pension fund's ability to integrate ESG. This ability stems from the historical origins of pension funds, their regulatory embeddedness, and the interpretation of fiduciary duty by the regulator. Historically, pension funds have been heavily influenced by social and political developments in their respective home countries, resulting in a diverse landscape of national pension systems around the world (Hammond and O'Brien 2023). The first pension system leads back to the German Empire in the late nineteenth century, when Chancellor Otto von Bismarck passed the Old Age and Disability Insurance Bill in 1889. In the UK, the Old Age Pensions Act of 1908 was the first piece of legislation that awarded pensioners aged 70 or above a basic allowance (Filgueira and Manzi 2017). The motivation of these early pension systems was driven

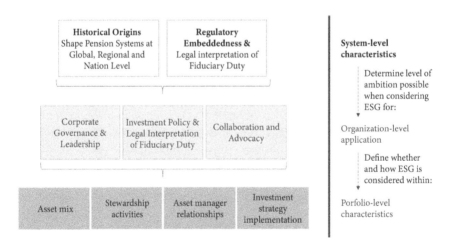

**Figure 3.2** Characteristics of pensions relevant for ESG

*Note*: This framework illustrates aspects of the institutional, organizational, and portfolio level, without a comprehensive representation of activities at each level. *Source*: Authors' elaboration.

by the Industrial Revolution and the growing importance of the working classes, which required governments to alleviate old-age poverty in light of rising life expectancies and failing familial support structures (Filgueira and Manzi 2017).

Much of today's debates around the structure and purpose of pensions, however, have their origins in the 1990s, when there was mounting uncertainty about the financial sustainability of the 'Pay-As-You-Go' public pension system in many of the OECD markets. As life expectancy rose and seniors comprised a greater share of the population, this triggered a debate about the funding of the pension plans as well as the move from DB to DC plans (Thurley and McInnes 2021). Eduard van Gelderen, Senior Vice President and Chief Investment Officer at PSP, described the shift in thinking related to this, saying that: 'there was a growing realization that pension capitalism was actually social capitalism, [...] and so early questions about stewardship and governance became questions about how to create a better world for pension plan members.'

Despite such shifts in thinking, integration of ESG-related considerations into pension fund management has made slow progress, encouraged by several national and international developments. The 2008 financial crisis, for example, gave rise to concerns about the stability of the financial market. In addition, platforms such as the United Nations (UN) Global Compact in 2000, and the UN Principles of Responsible Investing (PRI) in 2006, generated new pressure encouraging ESG considerations. In some jurisdictions, increasing stakeholder pressure also played a crucial role. In the UK, for example, several social movements accelerated the conversation around ESG in the late 1990s, where organizations such as Ethics for USS[5] specifically targeted pension funds to include environmental and social considerations into their investment decisions. As a response, USS adopted a sustainable investment policy in 1999.

Due to different historical experiences, pension regulation has evolved very differently in the three markets studied. In the US, the Employee Retirement Investment Security Act (ERISA) is cited as a challenge for pension funds seeking to integrate ESG factors, particularly in DC plans, as it gives little to no guidance on how this can be done (Fabian et al. 2023). To address this, a bill to amend ERISA was introduced by the Democrats in the Senate and House in May 2021, seeking to require that plans would have to consider ESG factors in a prudent manner consistent with their fiduciary duties (US Senate 2021). In the UK, the 2006 UK Corporate Governance Code and the 2021 UK Stewardship Code underscored the linkage of fiduciary duty and ESG as long-term risk factors. Additionally, since 2019, legislative measures from the UK Financial Conduct Authority (FCA) required pension trustees to set out in their investment policies how they include ESG considerations in investment decisions (Webb and

Brown 2019). Finally, in Canada, according to Section 78(3) of the Ontario Pension Benefits Act, Province of Ontario-governed pension plans have been required, since 2016, to state 'whether environmental, social, and governance (ESG) factors are incorporated into the plan's investment policies and procedures, and if so, how they have been incorporated.' As of now, only Ontario-governed pension plans and a few public sector pension plans have equivalent obligations. The Canadian regulatory authorities have not yet adopted the equivalent of a Canadian Stewardship Code for investment fiduciaries, but the Canadian Coalition for Good Governance,[6] an important voice on governance matters in Canada, published in 2017 seven stewardship principles that align with similar codes or principles in other countries, while reflecting on the unique nature of Canada's capital markets. These principles, supported by many large institutional investors, were intended to help institutions, investing in Canadian public equities, be active and effective stewards of their investments.

How pension plans can and want to consider ESG in investment decisions is highly dependent on the interpretation of fiduciary duty, both by the regulator and by the financial institution itself, a conclusion which regulates the relationship of a fund with its key stakeholders (Clark 2004; Clark and Monk 2011). Because pensions have a delegated authority to watch over their beneficiaries' retirement income with an intergenerational mandate, their fiduciary duty and legal constraints differ from other institutional investors. Yet, while the concept of pension manager fiduciary duty is grounded in a relatively stable set of legal principles, the interpretation of fiduciary principles can be quite dynamic, evolving with 'societal expectations' in the past (Wood 2011). Recently, for example, the Canadian Business Corporations Act (CBCA)-Section 122 (1.1) was amended to codify the long-standing common-law principle that directors and officers of CBCA corporations are not required to consider only the interests of shareholders when acting in the best interests of the corporation. Instead, they may also consider, among other factors, the interests of employees, the environment, and the long-term interests of the corporation. Hawley et al. (2011) stress the need to rethink the concept of fiduciary duty.

To more closely link intergenerational timeframes of pension fund mandates with the interpretation of fiduciary duty, some contend that 'pension sector leaders should have a legal obligation to look beyond tomorrow, and to focus the capital at their disposal at the long term' (Ambachtsheer 2014: 9). Richardson and Peihani add that this can 'create leverage to require trustees to be considerate of the needs of future pension plan retirees, decades from now, who may be impacted by changing economic and environmental conditions' (2015: 450). Yet where an expanded legal definition of fiduciary duty already exists, as is true for some, not all, types of pensions in common-law countries, implementation is usually unmonitored and unaudited, often without impact on investment decisions (Quigley 2019a).

## The organizational level

This level of pension funds is embedded in and shaped by the regulatory environment, as described above. Ultimately, the regulatory environment decides on the level of ambition that a pension fund can have when integrating ESG. We find that the regulatory environment of pensions is not always a supporting factor for the integration of ESG, and that pensions confront strict and narrow mandates, which often make it difficult for them to incorporate factors other than those of a financial nature. Leadership and corporate governance, the investment policy of a fund, and fund manager willingness to advocate and collaborate are therefore key factors at the organizational level that determine a pension fund's ability to incorporate ESG into investment decisions. The following section discusses this in more detail.

## Corporate governance and leadership

Within the given mandate and legal structure of a pension fund, the corporate governance of a plan and its leadership can be vital catalysts for the adoption of sustainable investment strategies. While some legal mandates give pension boards and leadership very strict boundaries where they cannot purse ESG policies, others give them more freedom and/or impose certain responsibilities. Where the legal environment gives no clear guidance, proactive leadership from pension boards and executives can push and enable a sustainable investment agenda and strategy. In other instances, as in the UK, pension trustees cannot legally provide opinions or advice on a fund's investment strategy. Still, their guidance and standpoint on long-term risk and sustainable development can help catalyze the right decision within a fund.

At an organizational level, pension funds still face the inherent challenge of having a long-term commitment toward their members, while facing public and sponsor expectations of generating short-term returns. This tension requires a thoughtful investment policy, strategy, and a clear interpretation of fiduciary duty at the organizational level.

**Investment policy** Pension funds are increasingly publishing investment policies, referring to ESG as one of many material factors. While this is mandatory in jurisdictions like the UK, this practice is also found in the US and Canadian pension markets. The Global Stewardship Principles from the International Corporate Governance Network (ICGN 2016) and guidance from the UN PRI (PRI 2021b) have clearly made it easier for firms to issue statements of investment policies and beliefs. While there are concerns about greenwashing and 'box-ticking' in instances of mandatory inclusion of ESG in policies (Webb and Brown 2019), these documents can provide a good opportunity for boards and/or trustees to demonstrate that they are taking ESG risks and opportunities seriously.

According to the PRI, 'responsible investment can be integrated into investment policies in many ways, including high-level public statements, codes of business practice, a standalone responsible investment policy or by embedding responsible investment considerations into an organization's main investment policy' (PRI 2021a). A sustainable investing policy or strategy therefore need not start with an ambitious zero-carbon commitment, but instead it can start with simply signaling awareness and willingness to be a responsible steward of capital. In this way, ESG is becoming increasingly relevant for the purposeful use of voting rights, influencing company strategies to ensure that pay is aligned, that there is quality disclosure (e.g., by supporting standard-setting), and that advocating for legislation enables long-term investing. The importance of policies also ties to our previous discussion of definitions of success regarding the use of ESG in investment decisions. Ideally, an organization's responsible investment policy defines what this success looks like within a given legal structure.

**Collaboration and advocacy** The notion of investor stewardship, as outlined, for example, by the ICGN, highlights the importance of investor collaboration to enhance the outcome of stewardship activities, such as engagement with companies (ICGN 2016). The decision as to whether a pension fund is willing to collaborate with other institutional investors and, indeed, whether it will advocate for sustainability topics through lobbying or endorsement activities, must be made at an organizational level and depend on the openness and interest of a fund's leadership in ESG.

Indeed, pension funds are no stranger to collaborations with other market participants. Via global forums such as the Net-Zero Asset Owner Alliance, to more local groups such as the Maple 8, pension funds can increasingly communicate, share best practices, and collaborate. Yet due to their limited resources, not every pension fund can get involved in every collaboration or lobby for every relevant piece of legislation. Nevertheless, carefully chosen collaboration can actually increase efficiency, and well-placed advocacy can have spillovers.

On the advocacy side, public sector pension funds can collaborate with policymakers as well. The Maple 8, for example, met with the Canadian security regulators to engage on proxy voting. Furthermore, pension funds may support frameworks or organizations that they see as useful for advancing sustainable finance practices on a global level. CalPERS, for example, has taken a public stand to support various initiatives of sustainability disclosure standardization such as the IFRS consultation and the consultation on the Value Reporting Foundation (CalPERS 2020a; CalPERS 2020b). In 2021, as another example, ten Canadian pension funds offered public comments on the SEC Climate Change Disclosure Consultation (US SEC 2021).

## The portfolio level

Under the assumption that interpretation and guidance from board and leadership allow for considerations of sustainable finance, we next turn to several factors important for ESG integration at the portfolio level.

**Investment strategy and asset mix**  Pension funds are usually highly diversified funds that invest in public market bonds and equities and, increasingly, they make substantial allocations to private equity, real estate, and infrastructure investments. A 2020 study from Mercer UK showed that, on average, European pension funds had invested 22 percent in public equity, 47 percent in growth fixed income, 53 percent in real assets, and 14 percent in private equity. The same survey found that in 2020, 88 percent of these funds had considered integrating ESG into their investment policy, up 20 percent from the year before. ESG integration in multiple asset classes is therefore a current challenge for pension funds and their managers.

ESG integration in investment has its origins in the public equity markets (Eccles and Stroehle 2018), yet these discussions have increasingly become relevant in the fixed income and private equity markets as well (Schroders 2020). Integrating ESG considerations into these different asset classes, however, requires different approaches and a deep understanding of how each of these markets work. For example, the need to move with agility varies by investment. In public markets, for instance, investments tend to be liquid and stewardship tools, such as voting and engagement, permit investors to try to influence a company's direction (at least to some extent). Investors in public companies can generally react by selling their stock if, for example, concerns about long-term value or sustainability risks emerge. Of course, this is only true if the stock is not held in an index or index replication strategy.

In private markets, by contrast, and particularly in private equity, investments tend to be less liquid. Accordingly, pension funds must carefully assess the risk and long-term strategy of each holding. ESG considerations in private investments can therefore be useful when assessing private assets and the need for continuous stewardship. Moreover, many investors have traditionally held private equity for their high financial returns, with ESG not being a priority, but this is starting to change significantly (Zaccone and Pedrini 2020). Additionally, General Partners managing private equity funds are gradually integrating ESG into their investment and asset management decision-making; some have even launched 'impact funds,' which focus specifically on the creation of positive social impact, though these are still niche products.

In fixed income investments, ESG can inform a negative or positive screening of the investment universe, or flow into the fundamental analysis of an issuer. In this regard, ESG integration into fixed income can resemble the public equity side. Nevertheless, ESG in fixed income is meant to inform about a potential credit risk. Accordingly, the issues important for a fixed income analyst may be very different to those that are important to shareholders (CFA Institute 2019). So, while an investor may choose to divest from a company on the public equity side (e.g., due to an ESG scandal), there may be incentives to simultaneously buy the bonds of the very same company. This highlights how tradeoffs between financial and ESG considerations are structured differently in different asset classes.

**Relationships with asset managers**  Pension funds have the choice either to manage their assets in-house, or to hire asset managers to manage their assets externally. Either way, the balance is struck between cost and return, where the higher cost of an outside manager is anticipated to be offset by a higher expected investment return. Most recently, the trend toward external managers has stalled. In the US, for example, larger state and public pension funds have returned to managing at least part of their assets in-house (Aubry and Wandrei 2020), often driven by concerns about the fees of these managers and related after-fee returns. If assets are internally managed, the pension fund can, within its mandate, have full discretion over ESG integration. When assets are externally managed, the UN Principles of Responsible Investment suggest that pension funds integrate their sustainable investment priorities into manager selection, appointment, and monitoring (UN PRI 2013).

The choice of internal versus external management in different asset classes will impact how much direct influence a pension fund can have over how ESG is integrated into investment decisions. Pension funds can outsource everything from portfolio construction and investment decisions, to engagement with holding companies and proxy voting. The selection of an asset manager for these activities is therefore important from an ESG perspective. An early alignment on ESG priorities and expectations about transparency, reporting engagement, and, when applicable, voting, are key to ensuring that ESG is taken into consideration in a way that fits with the pension fund's investment policy. ESG factors can then also be integrated into the asset manager monitoring process, which catalyzes ongoing conversations and reviews. Furthermore, while pension funds are explicit long-term owners and increasingly formulate expectations for long-term risk management, including ESG, their mandates to, and reviews of, asset managers can in fact be quite short term. Accordingly, longer-term mandates and performance reviews are needed to enable external managers to effectively manage the ESG priorities of their clients.

Finally, in private equity, pension funds can sometimes have only a limited effect on their managers. Currently, private equity funds are often oversubscribed, so General Partners (GPs) can often pick and choose the clients with whom they wish to work. This inhibits ESG conversations, as it reduces the ability of Limited Partners (LPs) such as the pensions buying into a private equity fund to negotiate disclosure requirements around new practices such as ESG. To this end, the International Limited Partner Association represents one forum where a coordinated pension fund voice can help establish a process for the whole private equity industry. If every pension fund were to require the same standard disclosure from GPs, it could very likely be a 'game changer,' much more so than sporadic and uncoordinated LP requests. Additional groups, such as the UK Pension Coalition for Inclusive Capitalism and the International Corporate Governance Network, have called for standard contract formats for public external managers.

**Stewardship activities** Finally, pension funds can use active ownership and engagement activities to exert their influence and to maximize both financial and ESG value. Stewardship and ESG integration can be linked and complementary activities integral to responsible investing (PRI 2021). According to the ICGN, stewardship is 'the responsible management of something entrusted to one's care. This suggests a fiduciary duty of care on the part of those agents (...) acting on behalf of beneficiaries, who are often long-term savers or members of pension funds' (ICGN 2016: 4). Stewardship is meant to promote high standards of corporate governance, to preserve and enhance long-term value, and to enhance systemic market stability.

Engagement—which is one tool used for stewardship—can enhance investment decisions, communicate concerns, and foster relationships and constructive conversations with companies about their ESG strategies. Eccles et al. (20219) outlined several strategies of engagement to be used for ESG interactions with issuers and holdings. Some are top-down, including conservative and opportunist engagements. Here ESG scores and topical lenses are used to screen the entire portfolio and engage laggards and leaders. Bottom-up strategies focus more on long-term, constructivist interactions that build relationships between the pension fund and companies. Alternatively, activist strategies can be used to address topics perceived as critical and neglected (Eccles et al. 2019). Overall, stewardship and engagement allow pensions to take ESG positions and actions.

## A Case Study: PSP Investments

To add depth to our analysis, we undertook an in-depth case study of PSP Investments in Canada, analyzing just how the fund's historical origins and organizational characteristics link to its understanding of ESG and its responsible investment strategy. PSP Investments is one of Canada's largest pension investment managers: it is a Canadian Crown corporation that invests DB pension plan assets for the federal Public Service, the Canadian Forces, the Royal Canadian Mounted Police and the Reserve Force (the 'Pension Plans'). As of March 31, 2020, PSP Investments had C\$169.8 billion assets under management.

### History and legal context of PSP Investments

PSP has a unique mandate and a governance structure tailored to that mandate. To understand and appreciate PSP's unique governance framework, it is important to consider the historical context that led to the creation of PSP in 1999.

In the 1980s, the Auditor General of Canada released a series of reports on the finance and accounting practices associated with the various federal superannuation (pension) plans. Among the Auditor General's recommendations was a proposal to have the funds for federal employees gradually invested in marketable securities, in order to provide a sound financial basis for future benefits. In the mid-1990s, Canada undertook an important pension reform. The key driver for pension reform was concern surrounding the long-term financial sustainability of public pension plans in the face of the important expected pension payouts associated with an aging population and retiree longevity. These payouts were predicted to rise higher than could be financed on the basis of the 'Pay-As-You-Go' model. PSP was therefore created in 1999 by an Act of Parliament (the *Public Sector Pension Investment Board Act*) to invest the net contributions received from the Government from April 2000. Initially, this reform covered the Canadian Forces, the Public Service, and the Royal Canadian Mounted Police DB pension plans; since March 1, 2007, it included the Reserve Force DB pension plan. PSP was given a clear statutory mandate and has operated at arm's length from the Government of Canada.

### Mandate and nature of PSP Investments

PSP's mandate is to manage the pension funds transferred to it by the Government of Canada in the best interests of the contributors and beneficiaries, and to maximize investment returns without undue risk of loss, having regard to the funding, policies, and requirements of the Pension

Plans. The Government of Canada manages and administers the Pension Plans, and PSP is the exclusive provider of investment management services to the Pension Plans. The rationale for creating the PSP was to help sustain the Pension Plans by investing the amounts contributed in a professionally managed diversified portfolio of capital market investments.

## Review of the nature of the arm's length relationship

PSP's business and activities are managed and supervised by a board of Directors (the 'Board of Directors') appointed by the Government. In managing and supervising PSP, the Board of Directors does not receive directives, mandate letters, or follow other instructions from the Government. Indeed, the Board of Directors alone establishes the PSP's investment policies, standards, and procedures, although in doing so, the Board of Directors is required to have regard to the funding, policies, and requirements of the Pension Plans and their ability to meet their financial obligations. This is a factor differentiating PSP's governance, compared to certain peers whose directors are not involved in the setting of investment policies, nor do they have approval authority over investment decisions.

## Investment approach

In keeping with PSP's legislative mandate, the Board of Directors annually approves the Policy Portfolio, which represents long-term target asset allocation among broad asset classes. In addition to allocations to publicly traded equities and fixed income, PSP's Policy Portfolio includes an important allocation to private asset classes, such as real estate, private equity, infrastructure, natural resources, and credit investments. PSP is invested in both active and passive investment strategies managed in-house as well as by external managers and fund managers. PSP's portfolio diversified in terms of asset classes, and also in terms of geography, making PSP a true universal owner.

## Responsible Investment at PSP Investments
### ESG at PSP Investments

In 2018, the sponsors of the Pension Plans adopted a Funding Policy stating an expectation that PSP would report in its Statement of Investment Policy Standards and Procedures, as well as other publicly available documents, how ESG factors are incorporated into its investment practices (PSP Investments 2020b). It was the first time since PSP's inception that PSP was provided with an expectation on ESG matters from the Pension Plans sponsors. Nevertheless, PSP did not wait until 2018 to start its ESG journey. Rather, its first Social and Environmental Responsibility Policy—now known as the Responsible Investment Policy (PSP investments 2020b)—was adopted in 2001, and it has been regularly reviewed since then to adapt to a changing world and reflect its current practices. The earliest version of the policy read:

> In carrying out this duty [to discharge PSP Investments' investment mandate], the board of directors recognizes that a broad range of factors may be relevant in assessing whether particular investments may properly be expected to contribute to or be detrimental to PSP Investments' ability to achieve its objects and perform its duties. Among other things, the environmental and social impact of the behaviour of corporations and entities in which PSP Investments may invest may be one of a number of relevant factors that our investment professionals would wish to take into account in making investment decisions for the [Pension] Plans.
> (. . .)
> To assist it in assessing the factors that guide and inform its investment decisions, PSP Investments encourages corporations and other entities in which it may invest to disclose regularly to their investors and potential investors the details of all policies, practices and matters that may be material to shareholder value. It is our view that reasonable and timely disclosure should be made by the corporations and entities in which we invest of their positions on all matters that may materially affect shareholder value. Where social and environmental issues are relevant and material, we would expect that they be included in that disclosure. All shareholders have a right to know about the activities of the corporations and entities whose securities they hold that are pertinent to the value of their investments.
>
> (PSP Investments 2001: 1)

The direction set by the Board of Directors in 2001 was anchored in the belief that environmental and social matters were relevant to investment decisions, especially when they could affect PSP's ability to provide for the financial benefit of the contributors to the Pension Plans and the Pension Plans' ability to honor the pension promises made to their contributors. This belief was not imposed by pension plan sponsors or by regulation. Instead, it was shaped through dialogue and several discussions between the board and senior management regarding the success factors for a long-term investor. This underscores how leadership and governance have been key facilitators of ESG integration at PSP. On this foundation, ESG developed from a risk management tool in 2001, to what is now an integrated investment decision factor.

## Other ESG enablers and inhibitors

It is useful to note that the lack of ESG-related regulations in Canada, either requiring the adoption of specific ESG practices or prohibiting ESG integration, qualifies as an enabler of ESG policy. As opposed to a responsible investment approach being imposed by a regulator, it allowed for the development of an approach aligned with PSP's mandate, its investment strategy, and its total fund perspective. This enabler helped in building a strong level of conviction about ESG risks and opportunities within the organization.

Other key enablers of ESG implementation at PSP were related to the fund's long-term investment mandate and asset mix. For PSP, moving into the ESG arena was seen as indispensable when investing in less liquid investments such as private assets. Accordingly, PSP adopted an ESG strategy early on which would ensure that ESG factors would be integrated in the investment process, from both a risk and an opportunity lens.

The COVID-19 pandemic has now amplified the importance of ESG issues for investors like PSP who seek greater transparency about how organizations are managing their ESG risks and integrating them into their business strategy. PSP is committed to bridging the gap between an ESG qualitative narrative and quantitative factor-driven analysis. Furthermore, PSP seeks to address this inhibitor by collaborating with peers, industry regulators, academia, and investee companies. This is one of the reasons why PSP joined its voice with other Canadian pension plan investment managers, calling on companies and investors to provide consistent and complete ESG information to strengthen investment decision-making and better manage ESG risk exposures (PSP Investments 2020a). It was the first time that the CEOs of Canada's eight leading pension plan investment managers issued a statement, but not the first time that these organizations collaborated to more effectively deploy resources and encourage ESG best practices.

## PSP Investments' ESG strategy

To take into account the world of tomorrow, PSP factors ESG risks and opportunities into its investment processes—with a view to enhancing performance, steering capital toward more attractive areas, and mitigating potential issues. As part of its investment analysis and decision-making processes, PSP identifies material ESG risks and opportunities that could impact its investments' long-term financial performance. PSP also leverages its ownership positions to promote good governance practices, by exercising its proxy voting rights and actively engaging with boards and management of investee companies on material ESG risks and opportunities. When PSP allocates a portion of its capital to externally managed mandates and fund investments in public and private market portfolios, it engages regularly with its external partners on ESG topics throughout the investment lifecycle.

To ensure that the ESG integration approach for each externally managed mandate and fund investment is consistent with its Responsible Investment Policy and expectations, PSP has developed an in-house proprietary assessment framework that evaluates and ranks by quartile the overall external managers' and general partners' ESG practices. The quartile ranking helps the board by prioritizing engagement, sharing of best practices, and measuring progress of ESG integration in investment decision-making and asset management over time.

Responsible investment at PSP is an active process that addresses ESG factors across all asset classes. PSP's investment teams evaluate ESG risks and opportunities in order to make more informed investment decisions, by the dedicated Responsible Investment group housed in their Chief Investment Officer group. This group works to oversee and implement responsible investment activities across the total fund, provide guidance on ESG themes and trends, build internal capacity through ESG knowledge sharing, and collaborate with industry peers to drive systemic change on key ESG issues.

## Conclusion

This chapter has discussed the origins of ESG in pensions by reviewing the characteristics of pension funds and how they can integrate these ESG factors into investment decisions. Drawing on existing literature, a range of interviews, and an in-depth study of PSP Investments, we showed how different institutional, organizational and investment factors play a role. We identified three levels for whether and how pension funds can integrate ESG: *the institutional level*, which sets the historical and regulatory context of the interpretation of fiduciary duty; *the organizational level*, which decides how investment mandates are translated into policies, governance structures, and collaborations; and *the portfolio level*, which implements investment strategies through asset allocation, the mandates to asset managers, and stewardship activities.

When reviewing these characteristics, we note that pension funds are not a homogenous community. They have different mandates, legal environments, and governance structures to work with. Despite this diversity, pension funds share a common objective, which is to identify the best investments or investment strategies to generate investment returns so as to be able to pay pensions to their beneficiaries for generations to come. In so doing, the inherent long-term investment time horizon and the diversified portfolio structures are often seen as the two of the principal ESG enablers in pension funds, where the growing evidence about ESG materiality requires pension funds to integrate them as risk factors in investment decision-making. How these factors will ultimately be taken into consideration must depend on discretion of the pension fund, governance structures, leadership, and the plan's investment policy suitability for the fund's asset mix. The freedom of pension boards and leaders to do this, however, can be restricted through a lack of clear guidance on ESG expectations from plan sponsors or regulators. Additionally, regulators can inhibit the integration of ESG by placing large reporting burdens on pension funds, therefore making ESG an expensive use of resources.

Finally, pension funds have grown to be powerful forces in the investment market, and they have an opportunity to further catalyze the market-wide integration of ESG factors. To do so, they should focus not on what differentiates them, but rather what they have in common. All pension funds have limited resources, yet collaboration and coordination can be key enablers for them to speak with one voice, and to make that voice heard more loudly and persuasively. Possible targets of such coordination, like disclosure standards and standard mandates for external managers, can help facilitate a deeper integration of ESG in the entire investment chain.

## Acknowledgments

We are grateful to PSP Investments, the UK Universities Superannuation Scheme USS, and CalSTRS, who supported this research with their time and availability. Particularly, we thank Robert Eccles, Bob Baldwin, and Eduard van Gelderen for their invaluable input and support, and comments on an earlier version of this analysis. We also thank Olivia S. Mitchell and the Wharton Pension Research Council reviewers for their thoughtful comments and guidance. Finally, we are grateful to the Wharton Pension Research Council for inviting this research to be presented to the 2021 conference.

# Appendix

Interviews conducted for this chapter:

- PSP, Canada; January 2021
- CalSTRS, United States; January 2021
- Universities Superannuation Scheme USS, United Kingdom; January 2021

Other Interviews also drawn on:

- NYCC, United States; December 2020
- OTTP, Canada; December 2020
- PGGM, Netherlands; December 2020
- AP2, Sweden; December 2020
- AP3, Sweden; December 2020
- AP7, Sweden; December 2020
- AWARE, Australia; December 2020

## Notes

1. See the discussion of the 'Universal Ownership thesis' in this regard, as, for example, outlined in Quigley (2019a; 2019b), also discussed below.
2. The markets included in this study are Australia, Brazil, Canada, Chile, China, Finland, France, Germany, Hong Kong, India, Ireland, Italy, Japan, Malaysia, Mexico, Netherlands, South Africa, South Korea, Spain, Switzerland, the UK, and the US.
3. See the OECD Global Pensions Database, https://stats.oecd.org/Index. aspx?DatasetCode=PNNI_NEW.
4. This is calculated from the value of the US equity market (12/2020: US$50.6 trillion), the global equity market (12/2020: US$95 trillion), and the equity-held percentage of pensions in the US (32.7 percent of US$32.2 trillion in 2019). In the UK, the sum is based on 11 percent of US$3.6 trillion EUM relative to US$5 trillion, and in Canada on 21.8 percent of US$2.8 trillion EUM relative to US$3.2 trillion. Data from Toronto Stock Exchange, OECD Pension Stats, and Bloomberg Finance.
5. Today part of the organization Share Action, see https://shareaction.org/ uss/. Being a catalyst for this type of activism, Ethics for USS also led to the creation of the 'Fair Pensions' organization in collaboration with WWF, Amnesty International, and Friends of the Earth in 2005.
6. Representing the interests of institutional investors, the Canadian Coalition for Good Governance promotes good governance practices in Canadian public companies and the improvement of the regulatory environment, to best align the

interests of boards and management with those of their shareholders, and to promote the efficiency and effectiveness of the Canadian capital markets.

# References

Alda, M. (2019). 'Corporate Sustainability and Institutional Shareholders: The Pressure of Social Responsible Pension Funds on Environmental Firm Practices,' *Business Strategy and the Environment*, 28(6): 1060–1071.

Ambachtsheer, K. (2014). 'The Case for Long-termism,' *Rotman International Journal of Pension Management*, 7(2): 6–15.

Ambachtsheer, K. and R. Bauer (2013). 'Ten Strategies for Pension Funds to Better Serve Their Beneficiaries,' *Rotman International Journal of Pension Management*, 6(2): 44–52.

Atta-Darkua, V., D. Chambers, E. Dimson, Z. Ran, and T. Yu (2020). 'Strategies for Responsible Investing: Emerging Academic Evidence,' *The Journal of Portfolio Management Ethical Investing*, 46(3): 26–35.

Aubry, J.P. and K. Wandrei (2020). 'Internal vs. External Management for State and Local Pension Plans,' Brief, Center for Retirement Research at Boston College.

Bender, J., T.A. Bridges, C. He, A. Lester, and X. Sun (2018) 'A Blueprint for Integrating ESG into Equity Portfolios,' *The Journal of Investment Management*, 16(1): 44–58.

Bird, R. and J. Gray. (2013). 'Principles, Principals and Agents,' International Centre for Pension Management Working Paper.

Blitz, D. and L. Swinkels (September 19, 2019). 'Is Exclusion Effective?' Forthcoming, *Journal of Portfolio Management*. Available at SSRN: https://ssrn.com/abstract=3337779 or http://dx.doi.org/10.2139/ssrn.3337779

Broccardo, E., O.D. Hart, and L. Zingales (April 22, 2022). 'Exit vs. Voice.' Harvard Law School John M. Olin Center Discussion Paper # 1061, Available at SSRN: https://ssrn.com/abstract=3680815 or http://dx.doi.org/10.2139/ssrn.3680815

CalPERS (2020a). Comment Letter to the IFRS. Sacramento, CA: CalPERS. https://www.calpers.ca.gov/docs/legislative-regulatory-letters/comment-ifrs-dec-31-2020.pdf.

CalPERS (2020b). Comment Letter to SASB. Sacramento, CA: CalPERS. www.calpers.ca.gov/docs/legislative-regulatory-letters/comment-sasb-dec-31-2020.pdf.

CFA Institute (2019). 'Integrating ESG in Fixed-Income Investing.' Interview with Kathleen Bochman. Charlottesville, VA: CFA Institute. www.cfainstitute.org/en/research/multimedia/2020/integrating-esg-in-fixed-income-investing.

Clark, G.L. (2004). 'Pension Fund Governance: Expertise and Organizational Form,' *Issues & Policy*, 3(2): 233–253.

Clark, G.L. and A.H.B. Monk (2010). 'The Legitimacy and Governance of Norway's Sovereign Wealth Fund: The Ethics of Global Investment,' *Environment and Planning*, 42: 1723–1739.

Clark, G.L. and A.H.B. Monk (2011). 'Partisan Politics and Bureaucratic Encroachment: The Principles and Policies of Pension Reserve Fund Design and Governance,' Working Paper, International Centre for Pension Management.

Eabrasu, M. (2018). *Moral Disagreements in Business—An Exploratory Introduction.* Cham: Springer.

Eccles, R.G. and J.C. Stroehle (2018). 'Exploring the Social Origins of ESG Measures,' Oxford University Working Paper.

Eccles, R.G., L.E. Lee, and J.C. Stroehle (2019). 'The Social Origins of ESG? An Analysis of Innovest and KLD,' *Organizations & Environment*, 3(4): 575–596.

Fabian N., M. Homanen, N. Pedersen, and M. Slebos (2023). 'Private Retirement Systems and Sustainability: Insights from Australia, the UK, and the US.' In P.B. Hammond, R. Maurer, and O.S. Mitchell, eds., *Pension Funds and Sustainable Investment: Challenges and Opportunities.* Oxford: Oxford University Press, pp. 199–219.

Filgueira, F. and P. Manzi (2017). 'Pension and Income Transfers for Old Age. Inter- and Intra-generational Distribution in Comparative Perspective,' United Nations ECLAC, Social Policy Series, Santiago, Chile.

Giese, G., L.E. Lee, D. Melas, Z. Nagy, and L. Nishikawa (2019). 'Foundations of ESG Investing: How ESG Affects Equity Valuation, Risk, and Performance' *The Journal of Portfolio Management*, 45(5): 69–83.

Gond, J.P. and V. Piani (2013). 'Enabling Institutional Investors' Collective Action: The Role of the Principles for Responsible Investment Initiative,' *Business & Society*, 52(1): 64–104.

GPIF (2020). 'Our Partnership for Sustainable Capital Markets,' Public Statement, GPIF. www.gpif.go.jp/en/investment/Our_Partnership_for_Sustainable_ Capital_Markets.pdf.

Hammond, P.B. and A. O'Brien (2023). 'Pensions and ESG: An Institutional and Historical Perspective.' In P.B. Hammond, R. Maurer, and O.S. Mitchell, eds., *Pension Funds and Sustainable Investment: Challenges and Opportunities.* Oxford: Oxford University Press, pp. 17–57.

Hawley, J.P. and J. Lukomnik (2018). 'The Third, System Stage of Corporate Governance: Why Institutional Investors Need to Move Beyond Modern Portfolio Theory.' SSRN Working Paper. https://ssrn.com/abstract=3127767.

Hawley, J.P., K.L. Johnson, and E. Waitzer (2011). 'Reclaiming Fiduciary Duty Balance,' *Rotman International Journal of Pension Management*, 4(2): 4–16.

Hoepner, A., M. Rezec, and S. Siegl (2011). 'Does Pension Funds' Fiduciary Duty Prohibit the Integration of Any ESG Criteria in Investment Processes? A Realistic Prudent Investment Test,' SSRN Working Paper. https://papers.ssrn.com/sol3/ papers.cfm?abstract_id=1930189.

ICGN (International Corporate Governance Network) (2012). *Model Contract Terms between Asset Owners and Asset Managers.* London: ICGN. http://icgn.flpbks.com/ icgn_model-contract-terms_2015.

ICGN (2016). *Global Stewardship Principles: International Corporate Governance Network.* London: ICGN. www.icgn.org/sites/default/files/ICGNGlobalStewar dshipPrinciples.pdf.

Johnson, K.L. and F.J. de Graaf (2009). 'Modernizing Pension Fund Legal Standards for the Twenty-First Century,' *Rotman International Journal of Pension Management*, 2(1): 44–52.

Kecskés, A., S. Mansi, and P.A. Nguyen (2020). 'Does Corporate Social Responsibility Create Shareholder Value? The Importance of Long-Term Investors,' *Journal of Banking & Finance*, 112 (105217). https://www.sciencedirect.com/science/article/abs/pii/S0378426617302273

Kiernan, M.J. (2007). 'Universal Owners and ESG: Leaving Money on the Table?' *Corporate Governance: An International Review*, 15(3): 478–485.

Kölbel, J.F., F. Heeb, F. Paetzold, and T. Busch. (2020). 'Can Sustainable Investing Save the World? Reviewing the Mechanisms of Investor Impact,' *Organization & Environment*, 33(4): 554–574. https://doi.org/10.1177/1086026620919202

Mercer UK (2020). *Investing in the Future – European Asset Allocation Insights 2020.* Mercer UK. https://www.uk.mercer.com/content/dam/mercer/attachments/private/6010897a-WE%20EAAS%202020_FIN_KR.pdf.

Monks, R.A.G. and N. Minow (2004) *Corporate Governance.* 3rd ed. Oxford: Blackwell Publishing Ltd.

The Pensions Regulator (2022). *The Pensions Regulator: Making Workplace Pensions Work.* https://www.thepensionsregulator.gov.uk/

Plan Sponsor Council of America (2018). *63nd Annual Survey of Profit Sharing and 401(k) Plans.* Chicago, IL: Plan Sponsor Council of America. https://www.psca.org/research/401k/63rdAR.

PSP Investments (2001). *Responsible Investment Policy.* Canada: PSP.

PSP Investments (2020a). Companies and Investors Must Put Sustainability and Inclusive Growth at the Centre of Economic Recovery. Public Statement. Canada: PSP. https://www.investpsp.com/media/filer_public/documents/Nov_23_Maple_8_CEO_statement_Updated_for_CEO_signatures_EN.pdf.

PSP Investments (2020b). *Responsible Investment Policy.* Canada: PSP. https://www.investpsp.com/media/filer_public/02-we-are-psp/02-investing-responsibly/content-2/documents/Responsible_Investment_Policy.PDF.

PSP Investments (2020c). *Statement of Investment Policies, Standards and Procedures for Assets Managed by the PSP Investment Board.* Canada: PSP. www.investpsp.com/media/filer_public/07-contributors/00-main-page/content-5/SIPP_-_english.pdf.

Quigley, E. (2019a). 'Universal Ownership in Practice. A Practical Positive Investment Framework for Asset Owners,' Cambridge University Working Paper.

Quigley, E. (2019b). 'Universal Ownership in the Anthropocene,' Cambridge University Working Paper.

Richardson, B.J. and M. Peihani (2015). 'Universal Investors and Socially Responsible Finance: A Critique of a Premature Theory,' *Banking and Finance Law Review*, 30(3): 405–455. Available at SSRN: https://ssrn.com/abstract=2726381

Schroders (2020). *Institutional Investor Study. Sustainability.* London: Schroders. www.schroders.com/en/hk/institutional-service/insights/institutional-investor-study-2020/sustainability/.

Thinking Ahead Institute (2020). Global Pension Asset Study. Arlington, VA: Thinking Ahead Institute, Willis Towers Watson. https://www.thinkingaheadinstitute.org/research-papers/global-pension-assets-study-2020/.

Thurley, D. and R. McInnes (2021). 'Public Service Pensions: Facts and Figures,' HoC Briefing Paper Number 8487, May 11, 2021, House of Commons Library, London.

United Nations Principles of Responsible Investing (2013). Aligning Expectations. Guidance for Asset Owners on Incorporating ESG Factors into Manager Selection, Appointment, and Monitoring. London: PRI. https://www.unpri.org/download?ac=1614.

United Nations Principles of Responsible Investing (2021a). An Introduction to Responsible Investment Policy, Structure and Process. London: PRI. https://www.unpri.org/download?ac=10224.

United Nations Principles for Responsible Investing (2021b). About Stewardship. London: PRI. https://www.unpri.org/stewardship/about-stewardship/6268.article.

United States Security and Exchange Commission (2021). Statement of Support to SEC Climate Change Disclosures Regulation. Washington, DC: US SEC. https://www.sec.gov/comments/climate-disclosure/cll12-8906827-244153.pdf.

United States Senate (2021). A Bill To Amend the Employee Retirement Income Security Act of 1974 to Permit Retirement Plans to Consider Certain Factors in Investment Decisions. Washington, DC: US Senate. https://smithsenate.app.box.com/s/j4qos4wd7spa5epdimsbct3kwejalb1s.

Urwin, R. (2011) 'Pension Funds as Universal Owners: Opportunity Beckons and Leadership Calls,' *Rotman International Journal of Pension Management*, 4(1): 26–34.

Webb, S. and S. Brown (2019). *Pensions and ESG: The Evolving Legal and Regulatory Landscape. A Practical Guide.* London: Herbert Smith Freehills.

Woods, C. (2011). 'Funding Climate Change: How Pension Fund Fiduciary Duty Masks Trustee Inertia and Short-Termism.' In J.P. Hawley, S.J. Kamath, and A.T. Williams, eds., *Corporate Governance Failures.* Philadelphia, PA: University of Pennsylvania Press, pp. 242–278.

Zaccone, M.C. and M. Pedrini (2020). 'ESG Factor Integration in Private Equity,' *Sustainability*, 12(14): 5725.

# Chapter 4

# ESG Investing: Financial Materiality and Social Objectives

*Linda-Eling Lee*

US-domiciled assets under management (AUM) that incorporate environmental, social, and governance (ESG) or sustainability considerations reached nearly US$17.1 trillion as of the end of 2019, up 42 percent from the prior year, according to the US SIF Foundation (2020).[1] But what do we mean when we talk about 'ESG'? While more and more public funds globally have clearly articulated what it means for their respective institutions (Nikulina 2023), there continues to be confusion over what ESG investing is and how to implement it. Some hurdles include a lack of understanding and confidence in how ESG concepts are measured, when such concepts are material, and how to work with ESG data in the investment process when such data are very different in nature from traditional financial data.

This chapter aims to address these hurdles by providing an overview of the 'state of play' on ESG data. We focus on recent advances in measuring ESG concepts, emerging evidence on the link between ESG and financial performance of equities and corporate bonds, and approaches that funds have used to implement their ESG policies in light of these advances.

In what follows, we begin by setting the context for the multifaceted concepts of ESG and the evolution of ESG data used in capturing those concepts. Next, we summarize the four main sources of ESG data today, and we review recent empirical research that tests the economic rationale for how and when ESG has impacted equity and bond returns. We also highlight emerging research that explains how each of the underlying components of E, S, and G bear on financial performance, including the implications of current thinking about ESG data for practitioners and the principles for the construction and use of ESG scores or ratings. Further, we draw lessons for implementing ESG in portfolio construction as well as considerations for equity allocations. Finally, with the rapid growth in attention to climate risk, we note that this rapidly growing area introduces additional complexity, overarching risk, and opportunity, especially for long-term investors.[2]

Linda-Eling Lee, *ESG Investing: Financial Materiality and Social Objectives*. In: *Pension Funds and Sustainable Investment*. Edited by P. Brett Hammond, Raimond Maurer, and Olivia S. Mitchell, Oxford University Press. © Linda-Eling Lee (2023). DOI: 10.1093/oso/9780192889195.003.0004

## Evolution of ESG Data and Measurement

Among the most often-invoked phrases when discussing ESG are: 'ESG means different things to different people' and 'You can do good and still do well.' As with most popular sayings, there is a grain of truth to each. In fact, while different people often mean different things when they refer to 'ESG,' the concepts embedded in ESG are relatively well delineated, but also multifaceted. Accordingly, there is room for misunderstanding, as some people may emphasize one facet of ESG such as good labor policies, while other people could be talking about something else, such as environmental or governance issues. While some argue that the objectives of different types of ESG investors are separate and distinct, we find that a social values-oriented-investor approach to ESG does not differ materially from one focused on enhancing the risk-adjusted characteristics of a portfolio. Indeed, there has been empirical evidence suggesting significant overlap between serving the public good and doing well financially (Friede et al. 2015), though the overlap is not perfect and can sometimes be in conflict.

As has been described by others, the movement today, broadly referred to as sustainable, responsible, or ESG investing, had its genesis in faith-based and/or ethically conscious investors who sought to align their portfolios with their personal values (see, for example, Eccles and Stroehle 2018; Hammond and O'Brien 2023). In contrast, the use of ESG criteria as valuation tools (e.g., as a way of establishing firms' intangible value) came at a later stage. Today, while the *materiality-based* concept has become the dominant force in the adoption of ESG investing by most mainstream financial players (Giese et al. 2019a), the *values* approach still applies.

The ESG data and ratings that exist in the marketplace today reflect this dual legacy (Eccles et al. 2019). Since values-based investing first shaped early ESG investing, it continues to be reflected in both the underlying components as well as the aggregation of select E, S, and G components into a company-level ESG rating. Global institutional investors' adoption of the United Nations' Sustainable Development Goals (SDGs) in 2015 expanded and refined values-oriented goals, which were intended to provide 'a universal call to action to end poverty, protect the planet, and ensure that all people enjoy peace and prosperity by 2030' (UNDP 2015). The creation of the SDGs encouraged growing interest from investors and companies in how E, S, and G data can capture the positive contributions of companies to societal goals.

The materiality–values duality is often evident depending on which factors drive an investor's desire to measure ESG. On the one hand, investors and others primarily motivated by the values dimension wish to determine whether a company's behavior is aligned with social objectives. They are primarily interested in the characteristics that help identify how companies contribute to societal outcomes (i.e., negatively or positively). On the other hand, those primarily interested in financial materiality tend to focus on the bundle of characteristics that help investors identify the risks or opportunities for a company to create long-term financial value, regardless of their social values or goals.

ESG measures can be selected and constructed to reflect each of these dimensions, yet a single ESG score or rating typically does not reflect both dimensions at the same time. Accordingly, an investor must first define what aspect of ESG he or she aims to measure. Otherwise, it would be difficult to disentangle how and why ESG ratings vary: do they arise from *differences in intention* (i.e., which dimension of ESG he or she aims to capture), or from *differences in effectiveness* (i.e., how well different methodologies capture the same targeted ESG dimension)?

## What Counts as ESG Data?

There is far more information *about* companies' ESG ratings than is provided *by* specific companies. The idea that company disclosures are the only reliable source of ESG data is outdated, and it has prevented investors from realizing the potential of technological advances in measurement.

There are four broad categories of ESG data sources: company disclosures, media, alternative data sources, and modeled data. Historically, ESG data have been sourced primarily from company disclosures and from the media, but in recent years, alternative data sources and modeled data have gained traction as the quality and quantity of these data have improved. In addition, these sources measure different aspects of ESG and each has its strengths and weaknesses. For example, company disclosures and analysis of media reports are necessarily backward-looking, while media, alternative data, and modeled data are better suited to projecting where companies might be headed.

### Company disclosures

One topic that investors continue to rely on is information that companies provide about their human capital (e.g., employee demographics, workplace practices). There are few third-party data sources to inform investors about the labor-related dimensions of a company, making this the most critical area for investor engagement to improve transparency. Too much reliance on corporate disclosures in the construction of an ESG signal can lead to a size bias and a geographic bias. As a result, studies have often found that ESG ratings are positively correlated with company size.

## Media sources

Media sources are frequently used to identify negative events or controversies, and less frequently to identify positive ESG news that could be influenced by a company's public relations and marketing initiatives. Data science and artificial-intelligence techniques have vastly improved our ability to know what companies are doing or not doing in remote locations. These capabilities have allowed media to become a better source than in the past for verifying the robustness of company disclosures on ESG issues. Nevertheless, artificial intelligence can be noisy, and confirming the veracity and identifying bias in media content requires quality-control processes that involve expert human intelligence. Even a company with the resources and technological prowess of Facebook relies on an army of humans to judge content suitability.

## Alternative data sources

Alternative data sources on ESG include a broad set of new datasets including government databases on waste or safety or labor violations at very granular levels; weather maps and satellite data; and filings for everything from patents to litigation. As with artificial intelligence techniques, identifying and extracting the relevant components for an investment context requires extensive expertise and the ability to shape and match the data to address specific questions.

## Models and estimated data

ESG analysts frequently rely on models to fill in the gaps in corporate disclosures and normalize reported data to allow for apples-to-apples comparisons across firms. What has changed in recent years is that more sophisticated modeling techniques have allowed for projections, such as the future trajectory of emissions based on targets and track records of emissions reductions. Further, these techniques have allowed for assessments that companies themselves may not have the knowledge to disclose, such as the proximity of their operations to areas with sensitive ecosystems.

Just as the concept of ESG is multidimensional, the sources of ESG data are varied and growing. Increasingly, the greater availability of alternative data sources and better models will supplement increased corporate disclosure to build a more robust dataset to inform investment decisions.

## Emerging Evidence on ESG and Materiality

There has been no shortage of studies in recent years attempting to confirm or debunk a link between ESG and performance. A metastudy by Friede et al. (2015) reviewed more than 2,000 research papers examining the relationship between ESG investing and returns, which concluded that most offered a correlational analysis without providing either a specified dimension of ESG, which the ESG variable captured, or an economic rationale for why such a correlation would exist.

However, most of these studies were not designed to separate the two dimensions of ESG: social objectives and materiality. Studies that did so detected differences in effectiveness. In one such study, over a 20-year period, firms with good ratings on material sustainability issues significantly outperformed firms with poor ratings on these issues, while firms with good ratings on immaterial sustainability issues did not significantly outperform firms with poor ratings on the same issues (Khan et al. 2016). In a separate study, based on the May 2013 to December 2018 period, exclusionary screens based on values acted as a portfolio constraint and increased risk, whereas integrating financially focused ESG factors had a positive effect on risk-adjusted returns that outweighed the negative effect of the exclusions (Giese 2019).

More recently, research has sought to better understand the underlying transmission channels through which ESG could impact financial variables (Giese et al. 2019b). We highlight some of the key findings from several recent such studies below, and to ensure data consistency and alignment with a focus on financial materiality, these studies all use MSCI ESG Ratings as the key ESG input. These ratings are designed to capture only the relevant ESG 'Key Issues'[3] in a given industry and are selected based on a fundamental assessment of how financially relevant a given key risk is in a specific industry; that is, how likely it is that the key risk can influence companies' revenue or assets. As such, the number and weights assigned to Key Issues by sub-industry may vary in any given period and over time. The indicators in each Key Issue form a score for that Key Issue, which is used, in turn, to calculate scores for each of the environmental, social, and governance pillars. Ultimately, the separate pillar scores are combined into an aggregate MSCI ESG score, used in creating MSCI ESG Ratings (Giese et al. 2020). Recently, Serafeim and Yoon (2021) found that of the three ESG ratings services, MSCI ESG Ratings had the strongest predictive power in predicting ESG-related news, and thus provided the best signal in predicting future stock returns.

Below, we summarize recent research exploring the relationship between companies' ESG ratings and the performance of equities and corporate bonds. We also discuss research that explores the impact of ESG ratings on the cost of capital.

**Finding 1:** ESG has impacted company financial performance through three economic transmission channels: cash flow, systematic risk, and idiosyncratic risk. Higher ESG-rated companies were more profitable than their

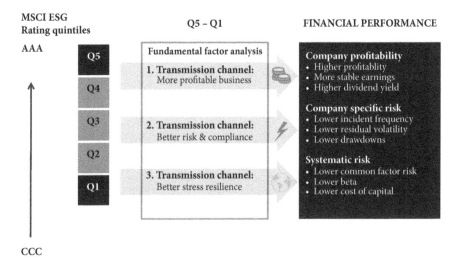

**Figure 4.1** ESG's impact on financial performance via economic transmission channels

*Source*: Author's calculations.

industry peers, paid more dividends, and experienced lower earnings volatility over the period December 2006 to December 2019. The transmission channels and target financial variables for each are described below, and a schematic of the concept appears in Figure 4.1.

(1) *The cash-flow channel*: Companies better at managing intangible capital (such as employees) may have been more competitive and hence more profitable over time.

(2) *Idiosyncratic risk*: Companies with stronger risk-management practices may have experienced fewer incidents, such as accidents, that triggered unanticipated costs.

(3) *Systematic risk*: Companies that used resources more efficiently may have been less susceptible to market shocks, such as fluctuations in energy prices.

We chose one target financial variable as a proxy for financial performance for each of the three channels, as shown in Figure 4.2. We selected gross profitability for the company profitability channel,[4] the frequency of experiencing larger than 95 percent losses over a three-year window for company-specific risk, and risk explained by MSCI's Global Equity Total Market Model (GEMLT) factors for systematic risk.

We have also examined whether mounting inflows into ESG investments have contributed to outperformance of standard MSCI ACWI ESG equity

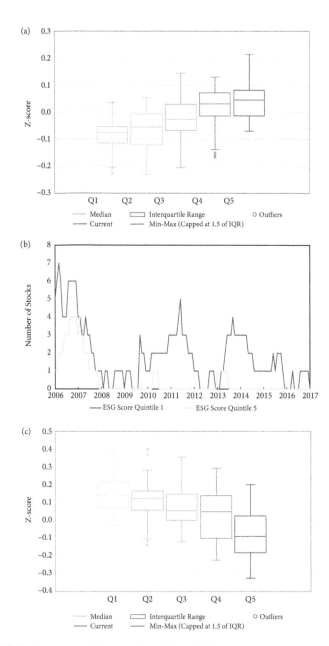

**Figure 4.2** Performance of target financial variables

*Notes*: (a) Gross profitability (z-score) of size-adjusted ESG quintiles is computed as most recently reported sales less cost of goods sold, divided by most recently reported company total assets. Data from December 31, 2006, to December 31, 2020. Distribution of monthly averages by quintiles. (b) For each period, we report the number of stocks that realized a more than 95 percent (%) cumulative loss over the next three years, taking the price at month end as the reference point for return calculation. Data from December 31, 2006, to December 31, 2020. (c) Systematic risk (or common factor risk) of size-adjusted ESG quintiles is computed as the volatility predicted by all the factors of the GEMLT model. Data from December 31, 2006, to December 31, 2020. Distribution of monthly averages by quintiles.

*Source*: Author's calculations.

indexes. Giese et al. (2021a) found no evidence that ESG-related returns stemmed from rising valuations of high-ESG-rated companies, over the period May 31, 2013, to November 30, 2020. Instead, the main source of ESG-related returns came from high-ESG-rated companies that displayed superior earnings growth and, to a smaller extent, higher investment returns compared with low-ESG-rated companies. These findings provide an economic rationale for categorizing ESG as a fundamental factor that typically derives returns from long-term earnings growth.

**Finding 2:** Extending our analysis to corporate bonds, we found that ESG considerations have been more helpful in mitigating downside risk than in capturing upside gains. We also found that ESG added value beyond credit ratings. For instance, Table 4.1 shows that the high-ESG-rated issuers (T3) experienced better risk-adjusted returns due to higher excess returns and lower excess risk, over our sample period. We also observe that the high-ESG-rated issuers also had significantly lower drawdowns during the downturn periods, indicating the inherent defensive characteristics of an ESG corporate bond strategy.

**Finding 3:** During a four-year study period, companies with high ESG scores, on average, experienced lower costs of capital compared with companies with poor ESG scores in developed markets. The relationship between company ESG scores was similar for both the cost of equity and debt.

To calculate the impact of ESG on both equities and debt issued in developed markets, we obtained monthly industry-adjusted ESG scores that underlie the MSCI ESG Ratings; next we classified the companies in the MSCI World Index (comprising developed-market constituents) into ESG-score quintiles, each with the same number of companies.[5] Our study period was from August 31, 2015, to January 29, 2021.[6] In the MSCI World Index,

TABLE 4.1 High ESG-Score bond issuers had more resilient excess returns

| | Excess return (%) | Excess risk (%) | Risk-adjusted excess return | Maximum drawdown (%) | Portfolio Beta |
|---|---|---|---|---|---|
| T1 (low) | 0.68 | 9.01 | 0.08 | 21.25 | 1.38 |
| T3 (high) | 1.08 | 4.51 | 0.24 | 10.57 | 0.69 |

*Note*: Average equal-weighted excess performance for low- and high-ESG-score terciles from January 2014 to July 2020. Return and risk numbers are annualized. Beta is calculated with respect to an equal-weighted (by issuer) universe. Sample universe restricted to issuers with available ESG scores.
*Source*: Author's calculations.

the average cost of capital[7] of the highest-ESG-scored quintile was 6.52 percent, compared with 6.81 percent for the lowest-ESG-scored quintile. The average cost of equity of the highest-ESG-scored quintile was 8.05 percent, compared with 8.71 percent for the lowest-ESG-scored quintile; similarly, the cost of debt was 2.88 percent and 3.72 percent for the highest- and lowest-ESG-scored quintiles, correspondingly.

Overall, companies with high ESG scores on average experienced lower costs of capital than companies with poor ESG scores (see Figure 4.3). The cost-of-capital channel was one way that firms' ESG profiles (as measured by MSCI ESG Ratings) could have been linked to corporate financing and investment decisions.

Much of what we have learned about the relevance of ESG for company performance so far applies to the universe of publicly listed equities and bonds. While little research has analyzed these issues for private assets, we can proceed by making certain assumptions. Within private equities, we can apply financially relevant ESG metrics from public companies to assets held in private equity funds. Similarly, the framework used to assess REITs (real estate investment trusts) in the public equities universe is largely applicable to direct real estate holdings. The key challenge with assessing private assets, then, is not the lack of a robust methodology, but a dearth of data. Of the four different sources of ESG data identified earlier, the most readily available source for private companies is the media, provided that the business is of a sufficient size. Given the potentially larger allocations that institutional investors expect to make to private assets in the future (MSCI Investment Insights 2021), there is some urgency to improving data availability in the private asset classes in order to achieve a total portfolio view of ESG exposures.

**Figure 4.3** Companies with high ESG scores on average had lower costs of capital
*Note*: Monthly averages were reported over the period from August 31, 2015, to January 29, 2021. On average, there were 1636 companies in the MSCI World Index during this period.
*Source*: Author's calculations.

# Implications for Practitioners
## Lessons for constructing an ESG rating

There are several ways to construct an ESG rating system. Some investors set out to construct a proprietary ESG rating methodology because they can customize the selection and weighting of ESG issues to better complement their unique process in security selection or portfolio construction. For example, if an investor's existing investment process already accounts for specific governance risks, she may want to construct a methodology that overweights the additional aspects of environmental or social risks that can be additive to the existing process.

Focusing on the 13 years of data used for MSCI ESG Ratings, we propose three lessons to incorporate when constructing an ESG rating that aims to capture financially relevant risks.

*Lesson 1*: Overreliance on data inputs from corporate disclosures can yield both geographic and size biases, potentially detracting from the rating's financial relevance.

Many studies have pointed out that most ESG ratings are positively correlated with company size (e.g., Boffo and Patalano 2020). A key driver of this correlation is the overreliance on corporate disclosures in the construction of a score. Our analysis of the MSCI ESG Rating broke each of the underlying ESG scores into two equally weighted components: (1) the issue risk-management score, which includes corporate disclosures on policies, practices, and performance, where available; and (2) the issue risk exposures scores, which consists only of data from third-party sources that are mapped to companies' estimated financial segments. As shown in Figure 4.4, the corporate disclosure-driven scores have maintained a stable positive correlation with company size, while the scores based on independent information have declined in correlation with size over time, potentially reflecting a rise in independent sources regarding companies' ESG exposure.

*Lesson 2*: Different risks have materialized over different time horizons. Hence, giving more weight to some issues than others in the rating construction will impact the time horizon over which a rating might indicate financial relevance.

As an example of this, we found that governance issues were consistently more significant for point-in-time financial fundamentals, while environmental and social issues contributed to stock-price performance over a longer period (Giese et al. 2020). We suggest that markets appear to price in ESG event risks quickly over a shorter time horizon, particularly environmental and social issues. Thus, when the focus of an ESG rating was to measure risks that can impact a company's short-term exposure to financial

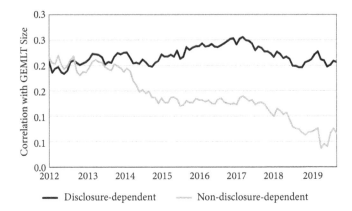

**Figure 4.4** Correlations between corporate and independent disclosures and size

*Note*: Disclosure-dependent score is the weighted average key issue management score, the non-disclosure dependent score is the weighted average key issue risk exposure score. Data from December 31, 2012 to August 31, 2020 (end date was subject to data availability).
*Source*: Author's calculations.

shocks, then governance indicators showed the best financial results. Yet, over longer time periods, a more balanced overall signal that aggregated industry-specific environmental and social issues was associated with better financial results than any of the individual pillar indicators, including the governance score.

*Lesson 3*: Weights play a big role. Specifically, ESG weightings have been neither static nor uniform over time, and ratings that capture industry-specific and dynamically evolving weights do better at predicting financial performance.

Static weighting has the benefit of being simple and transparent. Moreover, when an investor lacks specific views about the relative importance of environmental, social, or governance issues, this 'naïve' method could be appropriate. By contrast, selecting and weighting E, S, and G issues for each industry more precisely reflects industry exposures to relevant risks. Nevertheless, it has the drawback of introducing complexity and less comparability across industries. On average, each of the 158 Global Industry Classification Standard (GICS®)[8] sub-industries uses six ESG Key Issues in assigning weights in the MSCI ESG Ratings. The selection of Key Issues and their respective weights are readjusted on an annual basis.

In the short term, the equal-weighted approach gave higher weights to Governance Key Issues and showed slightly stronger financial results over a one-year window than the industry-specific approach of the MSCI ESG Rating. Yet, over a longer period of 13 years, we found that a hypothetical portfolio, constructed using the industry-specific approach to weight ESG issues, outperformed by 7.4 percent (cumulatively) one that equally weighted the ESG issues for all companies. Over time, the Social and Environmental Key Issues became more important, as they tended to unfold more slowly. Another important contributor to performance was that the industry-specific approach shifted dynamically as the weightings were rebalanced annually (Giese et al. 2020).

## Lessons for integrating ESG in portfolio construction

Broadly, there are two main methods for integrating ESG factors into portfolio construction:

*Select securities either for exclusion or inclusion*: Investors can use one or more ESG metrics that target the ESG characteristic to be excluded or included. This method could be applied to meet values-based objectives, such as excluding companies involved in tobacco production or in human rights controversies, or by including companies that meet a target diversity threshold. It could also be applied to financially driven objectives, such as excluding companies scoring poorly on corporate governance, or by including companies offering ESG-themed solutions such as green technologies.

*Re-weight securities*: Investors can give a greater weight to those reflecting a target ESG characteristic, at the expense of securities lacking that target ESG characteristic. This method could be applied to meet financially or impact-driven objectives, such as tilting toward companies with lower carbon intensity. A variant of reweighting is to employ optimization techniques to re-weight securities to maximize exposure to the target ESG characteristic, while adhering to pre-specific constraints such as sector, geographic, or factor exposure.

Comparing a targeted ESG profile and the portfolio's risk and return with those of the chosen benchmark is critical in selecting an approach. Today, those data are usually readily available for such comparisons. For example, commonly used global and regional equity benchmarks can be characterized by their carbon footprint, their percentage of female directors, and the percentage of companies with exposure to a range of business activities, from firearms to fossil fuels. We can examine such data alongside metrics on a benchmark's performance, risk, and investability (for a list of available ESG metrics, see Kouzmenko et al. 2020).

Once the method for integrating ESG has been chosen, the remaining specific portfolio construction issues need to be addressed. In so doing, we have generated several guidelines that are useful when implementing ESG into portfolios, including the following:

*Guideline 1*: ESG policies or mandates that impose a limited number of values-based exclusions have not incurred a large tracking error.

How much exclusion is too much? In looking at three model portfolios with increasingly stringent criteria, we found that excluding companies based on alleged corporate wrongdoing had slightly boosted returns but, as the exclusions increased, so did the tracking error, over the period from February 2007 to June 2017. Returns were also impaired as exclusions became more sweeping (Lee et al. 2017).

Examining the historical track record of ESG indexes also indicated that, when values-based exclusions were minimal and introduced few sector biases, the tracking error tended to be low. For example, the MSCI ACWI ESG Screened Index excludes stocks associated with controversies, including civilian and nuclear weapons, and tobacco, that derive revenue from thermal coal and oil sands extraction, and that are noncompliant with the United Nations Global Compact principles. As of February 26, 2021, the set of excluded stocks numbered 158 of the total index universe of 2964. Its tracking error to the parent MSCI ACWI Index was 0.47 (between May 31, 2012, and February 26, 2021).

*Guideline 2*: Portfolio construction methods that select or overweight better ESG performers within industries (i.e., best-in-class approaches) can lead to unintended factor exposures that may impact portfolio risk and return.

Equities research has found mild positive correlations between ESG ratings and factor exposures such as low volatility, larger size, and higher financial quality. While the level of correlation tends to be low, many of those relationships are stable and highly significant over time (Melas et al. 2016). An analysis of selected ESG indexes in 2020's volatile market also supports the finding that indexes with stronger ESG profiles tend to have higher exposure to low volatility; that exposure has been protective during sharp sell-offs but these firms have struggled to keep up during market rallies.

Advances in analytics allow investors to measure, rather than conjecture about, how much ESG has contributed to explaining portfolio risk and performance over and above these systematic exposures (Dunn et al. 2018). Factor models show that the explanatory power for ESG increased recently, in 2019 and 2020, based on a 13-year study period (Cano and Minovitsky 2021). When we look at corporate bonds, we find that higher ESG-rated bonds have typically offered exposure to higher-credit-quality bonds. Again, however, we can isolate the contribution from ESG, providing complementary information to what is offered by credit ratings (Mendiratta et al. 2020). Overall, the ability to consider the contribution of a portfolio's ESG exposure distinct from and alongside other intended and unintended exposures to traditional financial factors now offers investors a fuller understanding of portfolio characteristics and performance.

*Guideline 3*: While various ESG concepts are often correlated, targeting a desired outcome requires using specific inputs, where possible.

In constructing an equity portfolio, targeting a single ESG criterion, such as having more women on the corporate board, could result in unintended ESG benefits (not related to governance), such as better human capital practices (Eastman and Seretis 2018), or better carbon emissions management (Milhomem 2021). Yet when investors aim for a specific outcome, such as greater carbon efficiency, the input variable for portfolio construction should specifically measure companies' carbon efficiency, and not some other ESG criteria that could be broadly related.

To illustrate, two ESG indexes targeting higher overall ESG quality without an explicit carbon reduction goal have shown lower carbon intensity versus the benchmark. As of January 31, 2021, the MSCI ACWI ESG Focus Index and the MSCI ACWI ESG Leaders Index reported carbon intensity levels that represented approximately 31 percent and 36 percent reduction, respectively, versus the MSCI ACWI Index. Because carbon emissions are not used as a direct input into the index construction methodology, however, the carbon intensity is an *unintended byproduct* of the construction methodology that could conceivably differ in other time periods. By contrast, two ESG indexes that explicitly target a reduction in carbon intensity, among other climate-related objectives, showed lower carbon intensity *by design* and hence they seek to retain the reduction over time. The MSCI ACWI Low Carbon Target Index and the MSCI Climate Paris Aligned Index reported carbon intensity levels that represented approximately 70 percent and 80 percent reduction versus the MSCI ACWI Index, respectively.

*Guideline 4*: Allocators must choose between 'bottom-up' and 'top-down' approaches in integrating ESG across their total equity portfolios.

Investors face complex challenges in integrating ESG efficiently across multiple actively managed and indexed mandates across their portfolio. There are two basic approaches:

(1) A 'bottom-up' implementation addresses each portfolio one by one, leaving the policy (or reference) benchmark unchanged (at least initially). Historically, many asset allocators have followed this approach. From the perspective of an equities investor, Rao et al. (2021) explain that, on the plus side, this can lead to minimal disruption to existing actively managed ESG portfolios. On the minus side, this can lead to inconsistencies in ESG standards across portfolios, and thus generate sub-optimal outcomes at the total portfolio level. For example, in the

Rao et al. (2021) study, 1100 actively managed equity funds that had passed a series of screens for ESG criteria in September 2020 differed widely in how they measured up against the most common values-based criteria, such as those related to weapons or coal exposure.

(2)   A 'top-down' implementation starts with the adoption of an ESG benchmark to measure performance of both indexed and active mandates. This offers a more comprehensive approach that applies across all types of mandates, but it may require more significant changes to existing allocations. Such a 'top-down' method could be applied across both equity and fixed-income allocations, as has been demonstrated by leading institutions such as Swiss Re (2018), which adopted a top-down approach in an effort to improve risk-adjusted returns over the long run.

Allocators also may wish to weigh the potential costs of disrupting existing active mandates versus the benefits of adopting a consistent approach across their entire portfolios.

## Integrating Climate Risk

Looking forward, an increasingly urgent issue for investor attention will be how to integrate climate risk factors within the investment portfolio. Scientists have warned that the world's emissions are on track to exceed a tipping point that could lead to irreversible, catastrophic climate change (Sautner and Starks 2023). As policymakers grapple with measures to cut emissions and to protect us from severe weather changes, financial regulators are considering the implications for the allocation of capital and the stability of our financial system. Investors are only at the beginning stages of understanding the various paths that these changes could take in our physical world and in regulatory regimes.

The integration of ESG considerations as financially material factors into the investment process, of course, already includes important aspects of mitigating relevant environmental risks for specific industries. Yet because ESG reflects a range of social and governance issues in addition to environmental issues, a holistic ESG view, even one that focuses on capturing only financially material issues, will not substitute for a dedicated accounting of alternative climate scenarios, given the uncertainty around climate risks.

Implementing climate risk considerations into investment decisions may require an approach that supplements and differs from current approaches to implementing ESG. Different asset classes could face quite distinct dimensions of climate risk. Additionally, climate-related risks and opportunities likely will unfold differently across time horizons for different sectors and asset characteristics within an asset class. In fact, we see evidence in public equities that companies at the 'tails' of climate risk—those with assets at the highest risk of becoming obsolete or 'stranded' during the economic transition versus those representing potential solutions to hasten the transition—have started to face discernible stock-price valuation discounts and premiums, respectively (Giese et al. 2021b).

Furthermore, investors may need to account for feedback loops with the real economy; even a portfolio consisting of only the most 'green' or resilient holdings may not protect against a world in which assets not held in one's own portfolio take the world beyond an emissions tipping point. Hence, standard setters and policymakers are exploring new types of metrics that can account for the externalities, gauging, for example, the alignment of portfolios with a desired temperature pathway over the next several decades.[9] How to integrate these complex considerations—many of which are replete with uncertainties—will require new expertise in measuring exposures, constructing portfolios, and adjusting asset allocations. As standard setters have called for, harmonization of data disclosure requirements and adoption of consistent methodological principles in the construction of climate-related measurement will be needed to provide the critical ingredients necessary for the investment industry to marry climate and financial modeling.

## Conclusion

As ESG has entered the mainstream of investing, professionally managed assets that incorporate ESG considerations have grown dramatically in recent years. One key reason for this shift is the increasing evidence of how and when ESG factors have been financially material. We now see clearer distinctions between ESG motivations, especially between values-driven and financially driven objectives. These distinctions are fundamental in understanding why and how ESG measures differ. In addition, differing objectives can cloud views on whether ESG really has added value from a financial perspective. Despite a growing focus and empirical analysis on ESG from a financially relevant perspective, some confusion remains, as legacy approaches still exist that measure different objectives. By focusing on a clear and consistent measurement of ESG, we can obtain a more useful understanding of how it has contributed to financial performance. We believe that this is the way forward for ESG investing.

Our understanding of financial performance can be further improved by expanding data sources beyond corporate disclosures. Improvement of the underlying data holds great promise for constructing more precise measures across a range of ESG concepts. Even with imperfect data and evolving measurements, the available evidence, spanning over a decade, has supported the investment thesis. That is, industry-specific, financially relevant ESG information collected on a dynamic basis has improved returns by reducing risk and improving profitability. For investors implementing an ESG approach, emerging lessons on portfolio construction include the need to identify both intended and unintended outcomes in ESG and traditional financial factor exposures. Innovations in analytical tools have allowed more targeted applications and measurement of ESG characteristics alongside financial characteristics, improving transparency for investment managers and fund allocators. For asset owners considering implementing their ESG objectives across their portfolios, comparing the ESG and financial characteristics across the equity and fixed-income fund universe versus an appropriate ESG benchmark that reflects their investment objectives, can help inform decisions on whether to apply a bottom-up, fund-by-fund approach or a top-down approach.

Over the past decade, mounting evidence on how ESG has affected financial performance has persuaded many institutional investors to adopt ESG considerations into investment decisions (Lachance and Stroehle 2023). With climate risk, investors, companies, and the wider public may not have the luxury of another decade of wait-and-see. A shift of capital away from a carbon-dependent economy and the physical effects of our changing climate could affect the pricing of assets dramatically and in a compressed timeframe. Prudent investors would do well to pay attention to this next frontier of risks and opportunities.

## Acknowledgments

The author thanks Joel Chernoff for his contributions to this chapter.

## Notes

1. Measurements of ESG-related AUM vary widely, but several reports, including the 'Report on US Sustainable and Impact Investing Trends' from the US SIF Foundation (2020), as well as the Principles for Responsible Investment (PRI 2020), have found substantial increases in allocations to ESG investing, in part driven by strong performance during the COVID-19 pandemic.

2. This chapter draws on previous research that uses a broad range of time frames drawn from various papers. Some cover different time periods. We have updated in some instances where possible. This chapter is not intended to compare results across time periods nor is it meant to be representative of performance over any particular time. The analysis and observations in this report are limited solely to the period of the relevant historical data, back-test, or simulation stated. Past performance—whether actual, back-tested, or simulated—is no indication or guarantee of future performance. None of the information or analysis herein

is intended to constitute investment advice or a recommendation to make (or refrain from making) any kind of investment decision or asset allocation and should not be relied on as such.

3. In MSCI's ESG Ratings Key Issue Framework, thousands of data points are grouped across 35 ESG Key Issues that focus on the intersection between a company's core business and the industry-specific issues that may create significant risks and opportunities for the company. The Key Issues are weighted according to impact and time horizon of the risk or opportunity. All companies are assessed for Corporate Governance and Corporate Behavior. Please see https://www.msci.com/our-solutions/esg-investing/esg-ratings/esg-ratings-key-issue-framework. For the most current Key ESG Issues and their contribution to companies' ESG Ratings, please see https://www.msci.com/our-solutions/esg-investing/esg-ratings/materiality-map.

4. As we used a z-score format (which creates a standard unit of measurement), we were able to average these three quintile differences in one aggregated target function.

5. We controlled for size bias in ESG scores by using the residuals obtained from the cross-sectional regression of industry-adjusted ESG scores on size scores.

6. The study period of analysis is limited by data availability on the cost of capital.

7. The data on cost of capital was obtained from Thomson Reuters. It is the weighted average of the cost of equity, debt (after tax), and preferred stock. Cost of equity was derived from CAPM using the risk-free rate and equity risk premium of the company's country, and beta with respect to the country's primary index. Cost of debt took into account both short- and long-term debt, which is a 1- and 10-year yield on the credit curve of the company. Cost of preferred stock was the current dividend yield on preferred stock.

8. GICS, the global industry classification standard jointly developed by MSCI and Standard & Poor's.

9. See, for example, the Task Force report on Climate-related Financial Disclosures (2021a) and the TCFD Portfolio Alignment Team (2021b) report.

# References

Boffo, R. and R. Patalano (2020). *ESG Investing: Practices, Progress and Challenges*. Paris: OECD, ESG Investing: Practices, Progress and Challenges (oecd.org).

Cano, G. and S. Minovitsky (2021). Factoring in ESG. New York: MSCI. https://www.msci.com/www/blog-posts/factoring-in-esg/02343304664.

Dunn, J., S. Fitzgibbons, and L. Pomorski (2018). 'Assessing Risk Through Environmental, Social and Governance Exposures,' *Journal of Investment Management*, 16(1): 4–17. https://scholar.google.com/scholar?oi=bibs&cluster=3481056115109102315&btnI=1&hl=en

Eastman, M.T. and P. Seretis (2018). 'Women on Boards and the Human Capital Connection,' MSCI Research Insight. https://www.msci.com/www/research-paper/women-on-boards-and-the-human/0876228691.

Eccles, R.G. and J.C. Stroehle (2018). 'Exploring Social Origins in the Construction of ESG Measures,' SSRN Working Paper. https://papers.ssrn.com/sol3/papers.cfm?abstract_id=3212685.

Eccles, R.G., L.E. Lee, and J.C. Stroehle (2019) 'The Social Origins of ESG: An Analysis of Innovest and KLD,' Working Paper, Said Business School. https://papers.ssrn.com/sol3/papers.cfm?abstract_id=3318225.

Friede, G., T. Busch, and A. Bassen (2015). 'ESG and Financial Performance: Aggregated Evidence from more than 2,000 Empirical Studies,' *Journal of Sustainable Finance and Investment*, 5(4): 210–233.

Giese, G. (2019). 'Understanding MSCI ESG Indexes,' MSCI Research Insight. https://www.msci.com/documents/10199/5b8d92f4-5427-5c8b-e57c-86b7b1466514.

Giese, G., N. Kumar, Z. Nagy, and R. Kouzmenko (2021a). 'The Drivers of ESG Returns: A Fundamental Return Decomposition Approach,' MSCI Research Insight. https://www.msci.com/www/research-paper/the-drivers-of-esg-returns/02343319303.

Giese, G., L.E. Lee, D. Melas, Z. Nagy, and L. Nishikawa (2019a). 'Consistent ESG Integration through ESG Benchmarks,' *The Journal of Index Investing*, 10(2): 1–19. https://www.msci.com/our-solutions/esg-investing/foundations-of-esg-investing.

Giese, G., L.E. Lee, D. Melas, Z. Nagy, and L. Nishikawa (2019b). 'Foundations of ESG Investing: How ESG Affects Equity Valuation, Risk, and Performance,' *The Journal of Portfolio Management*, 45(5): 69–83. http://info.msci.com/foundations-of-ESG-investing-part1.

Giese, G., Z. Nagy, and L.E. Lee (2020). 'Deconstructing ESG Ratings Performance: Risk and Return for E, S and G by Time Horizon, Sector and Weighting,' MSCI Research Insight. https://www.msci.com/www/research-paper/deconstructing-esg-ratings/01921647796.

Giese, G., Z. Nagy, and B. Rauis (2021b). 'Foundations of Climate Investing: How Equity Markets Have Priced Climate Transition Risks,' *The Journal of Portfolio Management*, 47(9): 35–53.

Hammond, P.B. and A. O'Brien (2023). 'Pensions and ESG: An Institutional and Historical Perspective.' In P.B. Hammond, R. Maurer, and O.S. Mitchell, eds., *Pension Funds and Sustainable Investment: Challenges and Opportunities.* Oxford: Oxford University Press, pp. 17–57.

Khan, M., G. Serafeim, and A. Yoon (2016). 'Corporate Sustainability: First Evidence on Materiality,' *The Accounting Review*, 91(6): 1697–1724.

Kouzmenko R., S. Katiyar, and A. Gupta (2020). 'MSCI IndexMetrics®: An Analytical Framework for Factor, ESG and Thematic Investing,' *MSCI Research Insight*. https://www.msci.com/documents/10199/402635a5-fd5d-498e-985a-1bec8ff8d8b1

Lachance, S. and J. Stroehle (2023). 'The Origins of ESG in Pensions: Strategies and Outcomes.' In P.B. Hammond, R. Maurer, and O.S. Mitchell, eds., *Pension Funds and Sustainable Investment: Challenges and Opportunities.* Oxford: Oxford University Press, pp. 58–81.

Lee, L.E., Z. Nagy, and M.T. Eastman (2017). 'Do Corporate Controversies Help or Hurt Performance?' *Journal of Environmental Investing*, 8(1): 222–251. http://www.thejei.com/wp-content/uploads/2017/11/Journal-of-Environmental-Investing-8-No.-1.rev_-1.pdf.

Melas, D., Z. Nagy, and P. Kulkarni (2016). 'Factor Investing and ESG Integration,' MSCI Research Insight. https://www.msci.com/documents/10199/d13c8a0e-de0e-4313-82e2-0a197af30c34.

Mendiratta, R., H.D. Varsani, and G. Giese (2020). 'Foundations of ESG Investing in Corporate Bonds: How ESG Affected Corporate Credit Risk and Performance,' MSCI Research Insight. https://www.msci.com/documents/10199/19248715/Foundations-of-ESG-Investing-in-Corporate-Bonds-How-ESG-Affects-Corporate-Credit-Risk-and-Performance+(002).pdf.

Milhomem, C. (2021). 'Women on Boards: The Hidden Environmental Connection?' MSCI Blog. https://www.msci.com/www/blog-posts/women-on-boards-the-hidden/02361079223.

MSCI Investment Insights (2021). 'Global Institutional Investor Survey,' MSCI.com. https://www.msci.com/our-clients/asset-owners/investment-insights-report.

Nikulina, L. (2023). 'Global Pensions and ESG: Is There a Better Way?' In P.B. Hammond, R. Maurer, and O.S. Mitchell, eds., *Pension Funds and Sustainable Investment: Challenges and Opportunities*. Oxford: Oxford University Press, pp. 157–169.

Principles for Responsible Investment (PRI) (2020). 'COVID-19 Accelerates ESG Trends, Global Investors Confirm,' Unpri.org. https://www.unpri.org/pri-blog/covid-19-accelerates-esg-trends-global-investors-confirm/6372.article.

Rao, A., G. Giese, R. Subramanian, and Z. Nagy (2021). 'Better Together: Policy Benchmarks, Active Equity and ESG,' MSCI Research Paper. https://www.msci.com/www/research-paper/better-together-policy/02291648521.

Sautner, Z. and L. Starks (2023). 'ESG and Downside Risks: Implications for Pension Funds.' In P.B. Hammond, R. Maurer, and O.S. Mitchell, eds., *Pension Funds and Sustainable Investment: Challenges and Opportunities*. Oxford: Oxford University Press, pp. 137–156.

Serafeim, G. and A. Yoon (2021). 'Stock Price Reactions to ESG News: The Role of ESG Ratings and Disagreement,' Harvard Business School Working Paper 21-079. https://papers.ssrn.com/sol3/papers.cfm?abstract_id=3765217.

Swiss Re (2018). *Responsible Investments: The Next Steps in Our Journey*. Zurich: Swiss Re. https://www.swissre.com/Library/responsible-investments-the-next-steps-in-our-journey.html.

Task Force on Climate-related Financial Disclosures (2021a) *Proposed Guidance on Climate-related Metrics, Targets, and Transition Plans*. Basel: TCFD. https://assets.bbhub.io/company/sites/60/2021/05/2021-TCFD-Metrics_Targets_Guidance.pdf.

Task Force on Climate-related Financial Disclosures (2021b) *Measuring Portfolio Alignment: Technical Supplement*. Basel: TCFD. https://assets.bbhub.io/company/sites/60/2021/05/2021-TCFD-Portfolio_Alignment_Technical_Supplement.pdf.

UNDP (2015). *What are the Sustainable Development Goals?* New York: UNDP. https://www.undp.org/sustainable-development-goals.

US SIF Foundation (2020). *The US SIF Foundation's Biennial 'Trends Report' Finds That Sustainable Investing Assets Reach $17.1 Trillion*. Washington, DC: US SIF Foundation. https://www.ussif.org/blog_home.asp?Display=155.

**Part II**

**The Evolution of Pension ESG Investing**

# Chapter 5

## ESG and Expected Returns on Equities

The Case of Environmental Ratings

*Christopher C. Geczy and John B. Guerard Jr.*

Today, environmental concerns dominate environmental, social, and governance (ESG) criteria cited by investors as influencing portfolio decisions, measured both by numbers of investors and by the total amount of assets subject to environmental criteria. Until recently, other ESG criteria were dominant. The shift reflects a change in preferences or at least a heightened perception about the importance of climate change and related issues facing the environment, which might have an anthropogenic component.

For example, the US Social Investment Forum Foundation's *2020 Trends Report* (US SIF 2020) indicated that 'Environmental Considerations' was the leading ESG criterion by assets for money managers in 2020 with US$13.45 trillion out of approximately US$17 trillion aggregated across all investment vehicles, including separate accounts and undisclosed vehicles (US SIF 2020: 21, figure 2.4). The leading individual criterion is related to climate change. In addition, of the top 14 criteria listed, five fall in some way under the 'E' environmental umbrella. In contrast, in the 2007 Report (SIF 2007), environmental issues were ranked sixth, preceded by issues related to tobacco, Sudan, the MacBride Principles, human rights, community relations, and alcohol production, distribution, and sales (SIF 2007: 17, figure 3.4).

The challenge faced by pension fiduciaries is honoring the long-standing principle that their legal and ethical duties must focus on the financial betterment of beneficiaries, rather than on any other (perhaps private) benefit including sustainability, those related to the common good or the environment, or those related to social goals, if for any reason such consideration results in tradeoffs against risk-adjusted returns. For plans governed by ERISA, 1998 guidance from Robert Doyle, then Director of the Office of Regulations and Interpretations of the United States Department of Labor (US DOL), set a requirement of a side-by-side comparison of risk-adjusted

Christopher C. Geczy and John B. Guerard Jr., *ESG and Expected Returns on Equities*. In: *Pension Funds and Sustainable Investment*. Edited by P. Brett Hammond, Raimond Maurer, and Olivia S. Mitchell, Oxford University Press. © Christopher C. Geczy and John B. Guerard Jr. (2023). DOI: 10.1093/oso/9780192889195.003.0005 returns consistent with the Sharpe ratio, whenever socially responsible investments are considered for a plan:

> In discharging investment duties ... fiduciaries must, among other things, consider the role of the particular investment [in the] investment portfolio. Because every investment necessarily causes a plan to forgo other investment opportunities fiduciaries also must consider expected return on alternative investments with similar risks available to the plan ... If [those] requirements are met, the selection of a 'socially responsible' mutual fund as either a plan investment or a designated investment alternative ... would not, in itself, be inconsistent with ... fiduciary standards.
>
> (Doyle 1998: 2)

One of the challenges faced by those overseeing ERISA plans has been the perceived changes in guidance from the US DOL. For instance, reversing a stance articulated during the previous administration, Obama Administration Labor Secretary Thomas Perez said in October 2015: 'The question is this: Can an ERISA plan invest in projects or companies that serve the common good, while still keeping at the forefront the fiduciary principle of investing prudently and for the exclusive benefit of retirees and workers? I believe we can.' He also said that the '2008 [Bush Administration] guidance gave cooties to impact investing' (Perez 2015: np).

In turn, more recently, the Trump DOL articulated yet another shift in tone in a 2020 proposed rule:

> As ESG investing has increased, it has engendered important and substantial questions and inconsistencies, with numerous observers identifying a lack of precision and consistency in the ESG investment marketplace. There is no consensus about what constitutes a genuine ESG investment, and ESG rating systems are often vague and inconsistent, despite featuring prominently in marketing efforts
>
> (United States Department of Labor 2020)

This message raises further concerns about the fiduciary setting in which ESG criteria are considered, either via positive or negative screening, activism, engagement activities, or in other ways.

We address the important question about whether environmental scores, widely referenced and utilized, contain information directly related to expected returns and long-standing models for their forecasts that have survived multiple-comparison tests and out-of-sample tests alike. The results bridge concerns trustees would naturally have when making the required side-by-side comparisons of investments or portfolios selected, so as to have certain ESG characteristics with those that do not. Specifically, they meet the requirement of no decline in expected returns, holding risk constant,

TABLE 5.1  Reasons institutional investors report considering ESG factors, 2020 (US SIF Foundation)

| Reason | Number of Money Managers | % of Managers Responding | ESG Assets US Dollars (in billions) |
|---|---|---|---|
| Risk | 95 | 84% | $2,062 |
| Client Demand | 92 | 81% | $3,569 |
| Social or Environmental Impact | 90 | 80% | $3,476 |
| Returns | 82 | 73% | $2,355 |
| Mission | 79 | 70% | $2,445 |
| Fiduciary Duty | 72 | 64% | $3,557 |
| UN Sustainable Development Goals | 52 | 46% | $406 |
| Regulatory Compliance | 24 | 21% | $3,345 |
| Total Responding | 113 | | $3,621 |

*Note*: The table presents responses from 65 institutional investors who were asked to list the reasons they consider ESG factors among a series of possibilities. The table is ordered by the total ESG assets managed or held by these institutions. Assets and numbers of money managers may overlap since respondents could and did list more than one reason.
*Source*: Authors' adaptation of US SIF 2020 Trends Report, figure 3.13.

as set out by Robert Doyle in 1998, and attendant to the basic notion of financial fiduciary duty also in non-ERISA settings.

Recent surveys also indicate that asset managers and investors may reference ESG characteristics in ways that defy the traditional 'constrained opportunity set' interpretation of the incorporation of ESG characteristics in investment decisions. For instance, in a recent assessment of the reasons institutional investors reported considering ESG factors (Table 5.1), the most cited reason was Risk (84 percent), followed by Client Demand (81 percent), Social or Environmental Impact (80 percent), Returns (73 percent), Mission (70 percent), Fiduciary Duty (64 percent), UN Sustainable Development Goals (46 percent), and Regulatory Compliance (31 percent) (US SIF 2020: 28, figure 2.13). One interpretation of this ordering is that ESG criteria contain information important for investment selection, apart from the typical non-pecuniary or purpose-related reasons mentioned for screening or portfolio tilts toward 'good actor' firms in equity portfolios. When information on public investments is not limited to formal filings or releases governed, say, by Generally Accepted Accounting Principles (GAAP), other sources of information that would otherwise be difficult or expensive to collect and assess, including proprietary analysis-based ESG scores, may be valuable in assessing the cross-section of public firms.

The proprietary analysis-based ESG scoring used in this study is MSCI ESG KLD STATS, a 1991–2017 database of firm ESG ratings, today subsumed in MSCI ESG Ratings (MSCI ESG Research Inc. 2015). The inception of the ratings system was followed by the launch of the Domini 400 Social Index (today the MSCI KLD 400 Social Index), to rate companies whose stocks were in the index. We show that firm ESG characteristics computed via normalized MSCI KLD environmental scores interact with forecasted expected returns of US equities estimated from long-standing models for expected return first articulated by Guerard and Stone (1992), Bloch et al. (1993), Guerard et al. (1997), Guerard (1997a, 1997b) and further developed by Guerard et al. (2014, 2015). We focus on environmental characteristics because, especially for public firms, the potential cost of achieving high ratings in this category may be high, and because climate change is a major issue among SRI/ESG investors. The importance of using long-established models of expected return must be underscored. As Markowitz and Xu (1994), Lo and MacKinlay (1987), and Harvey et al. (2016) have pointed out, data mining biases in the absence of multiple-comparison test controls can lead to poor out-of-sample results. By relying on long-standing models developed before the KLD data rose to prominence, we may avoid some of the biases inherent in typical analysis.

Specifically, we find that firms with high ESG (environmental) scores have excess returns over those with low scores unconditionally, but also conditional on expected returns from models above with 'bagged' value, earnings, and momentum components articulated in the early 1990s. In addition, a battery of now-traditional risk-factor models including the CAPM, the Fama-French (1992) three-factor model, the Carhart (1997) extension, and a five-factor model that augments the Carhart model with the Fama-French Quality factor (Fama and French 2015) subsume neither environmental score-related return differentials nor expected return premia from the long-standing models. For pension trustees, or for the consultants and managers they hire, combining information from both inputs (expected return models and ESG criteria) might provide advantages in constructing equity portfolios. For those fiduciaries whose concerns center on risk and return considerations alone when selecting investments, our results suggest that incorporating non-GAAP information via earnings, price momentum, and ESG characteristics, along with a collection of weighted value measures, may collectively and individually add value rather than serve to induce the cost of a constraint on the investment universe.

# A Brief SRI/ESG Environmental Screen Literature Review

The empirical evidence is mixed on whether SRI/ESG portfolios incorporating constraints related to positive or negative screens induces a cost in investment performance or whether it is associated with additional gains.[1] The *Journal of Investing* has been an active SRI/ESG outlet for more than 20 years, starting with Luck and Pilotte (1993), Kurtz and DiBartolomeo (1996), and many of the Moskowitz Prize winners for research in socially responsible investing, including the first winner, Guerard (1997a). In this analysis, we apply the earnings forecasting model used in Guerard (1997a, 1997b) and the subsequent larger composite models of expected returns, Guerard et al. (2014, 2015), to show that incorporating ESG Environmental (ENV) criteria may potentially enhance stockholder returns. Specifically, we find that in certain implementations, incorporating the KLD environmental criteria enhances portfolio returns.

The Moskowitz Prize, awarded annually since 1996 for research in socially responsible investing, has recognized the environmental research analyses of Russo and Fouts (1997), Dowell et al. (2000), and Naaraayanan et al. (2020) among its winning studies. Russo and Fouts (1997) used the Franklin Research & Development Corporation (FRDC) environmental ranking. These authors report that in 1991 and 1992, in a 243-firm regression model using the return on assets (ROA) as the dependent variable, that ROA was positively and statistically associated with firm growth, industry growth, firm size, advertising intensity, and the FRDC environmental ranking.

Dowell, Hart, and Yeung (DHY 2000 hereafter) start their analysis with a universe of the S&P 500 Companies, operating in countries with per capita income below US$8,000 (in 1985 US dollars, relatively lower-income countries) during 1994–1997. They restrict their modeling to manufacturing firms and use the Investor Responsible Research Center (IRRC) environmental rating. The resulting universe is 89 firms. The dependent variable is Tobin's Q, measuring the firm Market Value of equity relative to the replacement costs of tangible assets, defined as book value of inventory plus the net value of physical plant and equipment. DHY (2000) study three ENV standards:

> ENV1 = Local ENV standard,
> ENV2 = US ENV standard, and
> ENV3 = Stringent ENV standard.

DHY (2000) report that 72 of the 89 firms never changed ENV strategies; 16 changed once; and one changed twice. Of these changes, 12 were positive and six were negative changes.

The DHY regressions show that Tobin's Q is positively and statistically associated with research and development expenditures, advertising intensity, and the IRRC environmental ranking. The smallest coefficient for ED2 (Table 5.3, regression 3-d) indicates that firms adopting their own stringent global environmental standards have a Tobin's Q that is higher than those using US standards abroad.

Naaraayanan, Sachdeva, and Sharma (NSS 2020 hereafter) study the New York City Pension System (NYCPS) Board Accountability Project (BAP, announced in November 2014) to hold boards accountable to long-term shareholders and give pensioners a voice concerning board diversity, climate change risks, and employee treatment. In the Russell 3,000 stock universe during the 2000–2013 time period, 62 of the 181 BAPs were environmentally based. NSS (2020) use the Thomson-Reuters (Asset4) ENV score. The reported regression results indicated that the return on assets was positively and statistically associated with the Fossil Fuel index return, form size, the market-to-book value ratio, and profitability. The authors did not find a statistically significant coefficient on the Thomson-Reuters environmental rating. Overall, the authors report that targeted BAP firms effectively reduced real Environmental Protection Authority (EPA)-measured toxic releases by a statistically significant amount. The BAP-targeted firms reduced their Toxic Release Inventory (TRI) and the Greenhouse Gas Reporting Program (GGRP) levels by up to 50 percent.

## Environmental Scores

Before the development of the KLD dataset in the early 1990s, which went on to become an industry standard, a large volume of ESG-related research focused on various ways to estimate the effects of ESG on company performance (for examples, see Gordon and Buchholz 1978; Aupperle et al. 1985; Rosen et al. 1991). To our knowledge, the first academic papers to validate and link KLD data with firm characteristics were by Ruf et al. (1993) and Graves and Waddock (1994).

KLD ratings started in 1991, covered about 650 companies, and were based on a –2 to +2 ratings system in nine categories, including negative screens. The current study utilizes the 2017 version of the database, in which rankings start December 1991, end December 2017, and contain binary values of 0 and 1 for strengths and weaknesses in seven categories and six controversy scores for more than 3,000 companies.

Over time, the KLD database has been enhanced, resulting from acquisitions and other methodology changes. For example, in 2000, the human rights category was added (Galema et al. 2008); in 2002, governance was added (Statman and Glushkov 2009); and in 2010, KLD decided to rank companies only on issues relevant for their industry instead of all issues.

From the early KLD studies (Sharfman 1996) and continuing to Statman and Glushkov (2009), among others, there has been an ongoing discussion about the challenges of creating a unique overall KLD-based score.

The simplest way that sums all strengths and subtracts all weaknesses incurs its own set of biases and imbalances driven by data structure rather than companies' ESG attributes. Dorfleitner et al. (2014) study the relation between ESG score performance and stock performance in various markets worldwide, reiterating global evidence of the positive association between firm ESG ratings and subsequent returns; however, the bias remains. The earlier literature attempted to address the implicit bias arising from weighting each issue equally. For example, in order to avoid treating each ESG strength and weakness as equally important, Waddock and Graves (1997) rely on the issues weighting scheme developed by Ruf et al. (1993). Because such weightings are highly subjective, they are no longer used in the more recent studies. For example, Employee Relations strengths are evaluated on ten individual variables, with a maximum score of 8, while Human Rights strengths are evaluated on three variables with a maximum score of 2. Hence, because of the uneven ranges, the raw score will be much more affected by the Employee Relations strengths vs. Human Rights strengths. The same issues affect the weights of strengths vs. concerns. An area having a larger number of evaluated metrics will receive a higher implied weighting in the overall raw calculations.

Another challenge arises because of the changing coverage of the KLD dataset over time. Specifically, as the number of strengths and weaknesses changes in each category, summing the raw strengths and weakness, as was the earlier practice, creates score dynamics that are influenced by the dataset construction, rather than by the company's changing ESG policies. Kempf and Osthoff (2007) address this problem by normalizing the net scores within each of the six categories. In addition, they introduce a way to transform the weakness measure into the same direction as the strengths.

Manescu (2011) adds an additional refinement that normalizes strengths and weaknesses separately because the number of each sub-strength and sub-weakness are different and also vary across time.

## Modifying the KLD Environmental Score Data

Inside each of (now) seven subcategories (Governance, Community, Diversity, Employee Relations, Environment, Human Rights, and Product Safety), KLD provides binary ratings on multiple individual measures of strengths and concerns criteria. For each of the seven categories and for each company in each year, the Category Raw Net Score is the sum of category strengths minus the sum of category weaknesses. The Total Raw Net Score is the sum of the strengths across all categories minus the sum of all the weaknesses across all categories. There is a Total Net Score only if both strength and weakness exist. If strengths or weaknesses are missing entirely, the Net Score is missing for that company in that year and is not included in calculations.

To avoid the challenges of combining sub-score ratings across ratings subcategories, identified in the literature, and to focus simply on the Environment subcategory, we do not aggregate across subcategories, and we focus on yearly constitution of the rankings. Specifically, we separately sum the number of Environmental strengths and weaknesses a given company has in a given year, rejecting zeros as non-covered, and then consider the simple difference between the two by firm and by year. We then compute each firm's Environmental net score (ENV) as the difference between the number of Environmental strengths and weaknesses it has (again, without firms that have zeros). Finally, portfolio formation stratifies firms by their ENV score into quintiles yearly denoting Lo ENV and Hi ENV as the bottom and top quintiles firms.

By focusing on the Environment subcategory alone, we avoid the issue of combining different possible numbers of strength and weakness indicators in the different subcategories. By computing strengths and weaknesses summations separately and rejecting zeros that indicate non-coverage, and only then computing a total ENV score (the number of strengths minus the number of weaknesses), we avoid distortion induced by non-coverage. Finally, by focusing on the yearly cross-section of firms and defining Lo and Hi ENV firms as the bottom and top quintiles, we effectively dynamically adjust for changes in the underlying structure of the KLD data in a manner that takes the position of traders operating on information known to them at the time of portfolio formation.

## Composite Models for Expected Returns Modeling and Stock Selection

In a number of composite models for expected returns, we utilize modifications of the expected return models outlined by Bloch et al. (1993). These models synthesized cross-sectional relationships between (and among) documented anomalies. Graham and Dodd (1934), Williams (1938), Graham et al. (1962), Elton and Gruber (1972a, 1972b), Latané et al. (1975), Jacobs and Levy (1988), and Dimson (1988) tested and reported known anomalies, including the low PE or high earnings-to-price (EP), high book value-to-price, high cash flow-to-price, high sales-to-price, and net current asset value.[2] In addition, the model synthesizes small-size earnings forecasts, revisions, recommendations, breadth, earnings surprises, and dividend yield variables identified (see Banz 1981; Dimson 1988; Jacobs and Levy 1988; and Ziemba and Schwartz 1993 as anomalies).

The resulting model from Bloch et al. (1993) is referenced below as equation (1) relating total realized returns, TR, to eight selected variables. We refer to this model as the composite model, REG8:

$$TR = w_0 + w_1 EP + w_2 BP + w_3 CP + w_4 SP + w_5 REP + w_6 RBP + w_7 RCP$$
$$+ w_8 RSP + e_t \tag{1}$$

where:

EP = [earnings per share]/[price per share] = earnings-price ratio;
BP = [book value per share]/[price per share] = book-price ratio;
CP = [cash flow per share]/[price per share] = cash flow-price ratio;
SP = [net sales per share]/[price per share] = sales-price ratio;
REP = [current EP ratio]/[average EP ratio over the past five years];
RBP = [current BP ratio]/[average BP ratio over the past five years];
RCP = [current CP ratio]/[average CP ratio over the past five years]; and
RSP = [current SP ratio]/[average SP ratio over the past five years].

Given concerns about both outlier distortion and multicollinearity, Bloch et al. (1993) test the relative explanatory and predictive merits of alternative regression estimation procedures and find that controlling for both outliers and multicollinearity via robust regressions is important. Second, Bloch et al. (1993) quantify the survivor bias (including dead companies in the database) and find that it was not statistically significant in either Japan or the US for the period tested. Third, they investigate period-to-period portfolio revision and find that tighter turnover and rebalancing triggers led to higher portfolio returns for value-based strategies. Finally, Markowitz and Xu (1994) develop a test for data mining.[3] In addition to testing the hypothesis of data mining, the test can also be used to estimate and assess the expected differences between the best test model and the average of simulated policies.

Studies of the effectiveness of corporate earnings forecasting variables[4] reported in Cragg and Malkiel (1968), Elton et al. (1981), DeBondt and Thaler (1989), Wheeler (1994), and Guerard and Stone (1992) were reprinted in Bruce and Epstein (1994).[5] Analysts' forecasts of earnings per share (EPS), EPS revision, and the direction of EPS forecast revisions were incorporated into the Institutional Broker Estimation Services (I/B/E/S) in-print database in July 1972. The I/B/E/S database has computer-readable data from January 1976, domestically, and January 1987 for non-US.[6] We refer the reader to Brown (1998) which contains about 570 abstracts of I/B/E/S studies.

Guerard et al. (1997) report that analysts' forecast variables enhanced portfolio returns over the long run. CTEF, a composite model of earnings consensus forecasts, revisions, and breadth, the agreement among analysts' revisions (all from I/B/E/S), was highly statistically significantly correlated with stock returns. Guerard and Mark (2003) reported that CTEF, and a nine-factor model, denoted REG9 and composed of REG8 plus CTEF, was highly (statistically) significantly correlated with stock returns.

Guerard et al. (2012) and Guerard et al. (2014) added price momentum (PM), price at *t-1* divided by the price seven months ago, *t-7*, which we refer to as 7/1 momentum. This is different from, but correlated with, the PR1YR momentum definition using prior returns measured from *t-1* to *t-12* to classify momentum. They denoted the ten-factor stock selection model as United States Expected Returns (USER). They reported, among other results, that: (1) the EP variable had a larger average weight than the BP variable; (2) the relative PE, denoted RPE, the EP relative to its 60-month average, had a higher average weight than the PE variable; and (3) the composite earnings forecast variable, CTEF, had a larger weight than the RPE variable. In fact, in the USER model, only the price momentum variable, PM, had a higher weight than the CTEF variable (and only by 1 percent, at that).[7]

In what follows, we employ the USER model shown in equation (2), augmenting REG8:

$$TR_{t+1} = a_0 + a_1 EP_t + a_2 BP_t + a_3 CP_t + a_4 SP_t + a_5 REP_t + a_6 RBP_t + a_7 RCP_t$$
$$+ a_8 RSP_t + a_9 CTEF_t + a_{10} PM_t + e_t \qquad (2)$$

where:

EP = [earnings per share]/[price per share] = earnings-price ratio;
BP = [book value per share]/[price per share] = book-price ratio;
CP = [cash flow per share]/[price per share] = cash flow-price ratio;
SP = [net sales per share]/[price per share] = sales-price ratio;
REP = [current EP ratio]/[average EP ratio over the past five years];
RB = [current BP ratio]/[average BP ratio over the past five years];
RCP = [current CP ratio]/[average CP ratio over the past five years];
RSP = [current SP ratio]/[average SP ratio over the past five years];
CTEF = consensus earnings-per-share I/B/E/S forecast (FEP), revisions and breadth (BR),
PM = Price Momentum; and
e = randomly distributed error term.

The Guerard et al. (2014) USER model test substantiated the Bloch et al. (1993) approach. In addition to the fundamental ten-factor **USER** model, we isolate the following subset models to isolate particular effects in the models: **EWC** sets a1 through a10 = 10 percent, allowing tests out-of-sample optimization of USER weights. **EVALUE** sets a5 through a10 equal to zero and a1 through a4 equal to 25 percent, producing, in effect, a 'bagged' value model that naïvely blends traditionally estimated valuation ratios. **MQ** sets a1 through a8 = 0, isolating the CTEF earnings variable and 7/1 price momentum, which are equally weighted.

## Model Estimation

For each security, we use monthly total stock returns and prices from CRSP files, earnings book value cash flow, net sales from quarterly COMPUSTAT files, and consensus earnings-per-share, forecast revisions, and breadth from I/B/E/S files. We construct the variables used in (3) for each month starting in January 1990. The USER model is estimated using the weighted least squared latent root regression analysis of Bloch et al. (1993) to control for multicollinearity among signal regressors and to address outliers (analysis over the 60-month (five-year) moving window for each period to identify variables statistically significant at the 10 percent level). The model uses the normalized coefficients as weights over the past 12 months with the Beaton-Tukey bisquare outlier adjustment. We use the statistically significant coefficients to estimate the next month's expected return rank, $E_i$, for each security. The USER estimation conditions are virtually identical to those described in Guerard et al. (2012) and Guerard et al. (2014, 2015).[8]

## Empirical Results

Table 5.2 presents summary statistics for our sample, and Figures 5.1 and 5.2 plot the numbers of firms having the requisite input over time for the calculation of the overarching USER model value and for the earnings subcomponent, CTEF. The number of firms having full input variable values is closely followed by the number of firms having the earnings variable. The former ranges from about 1,000 firms in 1976, just a few years after the NASDAQ exchange went online, joining NYSE and AMEX exchanges in the data, to about 1500 firms in 1991, the beginning of the KLD data. The number of firms having CTEF information peaks in 1989 at approximately 2750, while the number of firms having complete data for USER peaks at about 2550. Both decline to just under 2,000 firms at the end of the sample period in December 2017. Figure 5.2 tracks the number of firms in the tails of the distribution defined in the Low and High Environmental ratings equal-weighted portfolios. A large spike is seen in 2013 when the number of firms covered by KLD was expanded to a large number of firms in the left tail of the environmental score distribution.

TABLE 5.2 Summary statistics for the USER model and CTEF variable

|  |  | Annualized Arithmetic Return | Annualized Geometric Return | Annualized Volatility | # of Firms | Average Value |
|---|---|---|---|---|---|---|
| USER | Q5 (High) | 15.8% | 14.5% | 20.5% | 347 | 6.70% |
|  | Q4 | 14.7% | 13.7% | 18.4% | 347 | 0.03% |
|  | Q3 | 14.6% | 13.8% | 17.7% | 346 | 0.00% |
|  | Q2 | 13.5% | 12.5% | 18.1% | 347 | 0.00% |
|  | Q1 (Low) | 13.0% | 11.1% | 22.0% | 347 | −5.28% |
|  | Q5–Q1 | 2.8% | 2.3% | 9.4% |  |  |
| CTEF | Q5 (High) | 15.8% | 14.9% | 18.8% | 366 | 25.43% |
|  | Q4 | 15.2% | 14.3% | 18.9% | 365 | 13.42% |
|  | Q3 | 15.1% | 14.1% | 19.0% | 364 | 0.09% |
|  | Q2 | 13.2% | 11.7% | 19.9% | 365 | −13.71% |
|  | Q1 (Low) | 11.1% | 9.3% | 20.9% | 366 | −24.54% |
|  | Q5–Q1 | 4.7% | 4.5% | 6.5% |  |  |

*Note*: The table shows summary statistics for quintile portfolios formed on the ten-factor US Expected Return model (USER) of Guerard (1997a, 1997b) and Bloch et al. (1993) incorporating earnings yield, book-to-market, cashflow-to-price, and sales-to-price ratios, along with these ratios scaled by the average ratios over the previous five years as well as CTEF and price momentum. CTEF measures consensus earnings per share from I/B/E/S forecasts, revisions, and breadth. The sample ranges from May 1995 through December 2017. The table presents the average annual unconditional returns for the quintile groups, the average geometric return, the annualized standard deviation (volatility), the number of firms in each quintile, and the average of the USER model variable or CTEF, respectively.

*Source*: Authors' computations.

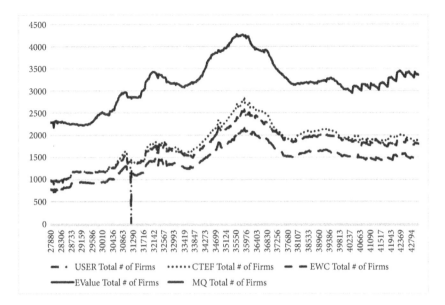

**Figure 5.1** Total number of firms counted in model and selected sub-components

*Note*: The number of firms counted is the intersection of WRDS Compustat, CESP, and IBES databases.

*Source*: WRDS Compustat, CRSP, and IBES databases.

Table 5.3 reports the baseline performance of five models of expected return via three encompassing risk-factor models from the academic literature estimated over the period March 1991 through December 2017. The five expected return models are subsumed in the USER model described above: USER, EWC, EValue, MQ, and CTEF. The EWC model naïvely equal weights inputs while the USER model optimizes the weights (with most of the period of the estimations being out of sample with respect to the optimized weights). The EValue model incorporates an equal weighting of the bagged, scaled price ratios articulated above, while the MQ model isolates the remaining variables (non-GAAP) formed using consensus earnings, earnings breadth, and earnings depth.

In Panel A of Table 5.3, quintile sorts on the encompassing USER model produce annualized alpha ranges from 3.2 percent to –0.1 percent in a one-factor CAPM using RMRF as the market measure. We see a U-shape pattern in one-factor market betas and inverted U-shapes in Adjusted R2s. The Q5-Q1 portfolio delivers an alpha of 3.3 percent with nearly zero-beta and adjusted R2. In the four-factor model of Carhart (1997), which embeds the Fama-French three-factor model, we see a similar pattern, except that across the CTEF quintiles, the momentum exposures are quite strong. Starting at a

TABLE 5.3  Baseline performance of five models of expected returns

**Panel 1**

**Multifactor Models Regressions (March 1991–December 2017)**

| | One-Factor Model (CAPM) | | | Fama-French/Carhart Four-Factor Model | | | | | | Fama-French/Carhart Plus Quality Five-Factor Model | | | | | | |
|---|---|---|---|---|---|---|---|---|---|---|---|---|---|---|---|---|
| | RMRF | Intercept | Adj R² | RMRF | SMB | HML | MOM | Intercept | Adj R² | RMRF | SMB | HML | MOM | Quality | Intercept | Adj R² |
| **USER** | | | | | | | | | | | | | | | | |
| Quintile 5 | 1.24 | 3.2% | 76.9% | 1.02 | 0.86 | 0.07 | -0.55 | 3.6% | 90.8% | 1.00 | 0.81 | 0.10 | 0.54 | -0.13 | 4.3% | 90.9% |
| Quintile 4 | 1.13 | 2.2% | 77.1% | 0.96 | 0.64 | 0.24 | -0.21 | 2.0% | 94.3% | 0.97 | 0.67 | 0.23 | -0.22 | 0.08 | 1.5% | 94.4% |
| Quintile 3 | 1.05 | 2.5% | 74.6% | 0.91 | 0.63 | 0.28 | -0.22 | 2.8% | 93.3% | 0.92 | 0.65 | 0.27 | -0.22 | 0.09 | 2.5% | 94.3% |
| Quintile 2 | 1.10 | 1.6% | 77.0% | 0.98 | 0.67% | 0.23 | -0.21 | 2.5% | 94.2% | 1.00 | 0.70 | 0.21 | -0.22 | 0.09 | 2.0% | 94.3% |
| Quintile 1 | 1.32 | -0.1% | 64.8% | 1.11 | 0.80 | 0.15 | -0.04 | 0.4% | 93.9% | 1.09 | 0.76 | 0.17 | 0.03 | -0.10 | 1.0% | 94.0% |
| L/S | -0.08 | 3.3% | 0.2% | -0.09 | 0.06 | -0.08 | -0.51 | 3.2% | 53.6% | -0.09 | 0.05 | -0.07 | -0.51 | -0.03 | 3.3% | 58.1% |
| **EWC** | | | | | | | | | | | | | | | | |
| Quintile 5 | 1.23 | 1.7% | 75.1% | 1.05 | 0.72 | 0.22 | -0.31 | 2.9% | 93.8% | 1.05 | 0.72 | 0.22 | -0.31 | 0.00 | 2.9% | 93.8% |
| Quintile 4 | 1.17 | 1.4% | 75.9% | 1.00 | 0.72 | 0.15 | -0.23 | 2.1% | 93.8% | 1.01 | 0.74 | 0.14 | -0.23 | 0.05 | 1.9% | 93.8% |
| Quintile 3 | 1.09 | 1.6% | 74.5% | 0.94 | 0.68 | 0.22 | -0.23 | 2.1% | 93.1% | 0.94 | 0.68 | 0.21 | -0.23 | 0.00 | 2.1% | 93.1% |
| Quintile 2 | 1.15 | 1.2% | 77.1% | 0.99 | 0.69 | 0.18 | -0.22 | 1.8% | 94.4% | 1.00 | 0.70 | 0.17 | -0.22 | 0.02 | 1.7% | 94.4% |
| Quintile 1 | 1.20 | 1.6% | 73.5% | 1.02 | 0.79 | 0.21 | -0.24 | 2.2% | 93.3% | 1.00 | 0.76 | 0.23 | -0.24 | -0.09 | 2.7% | 93.4% |
| L/S | 0.03 | 0.1% | 3.2% | 0.03 | -0.07 | 0.01 | -0.07 | 0.7% | 9.8% | 0.04 | -0.04 | -0.01 | -0.07 | 0.09 | 0.2% | 14.2% |
| **Evalue** | | | | | | | | | | | | | | | | |
| Quintile 5 | 1.13 | 3.0% | 67.0% | 0.91 | 0.74 | 0.12 | -0.36 | 5.0% | 89.2% | 0.89 | 0.70 | 0.14 | -0.36 | -0.13 | 4.7% | 89.3% |
| Quintile 4 | 1.06 | 2.4% | 69.4% | 0.89 | 0.75 | 0.11 | -0.18 | 3.0% | 89.3% | 0.87 | 0.71 | 0.13 | -0.18 | -0.09 | 3.5% | 89.4% |
| Quintile 3 | 0.97 | 2.9% | 69.1% | 0.82 | 0.65 | 0.13 | -0.19 | 3.6% | 88.0% | 0.80 | 0.62 | 0.14 | -0.19 | -0.08 | 4.0% | 88.0% |
| Quintile 2 | 1.04 | 2.1% | 70.7% | 0.88 | 0.71 | 0.15 | -0.19 | 2.6% | 89.9% | 0.87 | 0.68 | 0.16 | -0.18 | -0.07 | 3.0% | 89.9% |
| Quintile 1 | 0.98 | 2.3% | 69.5% | 0.83 | 0.68 | 0.08 | -0.17 | 2.9% | 88.9% | 0.80 | 0.63 | 0.11 | -0.16 | -0.14 | 3.7% | 89.1% |
| L/S | 0.15 | 0.7% | 18.2% | 0.09 | 0.06 | 0.04 | -0.19 | 2.0% | 44.5% | 0.09 | 0.07 | 0.03 | -0.19 | 0.00 | 1.0% | 55.4% |

**Panel 2**

**MQ**

| | RMRF | Intercept | Adj R² | RMRF | SMB | HML | MOM | Intercept | Adj R² | RMRF | SMB | HML | MOM | Quality | Intercept | Adj R² |
|---|---|---|---|---|---|---|---|---|---|---|---|---|---|---|---|---|
| Quintile 5 | 1.13 | 3.5% | 76.1% | 1.04 | 0.86 | 0.02 | -0.69 | 2.3% | 90.4% | 1.02 | 0.82 | 0.05 | -0.69 | -0.13 | 3.1% | 90.5% |
| Quintile 4 | 1.14 | 2.8% | 78.7% | 0.99 | 0.73 | 0.18 | -0.32 | 2.0% | 94.1% | 0.98 | 0.71 | 0.20 | -0.32 | -0.05 | 2.3% | 94.1% |
| Quintile 3 | 1.05 | 1.6% | 74.7% | 0.91 | 0.66 | 0.24 | -0.20 | 1.8% | 92.3% | 0.92 | 0.68 | 0.23 | -0.20 | 0.05 | 1.6% | 92.3% |
| Quintile 2 | 1.19 | 0.5% | 73.9% | 1.01 | 0.69 | 0.22 | -0.13 | 2.5% | 94.9% | 1.02 | 0.7 | 0.21 | -0.13 | 0.02 | 2.3% | 94.9% |
| Quintile 1 | 1.38 | -2.7% | 61.4% | 1.06 | 0.72 | 0.2 | 0.1 | 1.4% | 93.8% | 1.07 | 0.73 | 0.19 | 0.1 | 0.03 | 1.2% | 93.7% |
| L/S(Q5-Q1) | -0.26 | 6.2% | 6.0% | -0.02 | 0.14 | -0.18 | -0.80 | 0.9% | 71.0% | -0.05 | 0.09 | -0.14 | -0.79 | -0.16 | 1.8% | 35.4% |

**CTEF**

| | RMRF | Intercept | Adj R² | RMRF | SMB | HML | MOM | Intercept | Adj R² | RMRF | SMB | HML | MOM | Quality | Intercept | Adj R² |
|---|---|---|---|---|---|---|---|---|---|---|---|---|---|---|---|---|
| Quintile 5 | 1.15 | 2.1% | 79.4% | 1.02 | 0.62 | 0.16 | -0.14 | 2.3% | 92.6% | 1.04 | 0.65 | 0.14 | -0.15 | 9.2% | 1.7% | 92.7% |
| Quintile 4 | 1.17 | 2.6% | 77.7% | 1.02 | 0.70 | 0.16 | -0.19 | 3.0% | 94.1% | 1.01 | 0.70 | 0.16 | -0.19 | -0.5% | 3.0% | 94.1% |
| Quintile 3 | 1.12 | 2.9% | 70.0% | 0.94 | 0.77 | 0.12 | -0.22 | 3.8% | 89.8% | 0.92 | 0.73 | 0.14 | -0.22 | -9.9% | 4.4% | 89.9% |
| Quintile 2 | 1.23 | -0.6% | 74.1% | 1.04 | 0.80 | 0.17 | -0.29 | 0.5% | 94.4% | 1.03 | 0.78 | 0.18 | -0.28 | -5.1% | 0.8% | 94.4% |
| Quintile 1 | 1.27 | -2.5% | 71.3% | 1.04 | 0.83 | 0.13 | -0.37 | -0.5% | 93.2% | 1.02 | 0.80 | 0.15 | -0.36 | -8.6% | 0.0% | 93.2% |
| L/S | 0.12 | 4.6% | | -0.01 | -0.21 | 0.03 | 0.22 | 2.8% | | 0.02 | -0.14 | -0.01 | 0.22 | 0.18 | 1.8% | |

*Note:* The tables show performance and factor exposures of quintile portfolios formed on five expected return models: The ten-factor US Expected Return model (USER) of Guerard (1997a, 1997b) and Bloch et al. (1993) incorporates earnings yield, book-to-market, cashflow-to-price, and sales-to-price ratios, along with these ratios scaled by the average ratios over the previous five years as well as CTEF and price momentum. (CTEF measures consensus earnings per share from I/B/E/S forecasts, revisions, and breadth, and PM is 7/1 price momentum.) In addition, results are given for an equal-weighted model with the same characteristic variables (EWC), an equal-weighted naïve value-based model using just the scaled price ratios above (EVALUE), and MQ, an equal-weighted model including CTEF and price momentum. Monthly Quantile portfolio returns or L/S zero-investment portfolio returns are regressed on the one-factor US equity premium (RMRF) model (the CAPM), the Fama-French/Carhart four-factor model, and a Fama-French/Carhart five-factor model that includes the Fama-French quality factor.

*Source:* Authors' computations.

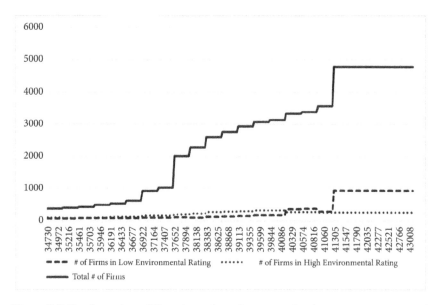

**Figure 5.2** Total number of firms in each environmental rating category compared to sample total

*Note*: The number of firms counted is the intersection of WRDS Compustat, CESP, and IBES databases.

*Source*: WRDS Compustat, CRSP, and IBES databases.

value of –0.55 and declining to –0.04 from the fifth to first quintile, momentum and CTEF sorts are quite highly correlated. The Q5-Q1 spread returns a strong negative loading on Carhart (1997) momentum but nothing on the remaining factor-mimicking portfolios.

In the five-factor model that adds quality, we see a similar pattern: USER quintiles produce strong patterns in momentum-mimicking portfolio loadings, while the Q5-Q1 spread produces a strong negative loading on momentum of –0.51 while the four-factor alpha is estimated to be 3.2 percent. As we will demonstrate below, the momentum loading derives from the 7/1 price momentum variable within the model and is, in that sense, an expected result. However, the four-factor alpha remains statistically significant and economically meaningful, indicating that USER encompasses information independent of the extended factor model. Moreover, the EWC and EValue results suggest that the contributions inherent in the definition of the USER model also add value. Because this model and its weightings were developed in advance of this time period, we are less worried about data mining than this finding would otherwise suggest.

MQ, which is a 50/50 combination of CTEF and price momentum, produces high alphas, but only for one-factor CAPM (6.2 percent). When momentum is accounted for in the four-factor model, the spread alpha is 90 bps and the momentum loading is a large −0.80 for the Q5-Q1 spread. When quality is introduced in the five-factor model, we see that momentum loadings are robust to the additional variable while the factor loading pattern is quite strong for both momentum and quality, but especially momentum. The five-factor alpha remains at 1.8 percent. In all of the one-, four- and five-factor models, we see the usual strong spread alpha (4.6 percent) which shrinks significantly when momentum and other zero-investment portfolio returns are included in the model where momentum subsumes the 7/1 momentum effect of the expected returns model. Finally, corresponding to the patterns above, the earnings composite variable CTEF survives one-, four- and five-factor regressions with positive and significant pricing error (alpha).

## The Interaction of Environmental Scores and Expected Return Models

Table 5.4 reports one-, three-, and five-factor model time series regressions in which, for each of the expected return models above (USER, EWC, EValue, MQ, and CTEF), returns from portfolios constructed based on their ENV and model numerical values are calculated. High and low ENV and model groups are defined yearly by the 30/40/30 criteria (see Fama and French 1992; Carhart 1997). Each year, the 30 percent of firms with the highest (low) normalized environmental scores are included in the high (low) ENV group. Independent firms are included in the high (low) USER groups yearly, based on their raw USER scores. Firms that are in both high environmental score and high USER score groups are characterized as High ENV + High USER and so on. Firms are equal-weighted within groups.

The results in Panel A of Table 5.4 generally demonstrate that High ENV have excess returns (alpha) holding USER constant, and that firms that have high expected returns via the models, along with high environmental scores, produce the greatest pricing errors (alphas) in the various factor model estimations. For example, in the CAPM (RMRF) regression in Panel A of Table 5.4, the High ENV + High USER portfolio produces an annualized intercept (alpha) of about 3.6 percent while the Low ENV + Low USER portfolio produces a historical alpha of 0.1 percent. The (High+High)—(Low+Low) spread produces a nearly zero-beta return (alpha) of about 3.5 percent. Moreover, when isolating the USER effect by going long and short along the USER dimension and examining the resulting ENV differentials, High ENV firms produce an 80 bps excess return while the Low ENV score portfolio produces an excess return of −0.40 percent, yielding an alpha of approximately 1.20 percent.

TABLE 5.4 The interaction of expected return models and ESG/KLD scores: The case of USER and Environmental scores

**Panel 1**

**Multifactor Models Regression Parameters (March 1995–December 2017)**

| USER | One-Factor Model (CAPM) | | | | | Fama-french/Carhart Four-Factor model | | | | | | | | Fama-Franch/Carhart Plus Quality Five-Factor Model | | | | | | | | |
|---|---|---|---|---|---|---|---|---|---|---|---|---|---|---|---|---|---|---|---|---|---|---|
| | RMRF | Intercept | Adj R² | TE | AR | RMRF | SMB | HML | MOM | Intercept | Adj R2 | TE | AR | RMRF | SMB | HML | MOM | Quality | Intercept | Adj R2 | TE | AR |
| HighENV+HighUSER | 0.95 | 3.6% | 69.9% | 9.4% | 0.38. | 0.94 | 0.29 | 0.41 | -0.07 | 4.6% | 78.7% | 8.0% | 0.57 | 1.01 | 0.38 | 0.26 | -0.19 | 0.22 | 1.8% | 77.1% | 9.5% | 0.19 |
| HighENV+LowUSER | 1.04 | 2.8% | 69.0% | 10.5% | 0.27 | 1.01 | 0.29 | 0.32 | -0.16 | 4.2% | 77.2% | 9.1% | 0.46 | 0.99 | 0.44 | 0.28 | -0.10 | 0.36 | 0.9% | 79.8% | 8.2% | 0.11 |
| LowENV+HighUSER | 1.11 | -0.3% | 64.0% | 12.6% | -0.02 | 1.13 | 0.16 | 0.57 | -0.10 | 0.4% | 72.5% | 10.8% | 0.04 | 1.10 | 0.35 | 0.60 | -0.29 | 0.44 | -2.8% | 80.5% | 10.0% | -0.27 |
| LowENV+LowUSER | 1.05 | 0.1% | 58.0% | 13.5% | 0.01 | 1.04 | 0.15 | 0.76 | -0.24 | 1.0% | 78.9% | 9.6% | 0.11 | 1.22 | 0.40 | 0.39 | -0.15 | 0.59 | -4.5% | 76.9% | 11.4% | -0.40 |
| HighENV: L/S USER | 0.06 | -0.4% | 0.7% | 8.6% | -0.05 | 0.09 | 0.00 | -0.18 | 0.14 | -0.7% | 15.5% | 7.9% | -0.08 | 0.12 | 0.05 | -0.21 | 0.13 | 0.15 | -1.8% | 15.7% | 8.2% | -0.22 |
| LowENV: L/S USER | -0.08 | 0.8% | 1.3% | 9.8% | 0.08 | -0.07 | 0.00 | 0.09 | 0.10 | 0.4% | 4.1% | 9.6% | 0.04 | -0.02 | 0.07 | 0.02 | 0.09 | 0.14 | -1.0% | 3.6% | 9.9% | -0.10 |
| (High+High)-(Low+Low) | -0.10 | 3.5% | | | | -0.10 | 0.14 | -0.35 | 0.18 | 3.5% | | | | -0.21 | -0.02 | -0.13 | -0.03 | -0.37 | 6.4% | | | |

| EWC | RMRF | Intercept | Adj R² | TE | AR | RMRF | SMB | HML | MOM | Intercept | Adj R² | TE | AR | RMRF | SMB | HML | MOM | Quality | Intercept | AdjR² | TE | AR |
|---|---|---|---|---|---|---|---|---|---|---|---|---|---|---|---|---|---|---|---|---|---|---|
| HighENV+HighEWC | 0.96 | 3.3% | 67.0% | 10.1% | 0.33 | 0.91 | 0.32 | 0.44 | -0.11 | 2.7% | 77.2% | 8.4% | 0.32 | 1.00 | 0.48 | 0.33 | -0.13 | 0.41 | 0.4% | 79.7% | 7.9% | 0.05 |
| HighENV+LowEWC | 1.03 | 3.0% | 72.0% | 9.7% | 0.31 | 0.96 | 0.28 | 0.25 | -0.14 | 3.3% | 77.6% | 8.7% | 0.38 | 1.00 | 0.34 | 0.20 | -0.15 | 0.17 | 2.3% | 77.9% | 8.6% | 0.27 |

| Evalue | RMRF | Intercept | Adj R² | TE | AR | RMRF | SMB | HML | MOM | Intercept | Adj R² | TE | AR | RMRF | SMB | HML | MOM | Quality | Intercept | AdjR² | TE | AR |
|---|---|---|---|---|---|---|---|---|---|---|---|---|---|---|---|---|---|---|---|---|---|---|
| LowENV+HighEWC | 1.13 | 0.0% | 64.7% | 12.5% | 0.00 | 1.10 | 0.18 | 0.56 | -0.18 | -0.4% | 75.7% | 10.3% | -0.04 | 1.22 | 0.40 | 0.40 | -0.21 | 0.59 | -3.8% | 79.3% | 9.5% | -0.40 |
| LowENV+LowEWC | 1.04 | -0.2% | 58.3% | 13.2% | -0.02 | 1.01 | 0.18 | 0.71 | -0.21 | -1.0% | 76.5% | 9.9% | -0.10 | 1.11 | 0.34 | 0.59 | -0.23 | 0.44 | -3.5% | 78.5% | 9.4% | -0.37 |
| HighENV:L/SEWC | -0.07 | -2.0% | 1.0% | 9.6% | -0.21 | -0.05 | 0.04 | 0.18 | 0.02 | -2.8% | 3.5% | 9.4% | -0.30 | 0.00 | 0.14 | 0.12 | 0.01 | 0.24 | -4.2% | 6.1% | 9.3% | -0.45 |
| LowENV:L/SEWC | 0.09 | -2.1% | 2.6% | 7.6% | -0.27 | 0.08 | 0.01 | -0.16 | 0.02 | -1.7% | 7.0% | 7.4% | -0.23 | 0.11 | 0.06 | -0.20 | 0.01 | 0.15% | -2.6% | 8.4% | 7.4% | -0.35 |
| (High+High)-(Low+Low) | -0.08 | 3.5% | | | | -0.10 | 0.14 | -0.27 | 0.09 | 3.7% | | | | -0.11 | 0.13 | -0.26 | 0.10 | -0.03 | 3.9% | | | |
| HighENV+HighE-VALU | 0.99 | 3.5% | 64.5% | 11.1% | 0.32 | 0.94 | 0.31 | 0.45 | -0.15 | 3.1% | 74.9% | 9.3% | 0.34 | 1.01 | 0.45 | 0.35 | -0.17 | 0.37 | 1.0% | 76.6% | 8.9% | 0.12 |
| HighENV+LowE-VALU | 1.03 | 2.9% | 72.8% | 9.5% | 0.31 | 0.97 | 0.29 | 0.25 | -0.13 | 3.1% | 78.2% | 8.5% | 0.36 | 1.01 | 0.37 | 0.19 | -0.14 | 0.21 | 1.9% | 78.8% | 8.4% | 0.22 |
| LowENV+HighE-VALU | 1.15 | 0.5% | 63.6% | 13.1% | 0.04 | 1.11 | 0.22 | 0.57 | -0.20 | 0.1% | 74.8% | 10.8% | 0.00 | 1.24 | 0.46 | 0.40 | -0.23 | 0.63 | -3.5% | 78.6% | 10.0% | -0.35 |
| LowENV+LowE-VALU | 1.03 | -0.3% | 58.6% | 13.1% | -0.03 | 1.01 | 0.17 | 0.69 | -0.21 | -1.1% | 76.4% | 9.8% | -0.11 | 1.10 | 0.33 | 0.58 | -0.23 | 0.43 | -3.5% | 78.4% | 9.4% | -0.38 |

*Continued*

## TABLE 5-4 Continued

|  | RMRF | Intercept | AdjR² | TE | AR | RMRF | SMB | HML | MOM | Intercept | AdjR² | TE | AR | RMRF | SMB | HML | MOM | Quality | Intercept | AdjR² | TE | AR |
|---|---|---|---|---|---|---|---|---|---|---|---|---|---|---|---|---|---|---|---|---|---|---|
| HighENV: L/sEVALU | -0.04 | -1.8% | 0.0% | 9.9% | -0.18 | -0.03 | 0.03 | 0.19 | -0.03 | -2.2% | 3.7% | 9.7% | -0.23 | 0.00 | 0.09 | 0.15 | -0.04 | 0.16 | -3.1% | 4.5% | 9.6% | -0.33 |
| LowENV: L/SEVALU | 0.12 | -1.6% | 4.8% | 7.9% | -0.20 | 0.10 | 0.06 | -0.13 | 0.00 | -1.1% | 8.0% | 7.7% | -0.15 | 0.14 | 0.13 | -0.18 | 0.00 | 0.20 | -2.3% | 10.6% | 7.6% | -0.3 |
| (High+ High)- (Low+Low) | -0.04 | 3.80% |  |  |  | -0.07 | 0.15 | -0.24 | 0.06 | 4.2% |  |  |  | -0.08 | 0.12 | -0.22 | 0.06 | -0.06 | 4.6% |  |  |  |

### Panel 2

| MQ | RMRF | Intercept | AdjR² | TE | AR | RMRF | SMB | HML | MOM | Intercept | AdjR² | TE | AR | RMRF | SMB | HML | MOM | Quality | Intercept | AdjR² | TE | AR |
|---|---|---|---|---|---|---|---|---|---|---|---|---|---|---|---|---|---|---|---|---|---|---|
| **HighENV+ HighMQ** | **0.9** | **3.5%** | **69.8%** | **8.9%** | **0.40** | **0.90** | **0.27** | **0.35** | **0.02** | **2.2%** | **76.0%** | **7.9%** | **0.28** | **0.98** | **0.41** | **0.25** | **0.00** | **0.38** | **0.0%** | **78.5%** | **7.5%** | **0.00** |
| HighENV+ LowMQ | 1.09 | 2.9% | 66.7% | 11.6% | 0.25 | 0.98 | 0.33 | 0.33 | -0.28 | 4.0% | 77.5% | 9.5% | 0.42 | 1.02 | 0.40 | 0.28 | -0.29 | 0.20 | 2.8% | 77.9% | 9.4% | 0.80 |
| LowENV+ HighMQ | 1.06 | 0.6% | 61.2% | 12.7% | 0.5 | 1.08 | 0.14 | 0.57 | -0.04 | -1.0% | 69.5% | 11.2% | -0.09 | 1.20 | 0.35 | 0.42 | -0.06 | 0.56 | -4.2% | 73.0% | 10.5% | -0.40 |
| **LowENV+ LowMQ** | **1.12** | **-0.9%** | **55.5%** | **15.0%** | **-0.6** | **1.03** | **0.23** | **0.71** | **-0.36** | **-0.5%** | **76.8%** | **10.8%** | **-0.05** | **1.13** | **0.04** | **0.58** | **-0.38** | **0.48** | **-3.3%** | **78.9%** | **10.3%** | **-0.52** |
| HighENV: L/SMQ | -0.19 | -1.7% | 5.7% | 11.3% | -0.15. | -0.08 | -0.05 | 0.01 | 0.29 | -4.1% | 22.3% | 10.1% | -0.40 | -0.04 | 0.02 | -0.03 | 0.28 | 0.19 | -5.1% | 23.2% | 10.0% | -0.51 |
| LowENV: L/SMQ | -0.06 | -1.0% | 0.1% | 12.4% | -0.8 | 0.05 | -0.08 | -0.15 | 0.32 | -3.0% | 21.6% | 10.9% | -0.27 | 0.07 | -0.05 | -0.17 | 0.31 | 0.09 | -3.5% | 21.6% | 10.9% | -0.32 |
| (High+ High)- (Low+Low) | -0.22 | 4.5% |  |  |  | -0.14 | 0.04 | -0.36 | 0.38 | 2.7% |  |  |  | -0.16 | 0.01 | -0.33 | 0.38 | -0.10 | 3.3% |  |  |  |

| CTEF | RMRF | Intercept | AdjR² | TE | AR | RMRF | SMB | HML | MOM | Intercept | AdjR² | TE | AR | RMRF | SMB | HML | MOM | Quality | Intercept | AdjR² | TE | AR |
|---|---|---|---|---|---|---|---|---|---|---|---|---|---|---|---|---|---|---|---|---|---|---|
| **HighENV+ HighCTEF** | **0.95** | **2.3%** | **69.9%** | **9.3%** | **0.25** | **0.95** | **0.22** | **0.37** | **-0.01** | **1.1%** | **75.3%** | **8.4%** | **0.13** | **1.05** | **0.39** | **0.24** | **-0.03** | **0.47** | **-1.6%** | **78.8%** | **7.8%** | **-0.20** |
| HighENV+ LowCTEF | 1.05 | 4.2% | 66.5% | 11.2% | 0.38 | 0.93 | 0.38 | 0.31 | -0.26 | 5.2% | 77.7% | 9.1% | 0.56 | 0.95 | 0.42 | 0.28 | -0.26 | 0.12 | 4.5% | 77.8% | 9.1% | 0.49 |
| LowENV+ HighCTEF | 1.09 | 1.2% | 60.8% | 13.1% | 0.09 | 1.07 | 0.15 | 0.56 | -0.15 | 0.4% | 70.9% | 11.2% | 0.04 | 1.19 | 0.37 | 0.40 | -0.18 | 0.58 | -2.9% | 74.4% | 10.5% | -0.27 |
| **LowENV+ LowCTEF** | **1.09** | **-1.6%** | **58.6%** | **13.8%** | **-0.12** | **1.05** | **0.22** | **0.72** | **-0.24** | **-2.2%** | **76.8%** | **10.3%** | **-0.21** | **1.14** | **0.39** | **0.60** | **-0.26** | **0.46** | **-4.8%** | **78.9%** | **9.8%** | **-0.48** |
| HighENV: L/SCTEF | -0.10 | -4.2% | 1.4% | 11.0% | -0.38 | 0.02 | -0.016 | 0.05 | 0.24 | -6.3% | 14.6% | 10.01% | -0.62 | 0.09 | -0.03 | -0.05 | 0.22 | 0.36 | -8.3% | 19.1% | 9.9% | -0.85 |
| LowENV: L/SCTEF | 0.00 | 0.4% | -0.4% | 10.3% | 0.04 | 0.02 | -0.07 | -0.17 | 0.08 | 0.3% | 4.1% | 10.0% | 0.03 | 0.05 | -0.02 | -0.02 | 0.08 | 0.13 | -0.4% | 4.5% | 10.0% | -0.04 |
| (High+ High)- (Low+Low) | -0.14 | 3.9% | | | | -0.10 | 0.00 | -0.35 | 0.23 | 3.30% | | | | -0.10 | 0.00 | -0.35 | 0.23 | 0.01 | 3.2% | | | |

*Note:* The tables show performance and factor exposures of portfolios formed using the ten-factor US Expected Return model (USER) of Guerard (1997a, 1997b) and Bloch et al. (1993) incorporating earnings yield, book-to-market, cashflow-to-price, and sales-to-price ratios, along with these ratios scaled by the average ratios over the previous five years as well as CTEF and price momentum. (CTEF measures consensus earnings per share from I/B/E/S forecasts, revisions, and breadth, and PM is 7/1 price momentum.) The monthly returns of high (low) KLD Environmental score firms with high or low USER rankings or L/S zero-investment portfolio returns are regressed on a one-factor US equity US equity premium (RMRF) model (the CAPM), the Fama-French/Carhart four-factor model, and a Fama-French/Carhart five-factor model that includes the Fama-French quality factor. TE is the unbiased residual standard deviation. AR is the appraisal ratio (Information Ratio with unconstrained beta).

*Source:* Authors' computations.

These results for the CAPM are robust across the additional factor models where interesting patterns in factor loadings emerge, indicating the interaction between ESG characteristics and traditional factor exposures. For example, while patterns in market betas remain intact in moving from the CAPM to the Carhart (1997) four-factor model, small-size effects emerge and in particular value (HML) factor loadings are significantly larger for High ENV + High USER portfolios than for Low ENV + Low USER portfolios. Specifically, the Fama-French HML (value less growth) factor loading for the (High+High)—(Low+Low) spread is –0.35, the momentum spread loading estimate is 0.18, and the intercept (pricing error or alpha) is an annualized 3.5 percent. In other words, perhaps as expected, firms that have low environmental scores seem to have a more pronounced value exposure than those with high scores, corresponding to received wisdom that ESG stock portfolios are generally tilted toward growth and away from the asset-heavy traditional value sectors and firms. These results are borne out by the five-factor model extending the Carhart (1997) model with the Fama-French Quality spread. Interestingly, quality subsumes the momentum loading and, to a lesser extent, value.

Part of the story behind the negative quality loading (–0.37 at the point estimate) in the regression is clear from the differences between the loadings on the Quality-mimicking portfolio spread, first holding ENV constant and then holding USER constant. For instance, the differential between High USER and Low USER loadings for High ENV is –0.14 (= 0.22–0.36), and for Low ENV, it is –0.15. In other words, USER correlates negatively with Quality, a fact that is known from previous literature that identifies USER as measuring expected profitability rather than realized profitability, which on average mean-reverts relative to expectations. Holding USER constant, for High USER, the spread in the quality loading between High ENV and low ENV is estimated as –0.22 (= 0.22–0.44) and for Low USER is 0.36–0.59 = –0.23. In other words, overall, equity portfolios load positively on the Quality factor portfolio, but Low ENV tends to load more strongly than High ENV, suggesting once again that positive environmental characteristics are negatively associated with realized measures of profitability, which is obliquely measured with respect to momentum and value, as is also known. Nonetheless, the alpha for the (High+High)—(Low+Low) spread is strong at an estimated 6.4 percent annualized value.

The evidence construed across model sub-components reinforces the story for the aggregate USER model. For instance, for the naïvely equal-weighted EWC model as well as the value-bagged model (EVALUE), the MQ model incorporating only price momentum and CTEF, and for CTEF itself, the CAPM and Carhart models load essentially the same with nearly identical intercepts. However, in the five-factor model, we see an inversion of the Quality loadings. In other words, in the unoptimized EWC model (recall that the input weightings in the USER model were optimized long ago, essentially out of sample, while the EWC model treats all inputs the same and the others break out sub-components) as well as the others, it is quite clear that Quality loadings are higher for High EWC, High EVALUE, High MQ, and High CTEF versus their Low counterparts. The information ratio optimization inherent in the definition of USER seems to weight components that invert the relationship. Nonetheless, the intercepts in all five-factor regressions remain economically and statistically significant for all models including for CTEF. Taken together, the results strongly suggest an interaction between ENV and various models for expected returns, which in turn indicates that when one is creating portfolios (ESG or not), one would do well to consider both sources of information and that ESG information in this important and currently very relevant case of environmental scores may be additive in creating portfolios.

## Conclusion

Using long-standing models for expected returns of US equities, we showed in this chapter that firm environmental ratings interact with those forecasted returns and produce excess returns both unconditionally and conditionally. Now-traditional factor models subsume neither environmental-related return differentials nor expected-return premia from those scores and models. In addition, combining information from both inputs (expected return models and ESG information) may provide an advantage in selecting investments, opening up the question of why? We speculated that the traditional inputs into quantitative estimates and models, namely data from accounting filings made under GAAP, are limited; and that information from earnings forecasts, their breadth, and their depth combine with ESG information to augment the information set referenced in successful strategies. For financial fiduciaries, this notion shifts the conversation about ESG reflecting only constraints to one of an expanded information and possibly investment opportunity set.

One troubling facet of the 1998 US DOL Doyle guidance is its sole emphasis on risk-adjusted return rather than on portfolio characteristics. As Geczy et al. (2021) point out, side-by-side comparisons of ESG and non-ESG investments may suggest that there is no expected risk-adjusted return difference between them, or even that ESG investments may outperform their non-ESG counterparts (or high- vs. low-scoring investments) and yet still lead to lower Sharpe ratios at the aggregate portfolio level. The critical feature for portfolios is not only whether a given high ESG-scoring investment outperforms a low-scoring one, but whether, in focusing or tilting toward firms with positive ESG characteristics, investment diversification is lost, especially if the 'tilt' ends up being Boolean (ESG in ... everything else out). It is surprising that guidance has not emerged framing this important point with more fidelity. After all, while we have shown that ESG scores can provide important information to investors about expected return, we have not shown that portfolios formed from *only* high scoring ESG firms maximize Sharpe ratios. Answering this key question in the broad cross-section of equities is fertile ground for research.

## Acknowledgments

The authors thank Alimu Abudu, Peter Cachion, Jamie Doran, Nancy Gao, Troy Wang, and Evan Xu for computational and outstanding research assistance. We also thank the MSCI KLD, Wharton Research and Data Services, and especially Olivia S. Mitchell, Sarah Kate Sanders, and the Pension Research Council staff and members for comments.

# Appendix

# KLD STATS[9]

MSCI KLD STATS ('KLD,' STATISTICAL TOOL FOR ANALYZING TRENDS IN SOCIAL AND ENVIRONMENTAL PERFORMANCE) is a dataset with annual snapshots of the environmental, social, and governance performance of companies rated.

## Strength and Concern (Positive and Negative Indicator) Ratings

KLD STATS covers indicators in seven major Qualitative Issue Areas including Community, Corporate Governance, Diversity, Employee Relations, Environment, Human Rights, and Product. It presents a binary summary of positive and negative ESG ratings. In each case, if KLD assigned a rating in a particular issue (either positive or negative), this is indicated with a one in the corresponding cell. If the company did not have a strength or concern in that issue, this is indicated with a 0. KLD STATS data are organized by year. Each year, RiskMetrics takes a snapshot of its ratings and index membership to reflect the data at calendar year end. Each spreadsheet contains identifying information about the company, index membership, a listing of positive and negative ratings, involvement in controversial business issues, and total counts for each area. Additionally, the data provide a summary count of all strengths and concerns the company received in a general category (either Qualitative Issue Area or Controversial Business Issue) in that year. The Environmental indicators are calculated separately but similarly to those in Geczy et al. (2020).

## ENVIRONMENT (ENV-)
### STRENGTHS

> *Beneficial Products and Services (ENV-str-A).* The company derives substantial revenues from innovative remediation products, environmental services, or products that promote the efficient use of energy, or it has developed innovative products with environmental benefits.
>
> *Pollution Prevention (ENV-str-B).* The company has notably strong pollution prevention programs including both emissions reductions and toxic-use reduction programs.
>
> *Recycling (ENV-str-C).* The company is either a substantial user of recycled materials as raw materials in its manufacturing processes, or a major factor in the recycling industry.

*Clean Energy (ENV-str-D).* The company has taken significant measures to reduce its impact on climate change and air pollution through the use of renewable energy and clean fuels, or through energy efficiency. The company has demonstrated a commitment to promoting climate-friendly policies and practices outside its own operations.

*Communications (ENV-str-E).* The company is a signatory to the CERES Principles, publishes a notably substantive environmental report, or has notably effective internal communications systems in place for environmental best practices. KLD began assigning strengths for this issue in 1996, and then incorporated the issue with the Corporate Governance: Transparency rating (CGOV-str-D), which was added in 2005.

*Property, Plant, and Equipment (ENV-str-F).* The company maintains its property, plant, and equipment with above average environmental performance for its industry. KLD has not assigned strengths for this issue since 1995.

*Management Systems (ENV-str-G).* The company has demonstrated a superior commitment to management systems through ISO 14001 certification and other voluntary programs.

## CONCERNS

*Hazardous Waste (ENV-con-A).* The company's liabilities for hazardous waste sites exceed US$50 million, or the company has recently paid substantial fines or civil penalties for waste management violations.

*Regulatory Problems (ENV-con-B).* The company has recently paid substantial fines or civil penalties for violations of air, water, or other environmental regulations, or it has a pattern of regulatory controversies under the Clean Air Act, Clean Water Act or other major environmental regulations.

*Ozone Depleting Chemicals (ENV-con-C).* The company is among the top manufacturers of ozone depleting chemicals such as HCFCs, methyl chloroform, methylene chloride, or bromines.

*Substantial Emissions (ENV-con-D).* The company's legal emissions of toxic chemicals (as defined by and reported to the EPA) from individual plants into the air and water are among the highest of the companies followed by KLD.

*Agricultural Chemicals (ENV-con-E).* The company is a substantial producer of agricultural chemicals, i.e., pesticides or chemical fertilizers.

*Climate Change (ENV-con-F).* The company derives substantial revenues from the sale of coal or oil and its derivative fuel products, or the company derives substantial revenues indirectly from the combustion of coal or oil and its derivative fuel products. Such companies include electric utilities, transportation companies with fleets of vehicles, auto and truck manufacturers, and other transportation equipment companies.

# Notes

1. The first commonly recognized paper on corporate social performance was by Milton Moskowitz (1972): he introduced the concept of social responsibility as a factor in the investment decision process and studied a handful of companies deemed to be acting according to corporate social responsibility practices and policies. Moskowitz (1997) reaffirmed his support of socially responsible investment (SRI) shortly after he established an award, the Moskowitz Prize, recognizing outstanding quantitative research in socially responsible investing. The Moskowitz Prize has been awarded annually since 1996, when Guerard (1997a, 1997b) won for research reporting no statistically significant costs associated with SRI. In contrast,Geczy et al. (2021), who were Honorable Mention awardees of the 2003 Prize competition, provided a detailed analysis demonstrating conditions under which SRI/ESG mutual fund portfolios created certainty equivalent costs relative to non-SRI/ESG portfolios.

2. The major papers on the combination of value ratios for the prediction of stock returns (including at least CP and/or SP) include those of Jacobs and Levy (1988), Chan et al. (1990), Fama and French (1992 and 1995), Bloch et al. (1993), Lakonishok et al. (1994). Haugen and Baker (1996) later produced highly cited variable testing which confirmed that fundamental variables enhanced portfolio returns over the long-run. Our point in this brief survey of anomalies is to acknowledge that Jacobs and Levy (1988), Chan et al. (1990), Bloch et al. (1993), and Ziemba and Schwartz (1993) were correct in their Berkeley Program in Finance and Q-Group presentations of the early 1990s on the inefficiencies of stock markets.

3. Bloch et al. (1993) wrote their manuscript in 1991. At the time of the original estimation of an eight-factor regression model, the international Institutional Brokers' Estimate System (I/B/E/S) was only four years old, having started in 1987. It lacked sufficient data for model building and testing, making it difficult for models with earnings forecasts to pass the Markowitz and Xu (1994) Data Mining Corrections test.

4. Expected earnings have been used as a proxy for a company's future cash flow in many studies. For a detailed analysis of analysts' consensus forecasts and share prices, see Elton et al. (1981).

5. The Bruce and Epstein (1994) and Brown (1998) works contain much of the rich history of earnings forecasting and resulting excess returns. Elton et al. (1981) developed the I/B/E/S database and published initial research using it. The Elton et al. (1981) paper is one of the more influential analyses in earnings forecasting and security analysis. Guerard et al. (1993) employed Toyo Keizai earnings forecasts in Japan because of the limitations of the non-US I/B/E/S database. The Toyo Keizai earnings forecasts enhanced portfolio returns by over 200 basis points annually. Analysts were aware of the return-enhancement of I/B/E/S forecasts in US stocks; see Guerard and Stone (1992), research sponsored by the Institute for Quantitative Research in Finance, the 'Q-Group,' circa 1985. Womack (1996), Guerard et al. (1997), Guerard et al. (2015), and Ball and Ghysels (2018), are among the thousands of studies of analysts' forecasting efficiency and how analysts' forecasts enhance portfolio return.

6. The newly created non-US I/B/E/S database did not have enough data in 1991–1994 to pass the Markowitz-Xu data mining test for its use in Japan.
7. Wall Street practitioners have embraced the 'low PE' approach for well over 50 years. This is a form of the contrarian investment approach associated with Bernhard (1959) and Dremen (1979, 1999). The authors believed in the low PE strategy, but not as an exclusive strategy. There is extensive literature on the impact of individual value ratios on the cross section of stock returns. We go beyond using just one or two of the standard value ratios (EP and BP) to include the cash-price ratio (CP) and/or the sales-price ratio (SP).
8. Guerard and Mark (2020) reported monthly Axioma attribution statistics which, in the case of CTEF, indicates that the forecasted earnings acceleration variable loads on Medium-Term Momentum (0.257), Growth (0.151), and Value (0.469), and that Mean-variance CTEF and USER portfolios produced approximately 300–350 basis points of Specific Returns for the 20-year time period, 1996–2016. In US portfolios, equally weighted 125 stock portfolios outperform Mean-variance (MV) 4 percent portfolios. In the Non-US and EAFE universes, Guerard and Mark (2020) reported that the CTEF ICs were higher than the USER ICs in their 10-, 5-, 3-, and 1-year time sub-periods. The CTEF and USER produced approximately 400–500 basis points of Active Returns and about 250 basis points of Specific Returns. The Non-US portfolios offer more stock selection than US portfolios, with the addition of the REG8 plus CTEF (denoted REG9) and USER factors. The t-statistic on the risk stock selection effect in Non-US portfolios was maximized with ranked CTEF. The t-statistics on the risk stock selection effect were statistically significant for USER, although the t-statistic on the risk stock selection effect in the Non-US portfolios was only statically significant at the 10 percent level. Guerard and Mark (2020) reported that only ranked CTEF was statistically significant in the US, whereas globally, ranked CTEF and USER were statistically significant in Total Active Returns and Risk Stock Selection Returns.
9. See Wharton Research Data Services, 'KLD on WRDS,' available at https://wrds-www.wharton.upenn.edu/documents/1154/KLD-on-WRDS.pdf.

# References

Aupperle, K., A. Carroll, and J. Hatfield (1985). 'An Empirical Examination of the Relationship between Corporate Social Responsibility and Profitability,' *The Academy of Management Journal*, 28(2): 446–463.

Ball, R. and E. Ghysels (2018). 'Automated Earnings Forecasts: Beat Analysts or Combine and Conquer?' *Management Science*, 64(10): 4936–4952.

Banz, R. (1981). 'The Relationship between Return and Market Value of Common Stocks,' *Journal of Financial Economics*, 9(1): 3–18.

Bernhard, A. (1959). *The Evaluation of Common Stocks*. New York: Simon & Schuster.

Bloch, M., J. Guerard, Jr., H. Markowitz, P. Todd, and G. Xu (1993). 'A Comparison of Some Aspects of the US and Japanese Equity Markets,' *Japan and the World Economy*, 5(1): 3–26.

Brown, L. (1998). 'Managerial Behavior and the Bias in Analysts' Earnings Forecasts,' SSRN Working Paper. https://papers.ssrn.com/sol3/papers.cfm?abstract_id=113508.

Bruce, B. and C. Epstein, eds. (1994). *The Handbook of Corporate Earnings Analysis: Company Performance and Stock Market Valuation.* Tokyo: Toppan.

Carhart, M. (1997). 'On Persistence in Mutual Fund Performance,' *Journal of Finance*, 52(1): 57–82.

Chan L.., Y. Hamao, and J. Lakonishok (1990). 'Fundamentals and Stock Returns in Japan,' Working Paper No. 45, Center on Japanese Economy and Business, Graduate School of Business, Columbia University.

Cragg, J. and B. Malkiel (1968). 'The Consensus and Accuracy of Some Predictions of the Growth of Corporate Earnings,' *Journal of Finance*, 23(1): 67–84.

De Bondt, W. and R. Thaler (1989). 'Anomalies: A Mean-Reverting Walk Down Wall Street,' *Journal of Economic Perspectives*, 3(1): 189–202.

Dimson, E. (1988). *Stock Market Anomalies.* New York: Cambridge University Press.

Dorfleitner, G., S. Utz, and M. Wimmer (2014). 'Patience Pays Off—Financial Long-Term Benefits of Sustainable Management Decisions,' SSRN Working Paper. https://papers.ssrn.com/abstractid=2533957.

Dowell, G., S. Hart, and B. Yeung (2000). 'Do Corporate Environmental Standards Create or Destroy Market Value?' *Management Science*, 46(8): 1059–1074.

Doyle, R (1998). *Advisory Opinion 1998-04A.* Washington, DC: United States Department of Labor, Pension and Welfare Benefits Administration.

Dremen, D. (1979). *Contrarian Investment Strategy: The Psychology of Stock Market Success.* New York: Random House.

Dremen, D. (1999). *Contrarian Investment Strategies: The Next Generation.* New York: Simon & Schuster.

Elton, E. and M. Gruber (1972a). 'Earnings Estimates and the Accuracy of Expectational Data,' *Management Science*, 18(8): B-367–B-481.

Elton, E. and M. Gruber (1972b). 'The Economic Value of the Call Option,' *Journal of Finance*, 27(4): 891–901.

Elton, E., M. Gruber, and M. Gu̇ltekin (1981). 'Expectations and Share Prices,' *Management Science*, 27(9): 975–1095.

Fama, E. and K. French (1992). 'The Cross-Section of Expected Stock Returns,' *Journal of Finance*, 47(2): 427–465.

Fama, E. and K. French (1995). 'Size and the Book-to-Market Factors in Earnings and Returns,' *Journal of Finance*, 50(1): 131–155.

Fama, E. and K. French (2015). 'A Five-Factor Asset Pricing Model,' *Journal of Financial Economics*, 116(1): 1–22.

Galema, R., A. Plantinga, and B. Scholtens (2008). 'The Stocks at Stake: Return and Risk in Socially Responsible Investment,' *Journal of Banking and Finance*, 32(12): 2646–2654.

Geczy, C., J. Guerard, Jr., and M. Samonov (2020). 'Warning: SRI Need Not Kill Your Sharpe and Information Ratios—Forecasting of Earnings and Efficient SRI and ESG Portfolios,' *Journal of Investing*, 29(2): 110–127.

Geczy, C., R. Stambaugh, and D. Levin (2021). 'Investing in Socially Responsible Mutual Funds,' *The Review of Asset Pricing Studies*, 11(2): 309–351.

Gordon, J. and R. Buchholz (1978). 'Corporate Social Responsibility and Stock Market Performance,' *Academy of Management Journal*, 21(3): 479–486.

Graham, B. and D. Dodd (1934). *Security Analysis: Principles and Technique*, 1st ed. New York: McGraw-Hill.

Graham, B., D. Dodd, and S. Cottle (1962). *Security Analysis: Principles and Technique*, 4th ed. New York: McGraw-Hill.

Graves, S. and S. Waddock (1994). 'Institutional Owners and Corporate Social Performance,' *Academy of Management Journal*, 37(4): 1034–1046.

Guerard, Jr., J. (1997a). 'Is there a Cost to Being Socially Responsible in Investing?' *Journal of Forecasting*, 16: 475–490.

Guerard, Jr., J. (1997b). 'Is there a Cost to Being Socially Responsible in Investing?' *Journal of Investing*, 6: 11–18.

Guerard, Jr., J. and A. Mark (2003). 'The Optimization of Efficient Portfolios: The Case for an R and D Quadratic Term.' In A. Chen, ed., *Research in Finance 20*. Bingley, UK: Emerald Group Publishing Limited, pp. 213–247.

Guerard, Jr., J. and A. Mark (2020). 'Earnings Forecasts and Revisions, Price Momentum, and Fundamental Data: Further Explorations of Financial Anomalies.' In C. Lee, ed., *Handbook of Financial Econometrics*. Singapore: World Scientific Handbook in Financial Economics, pp. 1151–1209.

Guerard Jr., J. and B. Stone (1992). 'Composite Forecasting of Annual Corporate Earnings.' In A. Chen, ed., *Research in Finance 10*. Greenwich, CT: JAI Press, pp. 205–230.

Guerard, Jr., J., M. Gultekin, and B. Stone (1997). 'The Role of Fundamental Data and Analysts' Earnings Breadth, Forecasts, and Revisions in the Creation of Efficient Portfolios.' In A. Chen, ed., *Research in Finance 15*. Greenwich, CT: JAI Press, pp. 69–91.

Guerard, Jr., J., H. Markowitz, and G. Xu (2014). 'The Role of Effective Corporate Decisions in the Creation of Efficient Portfolios,' *IBM Journal of Research and Development*, 58(4): 6:1–6:11.

Guerard, Jr., J., H. Markowitz, and G. Xu (2015). 'Earnings Forecasting in a Global Stock Selection Model and Efficient Portfolio Construction and Management,' *International Journal of Forecasting*, 31: 550–560.

Guerard, Jr., J., M. Takano, and Y. Yamane (1993). 'The Development of Efficient Portfolios in Japan with Particular Emphasis on Sales and Earnings Forecasting,' *Annals of Operations Research*, 45: 91–108.

Guerard, Jr., J., G. Xu, and M. Gultekin (2012). 'Investing with Momentum: The Past, Present, and Future,' *Journal of Investing*, 21(1): 68–80.

Harvey, C., Y. Lin, and H. Zhu (2016). '. . . and the Cross-Section of Expected Returns,' *Review of Financial Studies*, 29(1): 5–68.

Haugen, R. and N. Baker (1996). 'Commonality in the Determinants of Expected Results,' *Journal of Financial Economics*, 41(3): 401–439.

Jacobs, B. and K. Levy (1988). 'Disentangling Equity Return Regularities: New Insights and Investment Opportunities,' *Financial Analysts Journal*, 44(3): 18–43.

Kempf, A. and P. Osthoff (2007). 'The Effect of Socially Responsible Investing on Portfolio Performance,' *European Financial Management*, 13(5): 908–922.

Kurtz, L. and D. DiBartolomeo (1996). 'Socially Screened Portfolios: An Attribution Analysis of Relative Performance,' *Journal of Investing*, 5(3): 35–41.

Lakonishok, J., A. Shleifer, and R. Vishny (1994). 'Contrarian Investment, Extrapolation and Risk,' *Journal of Finance*, 49(5): 1541–1578.

Latané, H., D. Tuttle, and C. Jones (1975). *Security Analysis and Portfolio Management*. New York: The Ronald Press Company.

Lo, A. and A. MacKinlay (1987). 'Stock Market Prices Do Not Follow Random Walks: Evidence from a Simple Specification Test,' National Bureau of Economic Research Working Paper No. w2168. https://papers.ssrn.com/abstractid=346975

Luck, C. and N. Pilotte (1993). 'Domini Social Index Performance,' *Journal of Investing*, 2(3): 60–62.

Manescu, C. (2011) 'Stock Returns in Relation to Environmental, Social and Governance Performance: Mispricing or Compensation for Risk?' *Sustainable Development*, 19(2): 95–118.

Markowitz, H. and G. Xu (1994). 'Data Mining Corrections,' *Journal of Portfolio Management*, 21(1): 60–69.

Moskowitz, M. (1972). 'Choosing Socially Responsible Stocks,' *Business & Society Review*, 1: 71–75.

Moskowitz, M. (1997). 'Social Investing: The Moral Foundation,' *Journal of Investing*, 6(4): 9–11.

MSCI ESG Research Inc. (2015). *MSCI ESG KLD STATS: 1991–2014 Data Sets*. https://www.wiso.uni-hamburg.de/bibliothek/recherche/datenbanken/unternehmensdaten/msci-methodology-2014.pdf.

Naaraayanan, L., S. Sachdeva, and V. Sharma (2020). 'Real Effects of Environmental Activist Investing,' European Corporate Governance Institute, Finance Working Paper No. 743/2021. https://ssrn.com/abstract=3483692.

Perez, T. (2015). *United States Secretary of Labor's Remarks at Oct. 22, 2015 News Conference on Interpretive Bulletin 2015-01 Relating to the Fiduciary Standard under ERISA in Considering Economically Targeted Investments*. Washington, DC: US Department of Labor, Employee Benefits Security Administration.

Rosen, B., D. Sandler, and D. Shani (1991). 'Social Issues and Socially Responsible Investment Behavior: A Preliminary Empirical Investigation,' *The Journal of Consumer Affairs*, 25(2): 221–234.

Ruf, B., K. Muralidhar, and K. Paul (1993). 'Eight Dimensions of Corporate Social Performance Determination of Relative Importance Using the Analytic Hierarchy Process,' *Academy of Management Proceedings*, 1993(1): 326–330.

Russo, M. and P. Fouts (1997). 'A Resource-Based Perspective on Corporate Environmental Performance and Profitability,' *Academy of Management Journal*, 40(3): 534–559.

Sharfman, M. (1996). 'The Construct Validity of the Kinder, Lydenberg and Domini Social Performance Ratings Data,' *Journal of Business Ethics*, 15: 287–296.

Social Investment Forum (SIF) (2007). *2007 Report on US Sustainable and Impact Investing Trends*. Washington, DC: Social Investment Foundation.

Statman, M. and D. Glushkov (2009). 'The Wages of Social Responsibility,' *Financial Analysts Journal*, 65(4): 33–46.

United States Department of Labor (2020). *Proposed Rule: 29 CFR Part 2550 RIN 1210-AB95*, Financial Factors in Selecting Plan Investments. https://www.napa-net.org/sites/napa-net.org/files/financial-factors-in-selecting-plan-investments-proposed-rule.pdf.

US Social Investment Forum (SIF) (2020). *Report on US Sustainable and Impact Investing Trends*, 13th ed. (2020). Washington, DC: US SIF Foundation.

Waddock, S. and S. Graves (1997). 'The Corporate Social Performance-Financial Performance Link,' *Strategic Management Journal*, 18(4): 303–319.

Wharton Research Data Services. KLD on WRDS. https://wrds-www.wharton.upenn.edu/documents/1154/KLD-on-WRDS.pdf.

Wheeler, L. (1994) 'Changes in Consensus Earnings Estimates and their Impact on Stock Returns.' In B. Bruce and C. Epstein, eds., *The Handbook of Corporate Earnings Analysis*. Chicago, IL: Probus Publishing, 63–84.

Williams, J. (1938). *The Theory of Investment Value*. Cambridge, MA: Harvard University Press.

Womack, K. (1996) 'Do Brokerage Analysts' Recommendations Have Investment Value?' *Journal of Finance*, 51(1): 137–167.

Ziemba, W. and S. Schwartz (1993). *Invest Japan*. Chicago, IL: Probus Publishing.

# Chapter 6

# ESG and Downside Risks

Implications for Pension Funds

*Zacharias Sautner and Laura T. Starks*

Analyzing a firm from an environmental, social, and governance (ESG) perspective allows pension fund managers to potentially identify risk exposures that would be missed using only traditional investment analysis. The types of risks most likely to be uncovered using an ESG lens can be categorized as reputation risk, human capital management risk, litigation risk, regulatory risk, corruption risk, and climate risk. In addition, the components of risk (e.g., systematic risks, tracking error, and downside risks) can be affected differentially by ESG issues. Some of the risks, notably climate risk, have changed in importance over time and even for others, such as corruption risk, the ESG lens can provide a heightened way in which to examine the effects of the risks on pension portfolios.[1]

Due to their long-term horizons, pension funds face enhanced exposures to the long-lived effects of many ESG risks, especially those that arise from climate change. In addition, the long-term nature of pension funds combined with the potential consequences of being underfunded leaves their portfolios, particularly those for defined-benefit plans, more exposed to the repercussions of downside risks, that is, to sharp declines in asset values. Specifically, many pension funds face large liabilities toward their beneficiaries, and the failure to meet those liabilities because of significant negative ESG-related events carries large penalties. Thus, with wealth protection being an important dimension, pension funds should have a strong preference to identify and address ESG-related downside risks. Downside risks have also become important for pension fund managers from a more general portfolio construction perspective, as mounting evidence shows that asset returns are typically skewed. Left-skewed asset returns, in particular, violate a key assumption of the standard mean-variance investment framework, and asset allocation models have, in turn, been developed that explicitly incorporate the resultant downside risks.

Zacharias Sautner and Laura T. Starks, *ESG and Downside Risks*. In: *Pension Funds and Sustainable Investment*. Edited by P. Brett Hammond, Raimond Maurer, and Olivia S. Mitchell, Oxford University Press. © Zacharias Sautner and Laura T. Starks (2023). DOI: 10.1093/oso/9780192889195.003.0006

In this chapter, we first review different types and sources of ESG-related risks, with a focus on climate-related downside risks. We then report evidence on institutional investors' perspectives on the importance of climate-related downside risks and how such risks are priced in financial markets. We also demonstrate whether and how institutional investors address climate-related risks in the investment process.

## Types of ESG-related Risks
### Reputation risk

ESG issues pose significant reputational risks to the firms in which pension funds invest. The increasingly public discussion of firms' ESG activities through internet media sources and social media have created the possibility that management missteps in these areas result in material effects on firms' reputations. Moreover, the effects of reputational risk on market value can be quite large, given that estimates of the value of intangible assets for firms in the S&P 500 have increased from about 17 percent in 1975 to 90 percent in 2020 (Ocean Tomo 2020).[2] In a recent survey, firms were asked to rank their top three most important subclasses of intangible assets beyond intellectual property and information assets (Ponemon 2020). Among the top responses, 69 percent of the firms stated their third-party relationships, such as with customers, suppliers, vendors, and supply chains, and 47 percent stated their brand as being the top three most important subclasses of intangible assets. These two types of intangible assets would be particularly vulnerable to reputational penalties imposed on a firm because of ESG controversies or poor ESG practices.

Further evidence that ESG reputation risk can be significant is reflected in the fact that most of the ESG ratings agencies now include some type of controversy rating to ensure that their client investors are aware of the existing controversies that can affect a firm's reputation. For example, Sustainalytics states that ESG controversies ratings identify 'companies involved in incidents and events that may pose a business or reputation risk to a company due to the potential impact on stakeholders or the environment' (Sustainalytics 2021: 1). In fact, because of their contributions to a firm's ESG risk exposures, the controversies ratings have become a central part of most ESG ratings services. For example, a study by the EU Commission on sustainability-related ratings (European Commission 2020) has a section on 'Controversy Ratings.' This section specifically points to the different ESG ratings agencies, who provide news sentiment and controversy alerts so that investors become aware of the behaviors and practices of firms and countries that are not compatible with the investors' policies, and that could lead to reputational risks.[3] For some of the ratings agencies, a firm's controversy level is a significant part of the overall ESG score; for others it is reported as a separate score. In addition, for one agency, RepRisk, the controversy issues represent the total score. The EU Commission's study points out that 'Increasingly sustainability-related ratings providers are factoring controversies, allegations and negative news into their assessments of companies as a means of layering in risk exposure and signaling (potential) poor management' (European Commission 2020: 99). Again, these controversy ratings are consistent with the argument that using an ESG lens allows investors to go beyond traditional valuation models to assess risks that would not be captured by those models.

The controversy ratings have allowed ESG ratings agencies to give warnings, thus helping investors assess, or even avoid, firms with greater ESG risk exposure. For example, MSCI argues that in the two years prior to the emissions scandal, they had flagged Volkswagen on controversies related to product and service quality, bribery and fraud, and collective bargaining (MSCI 2015).

## Human capital management risk

Although human capital management risk has long been an aspect of ESG risk, it has come under heightened scrutiny during the COVID-19 pandemic because the pandemic highlighted firms' treatments of their employees. That is, the crisis highlighted how a firm's handling of social issues, of which human capital is a key component, affects firm performance. Recent evidence shows that investors became more concerned about how firms treat their human capital (Albuquerque et al. 2020; Cheema-Fox et al. 2020).

## Litigation risk

Litigation related to ESG issues can increase for firms considered to have poor ESG practices. For example, a number of jurisdictions (counties and cities) have filed lawsuits against oil firms, seeking compensation for climate change damages (e.g., New York City, Oakland, San Francisco, Boulder, San Mateo County, and Marin County). Recently, PG&E (Pacific Gas and Electric Company) had to file for bankruptcy as a result of legal claims related to the Californian wildfires, which exceeded US$10 billion. Similarly, BP had to pay more than US$18 billion to settle legal claims related to the oil spill at its Deepwater Horizon offshore drilling rig.[4]

## Regulatory risk

Regulatory risk recognizes that new (costly) regulations related to ESG can arise, and such regulations have been increasing over time. For example, according to an October 2018 report by Datamaran, during the previous three years ESG-related regulations grew by more than 100 percent in the UK, US, and Canada (Datamaran 2018). Recently, the EU established a new regulation that requires all financial market participants and financial advisors to disclose specific information on their approaches to the integration of a 'sustainability risk' into their investment decisions. They also have to disclose the extent to which their decision-making process and their investment products take into account the consideration of 'sustainability factor' adverse impacts. A 'sustainability risk' is defined as an 'environmental, social or governance event or condition that, if it occurs, could cause an actual or potential material negative impact on the value of the investment.'[5] Regulatory risk is a particularly important component of climate risk (along with physical risk and technological risk) and will be discussed in more detail below.

## Corruption risk

The risks related to corruption lead to both financial and reputational risks. Beck et al. (2005) provide evidence that corruption can hamper firm growth. In line with this evidence, institutional investors consider corruption risk to be a highly important risk. In a recent PwC survey of institutional investors, the investors identified anti-corruption along with climate change as their top two ESG concerns (PwC 2016).

## Climate risk

As pointed out by Litterman (2016) and Krueger et al. (2020), climate risk can negatively affect asset values, particularly for long-term investors such as pension funds. Thus, climate risk is an important consideration for the asset allocation and risk management of pension funds. Climate risk can originate from physical risks (e.g., sea-level rise, storms, or extreme temperature), regulatory risks (regulations to combat climate change), or technological risks (technological climate-related disruption), all of which can be financially material. The problem is that climate risk can be difficult to price and hedge due to its systematic nature, the fact that there does not exist sufficient disclosure by many firms that could be incorporated into the risk consideration, and the difficulty in finding suitable hedging instruments. Not surprisingly, institutional investors, corporate executives and policymakers have shown increased concerns regarding climate risk and climate-risk disclosure. Below we provide more discussion of different climate risks and their consequences on pension funds.

# Risk Components and ESG-related Risks
## Systematic risk

Systematic risk, that is, the risk that a firm has in common with the market, can contain ESG elements. Notably, Bénabou and Tirole (2010) point out that firms with higher ESG characteristics may have different systematic risk exposures, either due to their resilience in periods of crisis or because the firms face a specific ESG risk factor. Given these systematic risk exposures, the firms would be expected to require different risk premia, and consequently, have different expected returns. Albuquerque et al. (2019) develop a theoretical model consistent with this idea. In their model, firms have a choice to engage in ESG activities in order to increase their product differentiation and enhance their profits. The primary prediction arising from the model is that better ESG activities decrease systematic risk and increase firm value. The authors empirically test this model and find support for the predictions.[6] In further empirical tests, they show that the profits for high-ESG-scoring firms are less correlated with the business cycle than the profits for low-ESG-scoring firms.[7]

## Tracking error

Integrating ESG considerations into a portfolio process does not always reduce all components of portfolio risk as omitting firms or industries because of ESG concerns (e.g., negative screening) can lead to increased tracking error in a portfolio (e.g., Branch et al. 2019). Institutional investors that track an index or are evaluated relative to an index may in turn be concerned about ESG-related track error.

## Downside risk

For some investors, firms with higher ESG profiles provide a type of protection against downside risk because these firms are considered to be better managed and in turn have lower exposure to ESG risks. Empirical evidence demonstrates that the tail-risk measures are closely linked to ESG risk, as firms with better ESG performance are less vulnerable to firm-specific negative events (e.g., Krueger 2015; Diemont et al. 2016). Because of this, one of the primary arguments for integrating ESG analysis into portfolio investment decisions is the claim that such integration will mitigate risk, particularly downside risk. Among the most potentially devastating risks are risks that arise from controversies. These controversies may arise from the E of ESG (e.g., emissions, toxic wastes, and environmental disasters) or the S (e.g., human rights, labor rights, customer privacy, and product safety) or the G (e.g., bribery, fraud).

Two recent cases where ESG-related downside risks materialized are the PG&E involvement in the California fires, which was primarily an environmental risk but also involved social and governance risk, and the Wells Fargo series of scandals, which were primarily social risks, given the effects on customers, but also include governance risks. Both cases involved more than a single event and *ex post* analyses of the subsequent events indicate that these events had large negative effects on the stock prices of the two firms, even after controlling for stock market movements. These two events provide examples of the ESG-related downside risks that can occur. In both cases, pension funds lost significant amounts of money from their investments in these firms.

## Climate-related Downside Risks
### Importance of climate-related downside risks

In recent years, there has been an increasing amount of research on the financial effects of climate risk, which should be of particular relevance to pension fund managers and sponsors because of the potential portfolio effects. Researchers have provided theoretical evidence that climate risk should have a large effect on financial markets and may be mispriced (e.g., Bansal et al. 2016; Daniel et al. 2016); empirical evidence that equity markets underprice climate risk and underreact to it (Hong et al. 2019); and empirical evidence that extreme weather uncertainty affects financial markets (e.g., Kruttli et al. 2021). Further, Pankratz et al. (2021) show that firms with increased exposure to high temperatures face reductions in revenues and operating income. With regard to firm value, evidence suggests that increased climate risk disclosure affects firm value (Krueger 2018); that firms' exposure to climate risk predicts their stock returns (Kumar et al. 2019); that investors demand greater compensation from firms with higher carbon emissions (Bolton and Kacperczyk 2021); and that exposure to regulatory climate shocks negatively correlates with firm valuations in recent years (Sautner et al. 2021).

Another possible concern for pension fund portfolio managers and sponsors lies in the evidence that potential sea-level rise is already affecting real estate prices (e.g., Bernstein et al. 2019; Baldauf et al. 2020; Keys and Mulder 2020).[8] These potential consequences of climate risk make it even more difficult for pension fund managers, because climate risk is quite difficult to hedge (Andersson et al. 2016).

This broad base of evidence suggests that institutional investors, and pension fund managers in particular, should be worried about climate change and the resulting risks for their portfolio firms. Direct evidence supporting the claim that climate risks are an important concern for investors comes from Krueger et al. (2020) (KSS henceforth). KSS conduct an international survey among institutional investors, with 23 percent identifying as being asset managers, 22 percent banks, 17 percent pension funds, 15 percent insurance companies, and 8 percent mutual funds. There was a range of institution sizes but the majority had assets under management of at least US\$1 billion, including 11 percent that had assets of more than US\$100 billion. The sample was global, with 32 percent located in the US, 17 percent in the UK and Ireland, 12 percent in Canada, 11 percent in Germany, 7 percent in Italy, and 5 percent in Spain (the rest are located elsewhere in the world).

In questions regarding the importance of climate risks relative to other risks, as Figure 6.1 shows, most of the survey participants believe financial risk to be the most important, and climate risks, among other risks, to be relatively less important. However, on an absolute basis, the responses reported in KSS suggest that climate risks are deemed to have material financial consequences for portfolio firms. Moreover, in a question about their temperature expectations, the majority of respondents indicated that they expect a rise in global temperatures, and a significant number

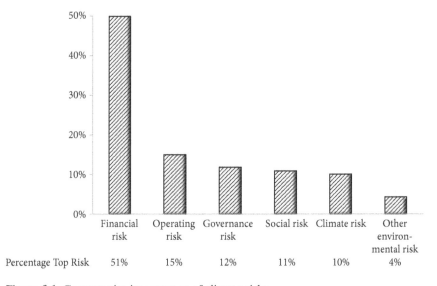

| Percentage Top Risk | 51% | 15% | 12% | 11% | 10% | 4% |

**Figure 6.1** Comparative importance of climate risks

*Note*: This figure reports the respondents' rankings of six major investment risks. Respondents were asked to rank the six risks from one to six, where one is the most important risk and six the least important risk. The figure reports the percentages of respondents that rank a risk as the most important risk.

*Source*: Krueger et al. (2020), Table 2.

believe that the temperature rise will exceed the Paris two-degree target. Further, their responses show that the majority believe that some climate risks, such as regulatory risk, have already been materializing. This is strong evidence, given theoretical evidence regarding the uncertainty of the time horizon over which climate risks would be materializing (e.g., Andersson et al. 2016; Barnett et al. 2020).

## Pricing of climate-related downside risks

Consistent with KSS's evidence that investors worry about climate risks, Ilhan et al. (2021) (ISV henceforth) demonstrate that uncertainty about climate-related downside risks began to be priced in financial markets. They argue that regulatory measures to limit carbon emissions, for example in the form of a carbon tax or limits on emissions, will have a significant financial impact on firms that produce large carbon emissions. Notably, for these types of firms, regulation that limits carbon emissions can lead to substantial increases in the cost of doing business or even to stranded assets. If banks reduce funding to carbon-intense firms, for instance, because of climate-related capital requirements, such firms may also experience constraints when financing future investment activities. At the same time, it is highly uncertain when and to what extent carbon-intense firms will be affected by future regulation. This climate policy uncertainty poses a challenge for investors in terms of adequately assessing how and when climate regulation will affect firms.

ISV address these issues empirically by exploring whether the option market prices climate policy uncertainty. Specifically, for their sample of S&P 500 firms, they test whether protection against downside tail risks through put options is more expensive for firms that emit more carbon. The benefit of examining traded options is that options-based measures reflect market participants' expectations of risk. Their primary measure to capture downside risk, *SlopeD*, reflects the steepness of the implied volatility slope; higher values of *SlopeD* indicate that deeper out-of-the-money put options are more expensive, and this reflects a relatively higher option protection cost against left-tail risks.

ISV provide a series of results documenting that climate policy uncertainty is priced in the option market. ISV's regression estimates, reproduced in Table 6.1, show that an increase in a firm's (log industry) carbon intensity by one-standard deviation increases *SlopeD* by 0.014 (see Column 1). This increase is meaningful as it equals about 10 percent of the standard deviation of *SlopeD*. Overall, ISV's evidence suggests that put options of carbon-intense firms are relatively more expensive, in particular for the far-left tail, as they protect investors against downside risks originating from climate policy uncertainty. ISV also show that the effect of carbon intensities on downside risk is amplified when the public pays relatively high

TABLE 6.1  Effects of carbon emission on downside risk

| Dependent variable: | *SlopeD* | *SlopeD* | *SlopeD* |
|---|---|---|---|
| | (1) | (2) | (3) |
| *log(Scope 1/MV firm)* | 0.006*** | | |
| | (3.39) | | |
| *Residual log(Scope 1/MV firm)* | | 0.003 | 0.005 |
| | | (0.81) | (1.06) |
| *log(Scope 1/MV industry)* | | | 0.006*** |
| | | | (3.76) |
| Model | Heckman | Heckman | Heckman |
| Controls | Yes | Yes | Yes |
| Year-by-quarter fixed effects | Yes | Yes | Yes |
| Level | Firm | Firm | Firm |
| Frequency | Monthly | Monthly | Monthly |
| Obs. | 18,664 | 18,664 | 18,664 |
| Adj. $R^2$ | n/a | n/a | n/a |

*Note*: This table reports regressions estimated at the firm-month level. *SlopeD* measures the steepness of the function that relates implied volatility to moneyness (measured by an option's Black-Scholes delta) for OTM put options with 30 days maturity. *Scope 1/MV firm* are a firm's Scope 1 carbon emissions (in metric tons of $CO_2$) divided by the firm's equity market value (in millions US$). *Scope 1/MV industry* is the Scope 1 carbon intensity of all firms in the same industry (SIC4) and year. It is defined as total Scope 1 carbon emissions (metric tons of $CO_2$) of all reporting firms in the industry divided by the total market capitalization of all reporting firms in the industry (in millions US$). *Residual log(Scope 1 MV/firm)* is the residual of an OLS regression with *log(Scope 1/MV firm)* as the dependent variable and *log(Scope 1/MV industry)* as the independent variable. The regressions in the table control for *log(Assets), Dividends/net income, Debt/assets, EBIT/assets, CapEx/assets, Book-to-market, Returns, Institutional ownership, CAPM beta, Volatility, Oil beta*, and a time trend (not reported). The sample includes all firms in the S&P 500 with data on carbon emissions disclosed to CDP. The table estimates the effect of emissions generated between 2009 and 2016 on option market variables measured between November 2010 and December 2017; *t*-statistics, based on standard errors clustered by industry (SIC4) and year, are in parentheses; n/a, not applicable; *$p$<0.1, **$p$<0.05, ***$p$<0.01. *Source*: Ilhan et al. (2021, table 4).

attention to climate change topics. The reason is that public attention to climate change topics increases the likelihood that pro-climate policies are adopted due to public scrutiny.

ISV use President Trump's election in 2016 as an event that reduced short-term climate policy uncertainty. While Trump signaled in his election campaign that climate-related policies would not become stricter, his opponent Hillary Clinton instead promised climate-friendly policies. ISV's tests in turn exploit that President Trump's election meant no change in the status quo of US climate regulation, whereas the election of Clinton would have meant the opposite. These arguments imply that for carbon-intense firms, the cost of insurance against downside risks associated with climate

TABLE 6.2 Effect of 2016 Trump election on climate-related downside risk

| Dependent variable: | SlopeD | SlopeD | SlopeD | SlopeD |
|---|---|---|---|---|
| Event window: | [−250; +250] | [−250; +250] | [−250; +250] | [−250; +250] |
| | (1) | (2) | (3) | (4) |
| Post Trump election x High Scope 1/MV Industry | −0.025** | −0.029** | −0.025*** | −0.020** |
| | (−2.18) | (−2.43) | (−2.88) | (−2.20) |
| Scope 1/MV industry high | 0.041* | 0.043* | | |
| | (1.67) | (1.77) | | |
| Post Trump election | −0.025*** | | | −0.022*** |
| | (−4.63) | | | (−4.33) |
| Model | DiD | DiD | DiD | DiD |
| Controls | Yes | Yes | Yes | Yes |
| Day fixed effects | No | Yes | Yes | No |
| Firm fixed effects | No | No | Yes | No |
| Industry fixed effects | No | No | No | Yes |
| Level | Firm | Firm | Firm | Firm |
| Frequency | Daily | Daily | Daily | Daily |
| Obs. | 200,897 | 200,897 | 200,897 | 200,897 |
| Adj. R-sq. | 0.062 | 0.091 | 0.294 | 0.184 |

*Note*: This table reports regressions estimated at the firm-day level. Results are from difference-in-differences regressions around the date of President Trump's election on November 9, 2016. *SlopeD* measures the steepness of the function that relates implied volatility to moneyness (measured by an option's Black-Scholes delta) for OTM put options with 30 days maturity. *Post-Trump election* equals one for all days after President Trump's election, and zero for all days before the election. *Scope 1/MV industry high* equals one for firms that operate in the top-10 industries based on *Scope 1/MV industry,* and zero otherwise. The regressions control for *Effective tax rate, Effective tax rate x Post-Trump election, log(Assets), Dividends/net income, Debt/assets, EBIT/assets, CapEx/assets, Book-to-market, Returns, Institutional ownership, CAPM beta, Volatility,* and *Oil beta* (not reported). The sample includes all firms in the S&P 500 with data on carbon emissions disclosed to CDP; *t*-statistics, based on standard errors double clustered by firm and day, are in parentheses; *p<0.1, **p<0.05, ***p<0.01.
*Source*: Ilhan et al. (2021, table 7).

policy uncertainty should have declined after the election of President Trump. Supporting this prediction, Table 6.2 demonstrates ISV's result that *SlopeD* for very carbon-intense firms indeed declined by 0.025 (Column 1) after President Trump's election, relative to less carbon-intense firms—a reduction equal to 12 percent of *SlopeD*'s standard deviation.

## Addressing climate-related downside risks

Given the uncertainty surrounding climate risk and ISV's evidence that climate-related downside risks are being priced, it is perhaps not surprising that investors started to address climate risks in their investment processes. In their global survey, KSS also asked the institutional investors which approaches, if any, they had taken to incorporate climate risks into their investment processes (they asked about the previous five years). The responses are provided in Table 6.3. As the table indicates, all but 7 percent of the investors have chosen 'some' approach for incorporating climate-risk management into their investment process.[9] The most common approach taken by the institutional investors (38 percent) is to analyze the carbon footprint of their portfolio firms. Further, 29 percent of the respondents attempt to reduce the carbon footprint of their investment portfolios. Another common approach, followed by 35 percent of the investors, is to analyze the stranded asset risks in their portfolios, that is, the risk of having an asset lose economic value earlier than anticipated due to climate change effects. Again, some of the respondents (23 percent) take this approach a step further by not only analyzing their portfolios' stranded asset risks, but also trying to reduce these risks (23 percent).

Over a third of the investors (34 percent) take an indirect approach because they believe that their general portfolio diversification serves as one method to incorporate climate risks into their portfolio process. In contrast, some investors (26 percent) take a direct approach by employing valuation models that specifically incorporate climate risks. Other direct approaches employed are to submit shareholder proposals to portfolio firms (25 percent), to hedge against climate risks (25 percent), or to employ negative screening (24 percent). It is striking that out of the list of 12 possible approaches offered to the respondents, the least frequently used method of dealing with climate risks is divestment, which is employed by 20 percent. The respondents could select more than one approach, and in further analyses we find that those who employ more approaches are those who are more concerned about the financial costs of climate change, those with longer horizons, and those who have a larger fraction of their portfolios managed using ESG analysis. Given the wide variety of approaches commonly employed, it appears that the investment industry is still trying to find out how to most effectively manage climate risks; this likely also applies to pension funds.

As we discuss below, Hoepner et al. (2021) provide evidence that shareholder engagement by investors can reduce downside ESG risks, especially those originating from climate change. The survey by KSS thus also asked investors what measures of engagement over climate-risk issues they have taken with any of their portfolio firms (during the past five years). Similar to the results in Table 6.3 of the heterogeneity of approaches taken to incorporate climate-related risks into their investment processes, the answers to this question, provided in Table 6.4, show that the respondents do not employ a

TABLE 6.3  Climate-risk-management approaches

| Climate-risk-management approaches taken in the past five years | Percentage that took this measure (%) | Significant differences in mean response vs. rows |
|---|---|---|
| | (1) | (2) |
| (1) Analyzing carbon footprint of portfolio firms | 38.0 | 4–14 |
| (2) Analyzing stranded asset risk | 34.6 | 5–14 |
| (3) General portfolio diversification | 33.9 | 6–14 |
| (4) ESG integration | 31.7 | 6–14 |
| (5) Reducing carbon footprint of portfolio firms | 29.3 | 1–2, 10–14 |
| (6) Firm valuation models that incorporate climate risk | 25.9 | 1–4, 12–14 |
| (7) Use of third-party ESG ratings | 25.6 | 1–4, 12–14 |
| (8) Shareholder proposals | 25.1 | 1–4, 12–14 |
| (9) Hedging against climate risk | 24.6 | 1–4, 13–14 |
| (10) Negative/exclusionary screening | 23.7 | 1–5, 13–14 |
| (11) Reducing stranded asset risk | 22.9 | 1–5, 13–14 |
| (12) Divestment | 20.2 | 1–8, 12–14 |
| (13) None | 7.1 | 1–12, 14 |
| (14) Other | 3.7 | 1–13 |

*Note*: This table reports the percentage of 410 respondents that in the previous five years took a given approach to incorporate climate risks into the investment process. Responses were not mutually exclusive. The table ranks results based on their relative frequency. Column (1) presents the percentage of respondents that took a certain measure. Column (2) reports the results of a *t*-test of the null hypothesis that the percentage for a given approach is equal to the percentage for each of the other approaches, where only differences significant at the 10 percent level are reported.
*Source*: Krueger et al. (2020, table 4).

unique approach to their engagement strategy, but that they employ a number of different methods. Moreover, the survey investors have a generally high level of engagement with their portfolio firms, as only 16 percent did not have any engagements over the period.[10] The most often used channel is to hold discussions with firm management regarding the financial

TABLE 6.4  Climate-risk engagement

| Direct engagement over climate-risk issues in the past five years | | Percentage that used this approach (%) | Significant difference in mean response vs. rows |
|---|---|---|---|
| | | (1) | (2) |
| (1) | Holding discussions with management regarding financial implications of climate risks | 43 | 2–10 |
| (2) | Proposing specific actions to management on climate-risk issues | 32 | 1, 6–10 |
| (3) | Voting against management on proposals over climate-risk issues at annual meeting | 30 | 1, 6–10 |
| (4) | Submitting shareholder proposals on climate-risk issues | 30 | 1, 6–10 |
| (5) | Questioning management on a conference call about climate-risk issues | 30 | 1, 6–10 |
| (6) | Publicly criticizing management on climate-risk issues | 20 | 1–5, 9 |
| (7) | Voting against re-election of any board directors due to climate-risk issues | 19 | 1–5, 9 |
| (8) | Legal action against management on climate-risk issues | 18 | 1–5, 9 |
| (9) | Other | 1 | 1–8, 10 |
| (10) | None | 16 | 1–9 |

*Note*: This table reports the percentage of 406 respondents that haven taken a particular approach of direct engagement over climate-risk issues in the previous five years. The table ranks results based on their relative frequency. Responses were not mutually exclusive. Column (1) presents the percentage of respondents that took a certain approach. Column (2) reports the results of a *t*-test of the null hypothesis that the percentage for a given approach is equal to the percentage for each of the other approaches, where significant differences at the 10 percent level are reported.
*Source*: Krueger et al. (2020, table 6).

consequences of climate risks for firms, which is used by 43 percent of the respondents. Thirty-two percent of the respondents propose specific actions to management on climate-risk issues. On the other hand, some of the investors choose to abandon the behind-the-scenes-approach and question management on a conference call about climate-risk issues (30 percent), publicly criticize management on climate-risk issues (20 percent), or submit a shareholder proposal on climate-risk issues (30 percent). A number of the investors (30 percent) vote at the annual meeting against management on proposals over climate issues. Smaller fractions vote against the re-election of any individual board directors due to climate-risk issues or take legal action against management over climate-related issues.

The investors reported that they usually received a response to their engagement, although the response could be a simple acknowledgment of the engagement rather than any actions by the firm to respond to the investor's concerns. The investors also indicated that if their engagement efforts were rebuffed, they typically did not escalate the engagement, try to hedge or divest from the firm. This lack of divestment due to failure of an engagement, combined with the lack of divestment for risk management purposes as discussed above, is striking given the ongoing debate regarding whether to divest from fossil fuel firms.

In the survey, the question of stranded asset risks due to climate change was also explored at a deeper level by asking the respondents the following: 'Responses to climate change may cause some assets to become "stranded"—i.e., unable to recover their investment cost, with a loss of value for investors. How large do you consider this risk in the following areas?' Then a list of industries was provided, which included coal producers, unconventional oil production (e.g., tar sands, fracking), conventional oil producers, natural gas producers, iron and steel producers, and conventional electricity producers. The results are provided in Table 6.5. The two industry sectors for which the largest percentage of respondents considered the risks to be very high were coal producers (25.1 percent of respondents) and unconventional oil producers (21.1 percent). In addition, 16.7 percent of the investors thought that conventional oil producers have a very high risk of stranded assets and the responses for the other types of producers were lower, but significant. Although it might be surprising that only 25.1 percent of the investors thought that the stranded asset risk was high in the coal industry, it should also be noted that the average response to the question is 2.73 (out of 4). This magnitude provides a stronger possibility that investors think stranded asset risk is high in the coal sector. There were also significant relations regarding the types of investor institutions who believe that the stranded asset risks are high in these sectors. For example, the investors more concerned about the financial effects of climate risks are the ones who believe that stranded asset risks are higher among oil and natural gas producers. In addition, for most of the sectors, investors who engage portfolio firms more over climate-risk topics, those with a higher share of investments under ESG principles, and those with a higher passive investment share, view stranded asset risks to be higher.

The survey evidence by KSS shows that a number of investors engage with their portfolio firms on climate issues. To understand whether such engagement can reduce downside risks, Hoepner et al. (2021) employ proprietary data regarding the activities of a large investor, who specializes in engagements with firms on ESG issues for both its own account and those of others. Through an analysis of 1712 engagements across 573 targets worldwide over the 2005–18 period, the authors find that a successful engagement typically takes about three years.

The authors employ two measures to examine whether a shareholder engagement appears to affect the downside risk of the target firms. The first measure is the lower partial moment (LPM) of the second order, using a zero percent-return threshold, that is, the negative part of the return distribution of returns. The second measure is the investment's value at risk (VaR). Using these measures in two different empirical approaches (difference-in-differences and factor model), the authors provide evidence that a successful ESG engagement by the investor is followed by reductions in the target firms' downside risk. They further find that engagement over environmental topics delivers the highest benefits in terms of downside risk reduction, and environmental engagements primarily feature the theme of climate change. This finding is consistent with the survey evidence in KSS, which indicates as discussed above that engagement over climate change is an important channel through which some institutions attempt to tackle climate-related risks. The results by Hoepner et al. (2021) suggest that such engagements have the potential to deliver substantial benefits for investors. Using the factor model approach, Hoepner et al. (2021) also find that the downside risk factor associated with a firm tends to decrease after at least partially successful engagements. Similar evidence is obtained by Dyck et al. (2019) who demonstrate that institutional investors are able to improve the ESG profiles of portfolio firms.

## Conclusions

In this chapter, we have discussed the implications of ESG risks for pension fund portfolios. We argued that the long-term horizons of pension funds expose them to the long-lived effects of many ESG risks, especially those related to climate change. The potential consequences of being underfunded also leaves pension funds particularly exposed to ESG-related downside risks. We have demonstrated how downside risks may affect pension funds in the face of climate change. We provided evidence showing that institutional investors think that climate risks are imminent today and have important financial implications for their portfolio firms. We also showed

TABLE 6.5 Stranded asset risk

| Stranded asset risk | % with ('very high') score | Mean score | % with 'Do not know' | N | H₀: Mean Score = 1 | Significant differences in mean score vs. rows |
|---|---|---|---|---|---|---|
| | (1) | (2) | (3) | (4) | (5) | (6) |
| (1) Coal producers | 25.1 | 2.78 | 3 | 371 | *** | 2–6 |
| (2) Unconventional oil producers | 21.3 | 2.69 | 3 | 371 | *** | 1, 4–6 |
| (3) Conventional oil producers | 16.7 | 2.64 | 4 | 371 | *** | 1, 4–6 |
| (4) Natural gas producers | 11.9 | 2.46 | 3 | 370 | *** | 1–3, 5 |
| (5) Iron and steel producers | 11.7 | 2.40 | 5 | 369 | *** | 1–4 |
| (6) Conventional electricity producers | 10.5 | 2.42 | 4 | 371 | *** | 1–3 |

*Note:* This table reports the investors' responses to the question of how large they consider the risk that climate change causes some assets to become stranded, that is, unable to recover their investment cost, with a loss of value for investors. The survey listed six industries for which the respondents were asked to evaluate this risk. Respondents could indicate their views on a scale of one ('low') through four ('very high'). They could also indicate 'Do not know.' Column (1) presents the percentage of respondents indicating that stranded asset risk is 'very high.' The table ranks results based on this measure. Column (2) reports the mean score, where higher values correspond to higher stranded asset risk. Column (3) presents the percentage of respondents indicating 'Do not know.' Column (4) reports the number of respondents. Column (5) reports the results of a *t*-test of the null hypothesis that each mean score is equal to 1 (low stranded asset risk). Column (6) reports the results of a *t*-test of the null hypothesis that the mean score for a given reason is equal to the mean score for each of the other reasons, where significant differences at the 10 percent level are reported; *t*-statistics (reported in parentheses) are based on standard errors that are clustered at the investor-county level; \*\*\*, \*\*, \* indicate significance levels of 1 percent, 5 percent, and 10 percent, respectively.

*Source:* Krueger et al. (2020, table 10).

that these risks are priced in financial markets. Finally, we presented evidence on whether and how institutional investors address climate-related risks in the investment process. We showed that the investors tend to prefer to employ risk management and engagement strategies, rather than divestment, to address the climate risk in their portfolios. Overall, our evidence implies that pension funds should develop processes to identify, measure, and manage ESG-related downside risks, especially those related to climate change.

## Acknowledgments

We are grateful to our co-authors Andreas Hoepner, Emirhan Ilhan, Philipp Krueger, Ioannis Oikonomou, Grigory Vilkov, and Xiaoyan Zhou, as this chapter builds on some of our joint work.

## Notes

1. Some of the other authors cited in this chapter use the terminology CSR (corporate social responsibility) rather than ESG. We use the term ESG throughout this chapter rather than alternating between ESG and CSR.
2. The composition of firms in the S&P 500, particularly the largest firms, has changed during the period. The top five firms in 1975 were IBM, Exxon, Procter & Gamble, General Electric, and 3M. The top five firms in 2020 were Apple, Microsoft, Amazon, Alphabet, and Facebook. Obviously, the latter have significantly more of their assets in intangible assets.
3. The agencies the EU cites as providing the controversy information are RepRisk, Bloomberg Environmental & Social News Sentiment Scores, MSCI ESG Controversies, Sustainalytics Controversies Research and Reports, ISS Country Controversy Assessment, and Vigeo Eiris Controversy Risk Assessment.
4. See Gilbert and Kent (2015) and Gold (2019).
5. See Regulation (EU) 2019/2088 of the European Parliament and of the Council of November 27, 2019 on sustainability-related disclosures in the financial services sector.
6. In other tests on the relation between ESG scores and systematic risk, Oikonomou et al. (2012) provide evidence that ESG/CSR performance is negatively but weakly related to systematic firm risk. They conclude that corporate social irresponsibility is positively and strongly related to financial risk.
7. Some practitioners have a similar view on the systematic element of ESG risks. These practitioners maintain that since ESG are systematic risk factors, investing according to ESG risks would then be a form of smart beta. The implication of this view is that these risk factors are mispriced and, consequently, an investor could take advantage of this fact by constructing a portfolio with specific exposure to ESG risks.
8. It should be noted that Murfin and Spiegel (2020) provide contrasting evidence.
9. Note that respondents with more sophisticated tools would have been more likely to participate in the survey.

10. In a survey of institutional investors regarding their shareholder engagements, McCahery et al. (2016) find that 19 percent of the respondents did not engage with their portfolio firms.

## References

Albuquerque, R., Y. Koskinen, S. Yang, and C. Zhang (2020). 'Resiliency of Environmental and Social Stocks: An Analysis of the Exogenous COVID-19 Market Crash,' *Review of Corporate Finance Studies*, 9(3): 593–621.

Albuquerque, R., Y. Koskinen, and C. Zhang (2019). 'Corporate Social Responsibility and Firm Risk: Theory and Empirical Evidence,' *Management Science*, 65(10): 4451–4469.

Andersson, M., P. Bolton, and F. Samama (2016). 'Hedging Climate Risk,' *Financial Analysts Journal*, 72(3): 13–32.

Baldauf, M., L. Garlappi, and C. Yannelis (2020). 'Does Climate Change Affect Real Estate Prices? Only if You Believe in It,' *Review of Financial Studies*, 33(3): 1256–1295.

Bansal, R., D. Kiku, and M. Ochoa (2016). 'Price of Long-Run Temperature Shifts in Capital Markets,' NBER Working Paper No. 22529, National Bureau of Economic Research, Cambridge, MA.

Barnett, M., W. Brock, and L.P. Hansen (2020). 'Pricing Uncertainty Induced by Climate Change,' *Review of Financial Studies*, 33(3): 1024–1066.

Beck, T., A. Demirgüç-Kunt, and V. Maksimovic (2005). 'Financial and Legal Constraints to Growth: Does Firm Size Matter?' *Journal of Finance*, 60(1): 137–177.

Bénabou, R. and J. Tirole (2010). 'Individual and Corporate Social Responsibility,' *Economica*, 77(305): 1–19.

Bernstein, A., M.T. Gustafson, and R. Lewis (2019). 'Disaster on the Horizon: The Price Effect of Sea Level Rise,' *Journal of Financial Economics*, 134(2): 253–272.

Bolton, P. and M. Kacperczyk (2021). 'Do Investors Care About Carbon Risk?' *Journal of Financial Economics*, 142(2): 517–549.

Branch, M., L. Goldberg, and P. Hand (2019). 'A Guide to ESG Portfolio Construction,' *Journal of Portfolio Management*, 45(4): 61–66.

Cheema-Fox, A., B.R. LaPerla, G. Serafeim, and H. Wang (2020). 'Corporate Resilience and Response During COVID-19,' Harvard Business School Accounting & Management Unit Working Paper No. 20-108, Harvard Business School, Boston, MA.

Daniel, K.D., R.B. Litterman, and G. Wagner (2016). 'Applying Asset Pricing Theory to Calibrate the Price of Climate Risk,' NBER Working Paper No. 22795, National Bureau of Economic Research, Cambridge, MA.

Datamaran (2018). *Global Insights Report: The Three Big Wake-Up Calls for Boards.* London: Datamaran Ltd. https://www.datamaran.com/global-insights-report/.

Diemont, D., K. Moore, and A. Soppe (2016). 'The Downside of Being Responsible: Corporate Social Responsibility and Tail Risk,' *Journal of Business Ethics*, 137(2): 213–229.

Dyck, A., K. Lins, L. Roth, and H. Wagner (2019). 'Do Institutional Investors Drive Corporate Social Responsibility? International Evidence,' *Journal of Financial Economics*, 131(3): 693–714.

European Commission (2020). *Study on Sustainability-Related Ratings, Data and Research.* Brussels, Belgium: European Commission. https://op.europa.eu/en/publication-detail/-/publication/d7d85036-509c-11eb-b59f-01aa75ed71a1/language-en/format-PDF/source-183474104%E2%80%9D.

Gilbert, D. and S. Kent (2015). 'BP Agrees to Pay $18.7 Billion to Settle Deepwater Horizon Oil Spill Claims,' Wall Street Journal, July 2. https://www.wsj.com/articles/bp-agrees-to-pay-18-7-billion-to-settle-deepwater-horizon-oil-spill-claims-1435842739.

Gold, R. (2019). 'PG&E: The First Climate-Change Bankruptcy, Probably Not the Last,' *Wall Street Journal,* January 18. https://www.wsj.com/articles/pg-e-wildfires-and-the-first-climate-change-bankruptcy-11547820006.

Hoepner, A.G.F., I. Oikonomou, Z. Sautner, L.T. Starks, and X. Zhou (2021). 'ESG Shareholder Engagement and Downside Risk,' ECGI Finance Working Paper No. 671/2020, European Corporate Governance Institute, Brussels, Belgium.

Hong, H.G., F.W. Li, and J. Xu (2019). 'Climate Risks and Market Efficiency,' *Journal of Econometrics*, 208(1): 265–281.

Ilhan, E., Z. Sautner, and G. Vilkov (2021). 'Carbon Tail Risk,' *Review of Financial Studies*, 34(3): 1540–1571.

Keys, B. and P. Mulder (2020). 'Neglected No More: Housing Markets, Mortgage Lending, and Sea Level Rise,' NBER Working Paper No. 27930, National Bureau of Economic Research, Cambridge, MA.

Krueger, P. (2015). 'Corporate Goodness and Shareholder Wealth,' *Journal of Financial Economics*, 115(2): 304–329.

Krueger, P. (2018). 'Climate Change and Firm Valuation: Evidence from a Quasi-Natural Experiment,' Swiss Finance Institute Research Paper No. 15-40, Swiss Finance Institute, Geneva, Switzerland.

Krueger, P., Z. Sautner, and L.T. Starks (2020). 'The Importance of Climate Risks for Institutional Investors,' *Review of Financial Studies*, 33(3): 1067–1111.

Kruttli, M.S., B.R. Tran, and S.W. Watugala (2021). 'Pricing Poseidon: Extreme Weather Uncertainty and Firm Return Dynamics,' Finance and Economics Discussion Series 2019-054, Board of Governors of the Federal Reserve System, Washington, DC.

Kumar, A., W. Xin, and C. Zhang (2019). 'Climate Sensitivity and Predictable Returns,' Working Paper, University of Miami, Miami, FL.

Litterman, B. (2016). *Climate Risk: Tail Risk and the Price of Carbon Emissions—Answers to the Risk Management Puzzle.* Hoboken, NJ: John Wiley & Sons.

McCahery, J., Z. Sautner, and L.T. Starks (2016). 'Behind the Scenes: The Corporate Governance Preferences of Institutional Investors,' *Journal of Finance*, 71(6): 2905–2932.

MSCI (2015). 'Volkswagen Scandal Underlines Need for ESG Analysis,' MSCI ESG Research: Volkswagen Rating. https://www.msci.com/volkswagen-scandal.

Murfin, J. and M. Spiegel (2020). 'Is the Risk of Sea Level Rise Capitalized in Residential Real Estate?' *Review of Financial Studies*, 33(3): 1217–1255.

Ocean Tomo (2020). *Intangible Asset Market Value Study.* Chicago, IL: Ocean Tomo. https://www.oceantomo.com/intangible-asset-mRRarket-value-study/.

Oikonomou, I., C. Brooks, and S. Pavelin (2012). 'The Impact of Corporate Social Performance on Financial Risk and Utility: A Longitudinal Analysis,' *Financial Management*, 41(2): 483–515.

Pankratz, N.M., R. Bauer, and J. Derwall (2021). 'Climate Change, Firm Performance and Investor Surprises,' Working Paper, UCLA, Los Angeles, CA.

Ponemon (2020). *Financial Impact of Intellectual Property & Cyber Assets*. Traverse City,
MI: Ponemon Institute. https://www.aon.com/getmedia/6e200c08-c579-4333-
b5f2-385ab6fbefde/Financial-Impact-of-Intellectual-Property-.

PwC (2016). *Redefining Business Success in a Changing World: CEO Survey*. London: PricewaterhouseCoopers. https://www.pwc.com/gx/en/ceo-survey/2016/
landing-page/pwc-19th-annual-global-ceo-survey.pdf

Sautner, Z., L. van Lent, G. Vilkov, and R. Zhang (2021). 'Firm-Level Climate Change
Exposure,' ECGI Finance Working Paper No. 686/2020, European Corporate
Governance Institute, Brussels, Belgium.

Sustainalytics (2021). *Controversies Research*. Amsterdam, Netherlands: Sustainalytics. https://connect.sustainalytics.com/controversies-research?_ga=2.55991083.
1214062825.1618239466-1283216333.1618239466.

# Chapter 7

# Global Pensions and ESG

*Is There a Better Way?*

*Luba Nikulina*

Environmental, social, and governance (ESG) factors entered our lives in the 1960s, when investors started to exclude stocks or entire industries from their portfolios based on their business activities, such as tobacco production or involvement in the South African apartheid regime. ESG influence has been growing ever since, particularly in the last five years, as the world has faced an increasing number of societal and planetary challenges such as climate change, inequality and, more recently, the global pandemic.

The Business Roundtable (2019), whose members are CEOs of major US companies, declared that 'companies should serve not only their shareholders, but also deliver value to their customers, invest in employees, deal fairly with suppliers and support the communities in which they operate.' The concept of multi-stakeholder capitalism is increasingly gaining prominence in society. As Peter Drucker (1973: np) observed almost 50 years ago: 'Any institution exists for the sake of society and within a community. It, therefore, has to have impacts; and one is responsible for one's impacts.'

This chapter explores whether a similar logic regarding multiple stakeholders, impact responsibility, and systems-level engagement applies to global pension funds.

## Scale and Influence of Global Pension Assets

Global asset owners controlled around US\$154 trillion at the end of 2020.[1] This sum includes a range of asset owners: pension funds, sovereign wealth funds, insurers, endowments, and foundations. Most of them have long-term, and often infinite, time horizons. More than 70 percent of these assets are managed via the global asset management industry. For the purposes of this chapter, we focus on pension funds, with the acknowledgment that other pools of capital will also be impacted, and hence have a role to play in the global sustainability arena.

Luba Nikulina, *Global Pensions and ESG*. In: *Pension Funds and Sustainable Investment*. Edited by P. Brett Hammond, Raimond Maurer, and Olivia S. Mitchell, Oxford University Press. © Luba Nikulina (2023).
DOI: 10.1093/oso/9780192889195.003.0007

TABLE 7.1  Largest pension funds (in US$ million)

| Rank | Fund | Market | Total Assets |
|------|------|--------|--------------|
| 1 | Government Pension Investment | Japan | $1,555,550 |
| 2 | Government Pension Fund[1] | Norway | $1,066,380 |
| 3 | National Pension | South Korea | $637,279 |
| 4 | Federal Retirement Thrift[2] | US | $601,030 |
| 5 | ABP | Netherlands | $523,310 |
| 6 | California Public Employees[2] | US | $384,435 |
| 7 | National Social Security[1] | China | $361,087 |
| 8 | Central Provident Fund | Singapore | $315,857 |
| 9 | Canada Pension[3] | Canada | $315,344 |
| 10 | PFZW[3] | Netherlands | $243,839 |
| 11 | California State Teachers[2] | US | $243,311 |
| 12 | Employees Provident Fund | Malaysia | $226,101 |
| 13 | Local Government Officials | Japan | $224,006 |
| 14 | New York State Common[2] | US | $215,424 |
| 15 | New York City Retirement[2] | US | $208.458 |
| 16 | Florida State Board[2] | US | $173,769 |
| 17 | Employees' Provident | India | $168,095 |
| 18 | Ontario Teachers | Canada | $159,666 |
| 19 | Texas Teacher | US | $157,632 |
| 20 | ATP | Denmark | $144,983 |

*Note*: [1] Estimate; [2] as of September 30, 2019; [3] as of March 31, 2020.
*Source*: Thinking Ahead Institute (2021).

According to Thinking Ahead Institute's (2020a) study, pension funds are the biggest asset-owning group, representing 37 percent of the total assets or US$57 trillion (see Table 7.1). The US is by far the largest pensions market, with around US$32.5 trillion, followed by Japan (US$3.6 trillion) and the UK (US$3.5 trillion). The concentration of global pension assets is significant in developed economies, with roughly US$43 trillion or 84 percent of global pension assets in the seven largest markets of Australia, Canada, Japan, Netherlands, Switzerland, UK, and US. To put global pension assets in perspective, in 2019 the global GDP amounted to US$88 trillion (World Bank 2021).

Various governments have pledged to spend on a wide range of environmental, 'green' initiatives, which in total amount to more than US$4 trillion. Assuming they are implemented, this level of spending is more than double the size of every other major human endeavor ever undertaken.[2] Moreover, global pension assets have been growing faster than the global economy, in that pension assets grew at 15 percent in 2019 and 11 percent in 2020. In addition, there has been a consistent shift from defined-benefit (DB) to defined-contribution (DC) plans, with DC accounts currently representing 53 percent of total pension assets in the seven largest pensions markets. The key implication of this shift for ESG investing is that the fundamental time horizon of pension assets is increasing toward infinite (setting aside, for the moment, regulatory and governance constraints on DC funds). Lastly, asset allocations for global pension assets have changed significantly, with a reduction in public equity allocations and consequent home bias. This has been offset by an increase in the global scale of investing and alternatives allocations, such as real estate, private equity, and infrastructure, which almost reached 23 percent of total pension assets at the end of 2020. Global alternatives have been attractive for return reasons, offsetting some of their governance difficulties. Many new ESG investments will be global in nature, and they will be channeled through alternative investment channels. This trend in asset allocation, lengthening time horizons, and experience in global investing and alternatives, makes the global pension assets pool a valid and potentially active contributor to the unfolding theme of new large-scale ESG investments.

## Why Pension Funds Invest in ESG

For many years, ESG investing was characterized, as Roger Urwin, global head of investment content at consultancy Willis Towers Watson, put it, as a 'very slow moving but unstoppable train' (cited by Rust 2018: np). Somewhat surprisingly, and despite significant economic challenges, this focus on ESG has accelerated from 2020, as the global pandemic brought to the forefront of investors' attention the importance of global health and safety, and how interconnected our world has become. In addition, unrest over racial inequality in the US has increased the focus on social responsibility. As a result, the 'slow-moving train' of ESG investing has been gaining significant momentum more recently.

A first consideration for pension funds' ESG investing must be financial, in line with the most common definition of pension fund fiduciary duty to the members. Embedding ESG into investment decision-making allows better risk management and identification of investment opportunities. The performance of highly rated ESG stocks in 2020 put them in the spotlight, perhaps unsurprisingly, considering the negative impact of the coronavirus crisis on the financial performance of the fossil fuel industries. Inevitably and perhaps for the wrong reasons, this recent short-term performance differential has caught investors' attention and prompted the flow of capital into ESG funds. While there may be some short-term bounce-back as the global economy reopens, highly rated ESG stocks are likely still at the very early stages of their long-term rise.

It is possible that companies which move away from a short-term shareholder-centric approach to a longer-term perspective can create value for all stakeholders and will significantly outperform their peers. The performance differential between highest and lowest ESG rated stocks was more than 23 percent in 2020 according to Fidelity International (Tan and Moshinsky 2020). Hale (2021) estimates that sustainable equity funds finished 2020 with a clear performance advantage relative to traditional equity funds, with three out of four sustainable equity funds beating their Morningstar Category average.

Reputational considerations also drive pension funds' increasing attention to ESG investing. For many pension funds, especially the larger ones, it is important to be considered leaders rather than laggards in this area. There are also risks of legal action, as demonstrated in the recent case brought against the trustees of the Rest pension fund in Australia by one of its members on the grounds of the failure to adequately consider climate change risks. Rest agreed to an out-of-court settlement in their dispute, admitted that climate change represents a 'material, direct and current financial risk' to the fund, and committed to a range of actions to address that risk (Angwin and Edwards 2021).

Last but not least, increasing regulatory pressure is being brought to bear on pension funds to consider ESG factors in their investment policies and decisions, especially as the number of ESG-related policies and regulations has accelerated (PRI 2021b). The Principles for Responsible Investments (PRI) estimates that 95 percent of all ESG regulations were developed since 2000 (see Figure 7.1), and 2020 saw 124 new or revised policy instruments or 32 more than the previous year. Very few of those regulations are truly global in scope, underscoring how challenging it is to come up

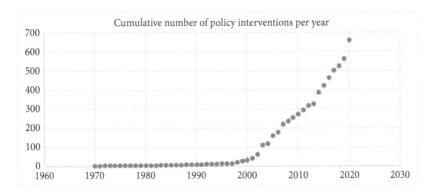

**Figure 7.1** Cumulative number of policy interventions per year

*Note*: 'Policy interventions' are new financial policies and regulations or updates of the existing policies and regulations by governments and regulatory bodies around the world.
*Source*: PRI (2021b). *Regulation Database*.

with a coordinated policy response to global challenges in an increasingly interconnected world. Instead of becoming better coordinated, however, the regulatory landscape has grown more diverse and fragmented of late. Accordingly, pension funds stand to benefit from a more coordinated global policy response to global challenges.

Insofar as ESG challenges tend to be global by nature, it will require a global effort and coordination on an unprecedented scale in order to address them. If left unresolved, some of these challenges can quickly become existential for humanity. There is a society-wide change taking place, with the world transitioning to a low-carbon economy while also addressing other social and environmental concerns, such as inequality and the loss of biodiversity. As global allocators and stewards of multigenerational capital, pension funds have a unique capacity to evaluate such challenges and to mobilize capital to address them.

## A 'Deeper Dive' into Climate Change

Some of the most acute global ESG challenges today include climate change, inequality, and loss of planetary biodiversity. It may be instructive to look deeper into the topic of climate change, since this has attracted meaningful global policy responses. Accordingly, its implications for pension funds could be indicative of future developments.

The global challenge of making an orderly transition to a low-carbon, climate-resilient economy has brought climate to the forefront of governmental, company, and investor agendas. Climate change action is supported by the global regulatory framework via the Paris Agreement, a legally binding international treaty on climate change adopted by 190 countries (United Nations Climate Change 2015). The main catalyst for action on a global scale has been the acknowledgment that climate risk has become a financial risk as well as opportunity (in addition to regulatory nudges, in many jurisdictions).

How public and private investments are allocated in the near term will determine whether global warming can be held below two degrees Centigrade and prevent associated catastrophic climate events. As noted by PRI (2021a: np) in their 'Inevitable Policy Response' statement:

> Financial markets today have not adequately priced-in the likely near-term policy response to climate change. The question for investors now is not if governments will act, but when they will do so, what policies they will use and where the impact will be felt ... a response by 2025 will be forceful, abrupt, and disorderly because of the delay.

In this context, any pension fund that does not take climate change into account is likely to ignore a major risk to pension savings and miss out on investment opportunities. If pension managers fail to consider risks and opportunities from climate change, or fail to exercise effective stewardship, their investment performance may suffer. Their members' savings may also suffer more immediate consequences from exposure to firms that are unprepared for the low-carbon transition. These developments pose new questions to pension managers, including whether they should think exclusively in the context of their own investment portfolios, or whether they should evaluate the overall global economy and how climate change will influence their performance more broadly. As a group of institutional investors, pension funds tend to have very long time horizons. As they are expected to deliver returns over many decades, if not infinitely, the argument can be made that the returns they seek can only come from a system which supports the funds' engagement with systemic risks and challenges beyond the near term. A related point is that, if there is one institution in the investment value chain where intergenerational equity should reign, it is a pension fund.

An example of the global leadership and coordination by asset owners is the UN-convened Net-Zero Asset Owner Alliance (2021), established in 2019. The group includes asset owners from a range of developed economies, and it has set itself an ambitious public commitment to transition its investment portfolios to net-zero greenhouse gas emissions by 2050. Sixteen of the current 35 Net-Zero Alliance members are pension funds from the US, UK, Sweden, Denmark, France, and Australia (see Table 7.2).

In addition to the fact that these entities' public commitments are quite bold, the alliance members have also set themselves ambitious interim targets to achieve these outcomes. The most common interim target is to reduce greenhouse gas emissions associated with their portfolios by half, and to double the amount of capital allocated to climate solutions by 2030. Pension funds can already invest new capital in assets and technologies that have both positive environmental impact and positive expected risk-adjusted return, such as renewable energy, transport electrification, and reforestation. There are also some promising new technologies on the horizon which still need to prove their effectiveness, both from an impact and return perspective, such as hydrogen fuel or carbon capture and storage technologies. Investment opportunities from addressing climate change will become more apparent as governments worldwide scale up their net-zero policies.

Alternatively, pension funds can divest from carbon-intensive businesses, or else engage with them to encourage their transition to carbon neutrality. While divestment is a powerful and sometimes required mechanism, it does not necessarily address the need to engage directly with non-green

TABLE 7.2 United Nations-convened Net-Zero
Asset Owner Alliance members

| | |
|---|---|
| 1 | Akademiker Pension (pension, Denmark) |
| 2 | Alecta (pension, Sweden) |
| 3 | Allianz (insurance, UK) |
| 4 | AMF Pension (pension, Sweden) |
| 5 | Aviva (insurance, UK) |
| 6 | AXA (insurance, France) |
| 7 | BTPS (pension, UK) |
| 8 | Cbus Super fund (pension, Australia) |
| 9 | CalPERS (pension, US) |
| 10 | Caisse des Depots (pension, Canada) |
| 11 | CDPQ (pension, Canada) |
| 12 | The Church of England (pension, UK) |
| 13 | CNP Assurances (insurance, France) |
| 14 | Dai-ichi Life Group (insurance, Japan) |
| 15 | Danica Pension (insurance, Denmark) |
| 16 | David Rockefeller Fund (foundation, US) |
| 17 | ERAFP (pension, France) |
| 18 | Folksam Group (insurance, Sweden) |
| 19 | FRR (pension, France) |
| 20 | KENFO (sovereign fund, Germany) |
| 21 | Generali (insurance, Italy) |
| 22 | Munich RE (insurance, Germany) |
| 23 | Nordea Life & Pension (insurance, Nordics) |
| 24 | P+ Pension (pension, Denmark) |
| 25 | PensionDanmark (pension, Denmark) |
| 26 | PFA (pension, Denmark) |
| 27 | PKA (pension, Denmark) |
| 28 | QBE (insurance, Australia) |
| 29 | SCOR (insurance, France) |
| 30 | St. James's Place (wealth, UK) |
| 31 | Storebrand (insurance, Norway) |
| 32 | Swiss Re (insurance, Switzerland) |
| 33 | UNJSPF (pension, US) |
| 34 | Wespath (insurance, US) |
| 35 | Zurich (insurance, Switzerland) |

*Note*: Global asset owners setting and reporting on
ambitious interim targets for net-zero emissions by
2050.
*Source*: Net Zero Asset Owner Alliance (2021).

firms. Moreover, divestment of carbon-intensive assets simply transitions
ownership of these assets to some other, perhaps less environmentally con-
scientious, owners. For this reason, engagement with specific businesses
becomes critical for pension funds that believe that addressing systemic
challenges is part of their mission, though active engagement has not been

at the top of most pension funds' agenda until recently. The investment value chain will need to shift so that asset owners, as providers of capital, set the tone and agenda for stewardship activities which they may delegate to asset managers for execution.

These new types of new primary investments are challenging, however, since they have been relatively small and illiquid to date, whereas the systemic challenge of transitioning the low-carbon economy requires investments on a far larger scale. Drawing parallels with investors' experiences with renewable energy, initially the scale of early private investments in wind and solar energy was very small, complex, and heavily predicated on government tariffs and subsidies. Nevertheless, for those who had the capability to be early adopters, these investments more than justified the risk and associated cost of investing. Wind and solar energy are now a common staple in pension funds' repertoires, enabling them to achieve attractive risk-adjusted returns without government support. Similarly, the public–private partnerships, such as Operation Warp Speed in the US and Project Lightspeed in Germany, have recently developed, manufactured, and distributed COVID-19 vaccines in less than 12 months. Many other industries will need to follow a similar journey, where public capital will jump-start the path toward carbon neutrality, giving private capital an opportunity to follow on acceptable risk-adjusted return terms.

It is also worth noting that the boundary between financial and nonfinancial considerations may become blurred and more challenging for pension funds to navigate in the future. For instance, setting targets for investment portfolios in terms of the reduction of carbon emissions could lead to unintended consequences, if decision makers put more weight on this target in the short-term compared to the long-run risk-return tradeoff. US public institutional investors facing strong regulatory pressure to invest more in infrastructure over time are now taking on more marginal deals in order to meet their nonfinancial objectives, which has led to underperformance (Andonov et al. 2021). In a similar vein, the use of economically targeted investments (ETIs), where fund managers take into consideration not only the investment return but also the economic benefits to the local community, was one of the most controversial issues facing public and private pension fund management in the US in the 1990s (Mitchell et al. 2008).

These risks of consequences, including potentially making suboptimal investment decisions, are substantial, and they must be acknowledged and clearly communicated. Even in the multi-stakeholder world, the primary purpose of pension funds continues to be their capacity to generate returns for their members. Finding a way to play an active role in, and deliver positive outcomes from, financing this economic transition is a key challenge for global pension funds, and addressing this challenge requires mindsets to work in ways that are not only systemic but transformational.

## Universal Ownership

The concept of universal ownership can be very useful when thinking about how pension fund managers could reset their mindsets and approaches. According to the PRI (2017), universal owners are large institutional investors who own highly diversified, long-term portfolios representative of global capital markets and which effectively hold a slice of the overall market. Consequently, their investment returns depend on market performance, including the costs of externalities. A sensible approach, in this instance, is to think about the overall economic system when making investments. To be successful in the longer term, universal owners must pursue the active ownership model focusing on engagement and stewardship, and they must also give more weight to intergenerational concerns and the sustainability of the global economy as factors affecting their future risk-adjusted returns.

Current definitions of what a universal owner is focus on size, long investment horizons, and a certain mindset. In practice, most large-asset owners today do not currently manage their funds in line with universal ownership principles, in part because they do not perceive themselves as large enough, do not have the long-term orientation, or they lack leadership buy-in to operate in this way. Five asset owners among the top one hundred have been identified in the 'universal owner' category, all of them pension funds: the Japanese Government Pension Investment Fund (GPIF), the Government Pension Fund (Norway), ABP (Netherlands), the California Public Employees Retirement System (US), and PFZW (Netherlands).

The Japanese Government Pension Investment Fund, as the largest pension fund in the world, offers some examples of how a universal owner can behave in a way that creates a positive impact on the entire system (Henderson et al. 2019). Its creation of new ESG indices, facilitation of corporate transparency, ESG disclosures, and engagement with asset managers requiring them to integrate ESG metrics into their investment processes, not only serveas a catalyst for broader-scale improvements in the financial markets in Japan, but also provide a role model for how to influence and change the system to other large-asset owners around the world.

Another example of a pension fund that has successfully developed systems-level thinking and engagement, while not having the size for universal ownership, is New Zealand's Super Fund. It currently holds around US$40 billion under management, having grown at over 10 percent per year for some time. It signed the Paris Pledge for Action in 2015, affirming its commitment 'to an emissions reduction target and regularly updating it' (New Zealand Super Fund nd). The Super Fund states that ESG has an impact on long-term returns and accordingly, it has embedded climate change into its investment strategies and ownership practices in the belief that it will improve its portfolio.

Ultimately, global pension funds are increasingly recognizing systemic risk as well as own portfolio risk, and they understand that their returns will be produced by a system that works, and those returns are worth more for their beneficiaries in a world worth living in. Pension funds can move from being silent and disengaged owners to active and purposeful owners, while still delivering on their key mission of securing financial futures for end savers worldwide.

## Role of Asset Managers

Asset managers are a critical link in the investment value chain, as they play a substantial role in managing and stewarding underlying assets on behalf of asset owners. This segment of the value chain has grown exponentially in the last few decades, both in the amount of capital and number of people involved, and has been able to provide much higher remuneration than asset owners. At the same time, investment performance is characterized by a very low signal-to-noise ratio and very long feedback loops that link outcomes with inputs into decision-making. As a result, the asset management industry has become extremely competitive, and the relationship between asset owners and asset managers is heavily influenced by short-term results that are rarely due to skill.

Like pension funds, asset managers have been responding to the recent developments in the ESG landscape, from both regulatory and investment perspectives, and they are boosting their ESG expertise and capabilities. Seventy-three asset managers have signed onto the Net-Zero Asset Managers Alliance, including many of the largest asset managers in the world: their assets represent US$32 trillion, more than one-third (36 percent) of the total assets under management worldwide. That said, asset managers' net-zero commitments tend to be stipulated by constraints put on them by their clients, the asset owners. This dynamic emphasizes the importance of the powerful 'voice from the top' of asset owners, yet asset owners still need support from asset managers to invest efficiently and effectively. They also need better measurement frameworks to ensure they are achieving the desired results. In any event, the current landscape reflects a work in progress rather than an endpoint.

To become more effective, the relationship between asset managers and asset owners would benefit from becoming more long-term and strategic in nature. Incentives and behaviors must be aligned across the investment value chain: for instance, asset owners need to outline investment mandates and incentives in a way that does not lead asset managers to short-term orientation in their mindsets and behaviors. Again, the Japanese GPIF provides a good example as it has completely restructured its active equity mandates, making them longer-term, while also aligning incentives (Henderson et al. 2019). Investors must also engage more actively with underlying businesses to encourage this transition since, to date, asset managers' capabilities devoted to stewardship have been modest compared to the task at hand. Miles and Shihn (2019) have estimated that dedicated stewardship resources represent around 1 percent of the total headcount in the asset management industry, while 99 percent is focused on research, valuation, and trading. Accordingly, the asset management industry has a unique opportunity to redefine its purpose and create value for all its stakeholders, including society at large.

## Finding a Better Way

A growing awareness of the need to look beyond immediate financial motives to create a sustainable future is prompting many leaders to focus more on culture, which includes multi-stakeholder capitalism and increased emphasis on purpose following the tragedy of the global pandemic. Pension funds, as the most sizable category of asset owners and ultimate allocators of capital, will therefore increasingly need to revisit their missions and beliefs to take on these wider ideals. While many expect these challenges to be longer term, there is also the risk of short-term repricing as new regulations reshape capital markets. For this reason, considering ESG factors is increasingly becoming a fiduciary duty, even in its most narrow definition.

Asset owners as a group, and pension funds in particular, often lack internal capabilities and are often under-resourced, precluding them from focusing on goals wider than immediate portfolio activities. One analysis of the investment value chain (Thinking Ahead Institute 2020b) suggested that asset owners represent only 10 percent of the total workforce employed in the investment industry, while bearing the ultimate responsibility for most of its capital. The same source noted that asset managers represent 60 percent of the total headcount, and other service providers account for around 30 percent. This allocation of resources does not appear aligned with where the ultimate power sits; to navigate the increasingly complex investment landscape and exercise genuine active ownership and stewardship rights, pension funds must devote more effort to defining their missions, beliefs, culture, and operating models.

## Conclusion

We have argued in this chapter that, aside from government spending, global pension assets represent the largest pool of capital on the planet, with the longest time horizon and multiple stakeholders across different generations. Many challenges facing our society are global in nature, and they can only be solved with a global and intergenerational mindset. Global pensions appear to have great potential to address these critical issues, yet the global investment value chain has mostly not heard a 'voice from the top.' Humanity would be remiss in not harnessing the power of this capital. Yet for this to happen, pension funds as investment organizations need to go through a transformational change that requires strengthened governance, greater system-wide collaboration, and substantive innovation.

## Notes

1. Unless stated otherwise, all estimates are from the research reported by the Thinking Ahead Institute, a global not-for-profit group founded by Willis Towers Watson (WTW) whose vision is to mobilize capital for a sustainable future. All numbers have been collated based on annual surveys run by TAI for the last ten years. Consequently, these numbers are more up to date compared with the estimates from OECD or World Bank.
2. The 'current pledge' includes spending by the US (US$2 trillion under the Biden administration), the EU (US$1.3 trillion from Green New Deal), and China (at least US$800 billion during 14th five-year plan. 'Other major human endeavours' include US Interstate Highway System, Saudi Arabia's NEOM, Xiongan New Area, the Apollo Program, the Great Wall of China, China Three Gorges Dam, Manhattan Project, Panama Canal, Suez Canal, and the US transcontinental railway.

## References

Andonov, A., R. Kräussl, and J.D. Rauh (2021). 'Institutional Investors and Infrastructure Investing,' Discussion Paper, Centre for Economic Policy Research, London. https://cepr.org/active/publications/discussion_papers/dp.php?dpno=15946.

Angwin, C. and C. Edwards (2021). *Pension Fund Agrees Settlement in Landmark Australian Climate Change Case, McVeigh v Rest.* London: Travers Smith LLP. https://www.lexology.com/library/detail.aspx?g=af3a2627-c9c3-41f1-8263-51ac1cd89007.

Business Roundtable (2019). *One Year Later: Purpose of a Corporation.* Washington, DC: Business Roundtable. https://s3.amazonaws.com/brt.org/BRT-StatementonthePurposeofaCorporationJuly2021.pdf.

Drucker, P. (1973). *Management: Tasks, Responsibilities, Practices.* New York: Harper & Row.

Hale, J. (2021). 'Sustainable Equity Funds Outperform Traditional Peers in 2020,' Morningstar Sustainability Matters, January 8. https://www.morningstar.com/articles/1017056/sustainable-equity-funds-outperform-traditional-peers-in-2020.

Henderson, R., G. Serafeim, J. Lerner, and N. Jinjo (2019). 'Should a Pension Fund Try to Change the World? Inside GPIF's Embrace of ESG,' Harvard Business School case 319-067, January 2019 (revised February 2020).

Miles, S. and A. Shihn (2019). *Investor Stewardship—One Hand on the Wheel*. London: Willis Towers Watson. https://www.willistowerswatson.com/-/media/WTW/Insights/2019/04/investor-stewardship-one-hand-on-the-wheel. PDF?modified=20190529171647.

Mitchell, O.S., J. Piggott, and C. Kumru. (2008). 'Managing Public Investment Funds: Best Practices and New Challenges,' *Journal of Pension Economics and Finance*, 7(3): 321–356.

Net Zero Asset Owner Alliance (2021). 'Global Asset Owners Setting and Reporting on Ambitious Interim Targets for Net-zero Emissions by 2050,' UN Environment Programme Finance Initiative, Principles for Responsible Investment. https://www.unepfi.org/net-zero-alliance/.

New Zealand Super Fund (nd). *Paris Agreement*. Auckland, NZ: New Zealand Super Fund. https://environment.govt.nz/what-government-is-doing/international-action/about-the-par-agreement/.

PRI (2017). Macro Risks: Universal Ownership. London: PRI. https://www.unpri.org/sustainable-development-goals/the-sdgs-are-an-unavoidable-consideration-for-universal-owners/306.article.

PRI (2021a). Inevitable Policy Response 2021: Policy Forecasts. London: PRI. https://www.unpri.org/inevitable-policy-response/the-inevitable-policy-response-2021-policy-forecasts/7344.article.

PRI (2021b). Regulation Database. London: PRI. https://www.unpri.org/policy/regulation-database.

Rust, S. (2018). *IPE Conference: The Intertwined Future of Retirement and Investment*. London: Investment & Pensions Europe. https://www.ipe.com/ipe-conference-the-intertwined-future-of-retirement-and-investment-/10028515.article.

Tan, B.J.-H. and J. Moshinsky (2020). 'Putting Sustainability to the Test: ESG Outperformance amid Volatility,' Fidelity White Paper, Fidelity International. https://eumultisiteprod-live-b03cec4375574452b61bdc4e94e331e7-16cd684. s3-eu-west-1.amazonaws.com/filer_public/e1/2d/e12d7270-0fc1-4f3f-88d1-e0c73eb5aefd/putting_sustainability_to_the_test_whitepaper_edition_vol_28. pdf.

Thinking Ahead Institute (2020a). Global Pension Assets Study 2020. Arlington, VA: Thinking Ahead Institute, Willis Towers Watson. https://www.thinkingaheadinstitute.org/research-papers/global-pension-assets-study-2020.

Thinking Ahead Institute (2020b). Top 100 Asset Owners, The Most Influential Capital on the Planet. Arlington, VA: Thinking Ahead Institute, Willis Towers Watson. https://www.thinkingaheadinstitute.org/research-papers/the-asset-owner-100-2020/.

Thinking Ahead Institute (2021). Global Pension Assets Study 2021. Arlington, VA: Thinking Ahead Institute, Willis Towers Watson. https://www.thinkingaheadinstitute.org/research-papers/global-pension-assets-study-2021/.

United Nations Climate Change. (2015). *The Paris Agreement*. Bonn, Germany: UNFCCC.

World Bank (2021). World Bank National Accounts Data, and OECD National Accounts Data Files. Washington, DC: The World Bank Group. https://data.worldbank.org/indicator/NY.GDP.MKTP.CD.

**Part III**

**Impacts of ESG on Pension Governance, Investments, Structures, and Reporting**

# Chapter 8

# Eliciting Pension Beneficiaries' Sustainability Preferences: Why and How?

*Rob M.M.J. Bauer and Paul M.A. Smeets*

Many employees across the globe entrust their pension contributions to occupational or employment-based pension funds. Jointly, these funds hold about US$50 trillion in assets under management (Willis Towers Watson 2020). Slightly less than half of these assets are managed in defined-benefit (DB) schemes, while the other half are managed in defined-contribution (DC) plans in which plan participants bear the investment risk. Irrespective of plan design, pension funds universally promise to deliver stable and adequate solutions for retirement incomes to participants.

In the large majority of cases, pension plan beneficiaries are not directly involved in any of the strategic choices made by these funds. This non-involvement holds for strategic decisions on the design and governance of DB and DC plans but also for strategic choices on the funds' investment programs. Notably, beneficiaries generally are not part of the debates on sustainable investments in which nonfinancial preferences oftentimes play a prominent role. For this reason, the central question we tackle in this chapter is whether pension plan participants should be involved in setting the agenda on the sustainable investments in their pension fund. If the answer to this question is affirmative, how and at what stage should they be involved in decisions?

The Global Financial Crisis in 2008 and the subsequent market response showed that informational asymmetries, misaligned incentives, and fuzzy chains of intermediation lead to substantially lower levels of trust in the financial sector (Waitzer and Sarro 2014). This lack of trust has encouraged regulators, legislators, and courts across the globe to bend the trajectory of many relevant laws into a direction that they believed better served the public interest. Moreover, it explains why many financial institutions, and pension funds in particular, have stepped up and joined collaborative approaches (e.g., Principle for Responsible Investments (PRI) and Climate Action 100+).[1] Through these vehicles, in the interests of their beneficiaries

Rob M.M.J. Bauer and Paul M.A. Smeets, *Eliciting Pension Beneficiaries' Sustainability Preferences: Why and How?*. In: *Pension Funds and Sustainable Investment*. Edited by P. Brett Hammond, Raimond Maurer, and Olivia S. Mitchell, Oxford University Press. © Rob M.M.J. Bauer and Paul M.A. Smeets (2023). DOI: 10.1093/oso/9780192889195.003.0008 and clients, they tackle global challenges such as climate change, inequality, and human rights' violations in the interactions with their portfolio companies and delegated asset managers. Many pension funds now have a full-fledged sustainable investment policy that they execute and report on. They increasingly 'walk the talk.'

Yet this proactive stance has not yet materialized as a stronger involvement of beneficiaries in the sustainable investment agenda of pension funds. Only in a very limited number of funds do the ultimate owners of the entrusted investments have direct involvement in decisions. The reasons for not 'democratizing' this process revolve around legal interpretations, cultural and societal perspectives, participants' low financial literacy levels, pension funds' capacity constraints, habit, or simply decision makers' unwillingness.

Nevertheless, it is becoming increasingly clear that pension funds cannot simply ignore the many calls for action by substantial parts of their membership. For example, half of UK universities have now committed to divesting their fossil fuel investments (*The Guardian* 2020). Universities have started dialogues with their individual endowments, and NGOs increasingly have engaged directly with pension funds and their participants. Fossil Free UK, for example, is in a continuous dialogue with the Universities Superannuation Scheme (USS) in the UK with the goal to screen for and exclude the fossil fuel industry from their investment portfolio and immediately freeze any new investment in fossil fuel companies (Fossil Free Campaign UK 2020). Another recent example of an NGO targeting pension funds directly is Tobacco Free Portfolios (TFP) (Tobacco Free Portfolios 2021). Many pension funds and asset managers, partially based on the interactions with TFP, have decided to divest from tobacco manufacturing companies. Across the globe, younger generations are calling on pension funds and other financial institutions to deploy capital in such a way that it has a positive effect on the trajectories of climate change. In some cases, pension funds proactively signal in their mission statement that they take this dialogue very seriously. PGGM, the Dutch pension delivery organization for the health-care sector, for example, states on its website: 'Our ambition: to provide for good pensions in a livable world' (PGGM 2020: np). Interestingly, only rarely is the direction of the sustainable investment program, including the inherent dilemmas involved, based on direct interaction with pension fund beneficiaries. In the majority of cases, pension boards alone handle the decision-making.

In what follows, we first discuss the context in which pension funds decide on a sustainable investment program and how they can integrate sustainability in their investment decisions. Next, we identify key factors accounting for different ways to integrate nonfinancial preferences in pension funds' investment processes, including the motivation to involve participants. We also largely focus on funds in the EU, the UK, and the US, and we devote special attention to the Netherlands where a pension fund gave its participants a real vote (Bauer et al. 2021). In a conclusion, we synthesize our findings and summarize our answer to our central question: How can we involve pension participants in a meaningful way when setting a pension fund's sustainable investment agenda?

## Why Measure Nonfinancial Preferences?

In a retail investment context, investors can individually choose which funds they buy or sell, and when. In the past three decades, many mutual funds have created sustainability profiles that allow individuals to choose funds that match their sustainability or nonfinancial preferences, at least to some extent.[2] A recent study using a natural experiment found causal evidence that market-wide, retail investors do value sustainability (Hartzmark and Sussman 2019). The authors reported that, when mutual funds were categorized by Morningstar as 'low sustainability,' they experienced significant net outflows. By contrast, when funds were categorized as 'high sustainability,' they experienced substantial net inflows. The authors concluded that their experimental evidence was consistent with positive affect influencing expectations of sustainable fund performance. Also, nonpecuniary motives influenced investment decisions. In the US context, then, nonfinancial motives do directly affect the demand for sustainable mutual funds. Earlier work (Bollen 2007; Riedl and Smeets 2017) showed that many retail investors are motivated by their strong social preferences, accepting lower expected returns on socially responsible investments and paying higher management fees.

Pension fund participants, in contrast to retail investors, generally do not have the freedom to join a plan that matches their sustainability preferences. There is no market-clearing mechanism that matches supply to demand for sustainable pension investments. In most countries, being a participant in a collective DB pension means joining the public sector, industry, or corporate plan offered by their plan sponsor; generally, they do not have an opportunity to make individual, discretionary investment choices. Here, the DB fund boards and management determine and execute strategic investment choices that include strategic decisions and directions related to sustainable investments. In a DC setting, by contrast, there are potentially more options for plan participants, which can vary from choosing the degree of risk-taking to the choice of investment funds. Nevertheless, in the DC space, the menu of funds and the actual selection of delegated asset managers who supply these funds are typically set by the plan boards and managers.

Since the start of the PRI movement in 2006, there has been a considerable growth in the assets under management (AUM) of PRI signatory institutions. Asset managers and asset owners that join the PRI generally have more socially conscious portfolio-level footprints, especially along the social and governance dimensions (Gibson et al. 2020). Nevertheless these differences are not large, which could be explained by the fact that some funds join the PRI for reputational reasons. In addition, differentiating between US and non-US investors, the authors conclude that US signatories do not have more socially conscious footprints, perhaps due to the different interpretation of fiduciary duties in the US market (Gibson et al. 2020).

## Three ways to implement sustainable investments

Pension funds have three distinct ways that they can integrate sustainability into their investment decision-making. First, they can develop a divestment (or exclusion) policy. Globally, many examples exist of pension funds that publicly declare their divestment of certain industries, such as the tobacco industry or the nuclear weapons industry (ABP 2018). These decisions are often based on the nonfinancial preferences of pension funds (i.e., their boards), but increasingly these divestment policies are also linked to financial considerations. The USS's recent divestment from tobacco manufacturing companies and thermal coal mining companies was motivated on its website as follows: '. . . the traditional financial models used by the market as a whole to predict the future performance in these sectors had not taken specific risks into account. These included changing political and regulatory attitudes and increased regulation that USS Investment Management consider will damage the prospects of businesses involved in these sectors in the years to come' (USS 2020: np).

A second way of integrating sustainability into the investment process is to complement financial information with nonfinancial (sustainability) information when making strategic decisions on asset allocation or buying and selling securities in the public and private asset space.[3] The key objective of these strategies is to improve the risk-adjusted returns of investments, meaning that many investors believe that financial markets have not yet fully priced material sustainability information. The jury is still out on this matter, but several excellent meta-studies and books exist on the topic (Edmans 2020; Matos 2020). Most prominent practical examples can be found in equity investments in both qualitative and quantitative strategies, but also in all other asset classes today. The integration of sustainability information varies from slightly tilting portfolios toward certain Sustainable Development Goals (FTSE Russell 2020), to positive and negative screening of portfolios; in its most extreme form, there can be mandates with a small, selected number of highly sustainable companies that investors perceive as positively contributing to both society and the bottom line.

A third way to interact with companies and investment vehicles on sustainability issues is to engage in active ownership strategies. Many pension funds have established voting guidelines that go beyond standard shareholder-oriented governance concerns, and that are executed by professional agencies in the interests of asset owners. Also, the level and intensity of private engagement with companies by pension funds has increased steadily in the past decade. Pension funds as a group are now voicing concern and demanding action on sustainability issues such as companies' compliance with the Paris Agreement (Climate Action 100+ 2021). Many other appearances of active ownership include filing shareholder proposals, class action lawsuits, and media campaigns. In some cases, failed engagement with companies may lead to divestment of the asset altogether. A good example of the latter case is the divestment of Walmart by the largest Dutch pension fund (ABP) in 2012 because of poor labor practices.

## A preference for engagement

A recent large-scale survey among institutional investors, with a substantial number of pension funds in the sample, found that respondents generally think that climate risks have important financial implications for firms they invest in (Krueger et al. 2020). The survey also showed that institutional investors consider climate risk for both financial and nonfinancial reasons; in fact, there was no single motive that explains why and how these investors incorporated these perceived risks into their investment decisions. Reputational concerns, legal considerations, and investment beliefs about the effect of climate change on risk and returns were the key drivers of spending resources on assessing climate risks and opportunities. The survey responses also showed that most respondents favored engagement over divestment and that larger investors engaged with companies along more dimensions.

This preference for engagement relates to studies showing that engagement can have a positive effect on performance, in some cases (Dimson et al. 2015; Azar et al. 2021; Kölbel et al. 2020). Successful engagements are followed by positive abnormal returns, and engagement success is more probable if the engaged company has reputational concerns and a higher capacity to implement change. This study also showed that collaboration among engaged investors was instrumental in increasing the success rate of environmental and social engagements. A recent PRI analysis of the effectiveness of coordinated engagement activities showed that a two-tier strategy combining lead investors with supporting investors was effective in successfully achieving the stated engagement goals, and was followed by improved target performance (Dimson et al. 2021).

Initiating and executing an engagement strategy raises another set of questions for pension boards, including: Which budget should be allocated to engagement activities? Which topics are worth engaging on? How can one measure the engagement's success? Which collaborative vehicles should be joined to ensure engagement is effective? Do the benefits of engagement outweigh costs? Is it strictly about financial benefits, or also about environmental or social benefits? As pension funds do not have unlimited resources, choices need to be made regarding what topics to prioritize and what companies to target first, and through what engagement channel.

## Prioritization

Pension fund boards need to prioritize sustainable investment activities, spanning from divestments to the integration of sustainability into investments, and the deployment of active ownership strategies. Subsequently, internal or external asset management organizations must execute these strategies in line with the board's priorities. Many of the decisions and priorities can involve weighing the importance of nonfinancial preferences, yet it is complex to disentangle financial from nonfinancial preferences. Board members may hold different beliefs about the effectiveness of divestment or engagement, along with the likelihood of having successful engagements, the potential spillovers of engagement activity from one company to another, the perceived willingness of companies to contribute to the renewable energy transition, the expected financial consequences in case of divestment, and the assessment of the long-term effect of selling these shares to other owners. Pension fund boards tend to expend much energy on this topic, including preferences regarding nonfinancial as well as financial criteria.

To return to our central question, should the ultimate owners of pension funds have a voice when pension boards make strategic investment decisions of a nonfinancial nature, or when these are motivated by nonfinancial criteria? To this we turn next.

## What Drives the Sustainable Investment Agenda?

In our view, there is no single response to the question of how to integrate sustainability into the investment process, and especially not how to involve the ultimate owners in this process. Market forces being absent, we first identify a set of exogenous factors that may lead to the observed heterogeneity in responses by pension funds across the globe (Gibson et al. 2020; Krueger et al. 2020).

## Legal and societal contexts

Pension funds operate in both legal and societal contexts, and these are key drivers in accounting for differences in their sustainable investment activities around the world. Laws relevant to pension funds, their interpretations and subsequent trajectories, differ markedly per jurisdiction, as do regulatory bodies' attitudes toward the sustainable investment topic. When browsing legal scholars' contributions to this discussion, references to the prudent person rule often occur (also known as prudent man, prudent investor, or prudent expert). The prudent person rule is linked to two key principles of Anglo-American trust law: prudence and loyalty (Maatman and Huijzer 2019). According to Kuiper and Lutjens (2011), the prudence principle can be applied to a pension fund as follows: Pension funds must manage the pension capital with the care, caution, expertise, and competence that may be demanded of a reasonably competent and reasonably acting pension fund. The loyalty principle requires trustees to give priority to the beneficiaries' interests under all circumstances. If trustees fail to do so, and thereby cause harm to beneficiaries, they are liable in principle.

In the Netherlands, three initiatives exemplify the development of the prudent person rule in the context of responsible pension investments. In 2010, the Dutch Committee on Investment Policy and Risk Management devoted particular attention to pension funds' social position, and it endorsed the view that socially responsible action must be an integral part of the pension funds' risk and investment policies. This committee explicitly mentioned that the participants' preferences must be embedded in the pension fund's policies (Frijns Report 2010). To our knowledge, this is the first time that involving beneficiaries is mentioned explicitly.

In 2018, a large number of Dutch pension funds, in cooperation with NGOs, trade unions, and government, signed the Agreement on International Responsible Investment for the Pensions Sector. It stipulated that:

> The implementation of this Agreement should contribute to, and may not prejudice, the fulfillment of the pension funds' fiduciary duty arising from Article 135(1) of the Dutch Pensions Act; the pension fund's board must ensure that there is support among participants for choices made regarding responsible investment. Taking material Environmental, Social and Governance (ESG) factors into account in investment decisions is consistent with risk assessment and risk management and is in line with the fiduciary duty of pension funds. Such factors can become material in the short, medium and long term.

(IRBC 2018: 5)

Signing this agreement meant that the Dutch pension regulator will check whether funds actually do comply with these promises.

In parallel, the European Union (EU) launched the EU Pension Directive (IORP II 2016) that claimed that environmental, social, and governance factors are important for pension funds' investment policy and risk management systems. Yet IORP II has no direct reference to investigating member preferences toward sustainable investments. Outside the Netherlands, very few concrete cases exist in Europe, whether in hard or soft law, where governments have requested, advised, or even proposed the involvement of beneficiaries in some stage of the setting of pension funds' sustainable investment policy. One rare example is a recent consultation document in which the EU put forward the question of whether the integration of beneficiaries' sustainability preferences in the investment strategies of occupational pension funds should be further improved. The majority of respondents (from all branches of society) answered 'don't know' (57 percent), about a third (32 percent) answered 'yes,' and a smaller subset of respondents (11 percent) said 'no' to this question (European Commission 2020a, 2020b).

How European law develops depends on further evolution of the prudent person rule. Anglo-American law describes a pension fund trustee's fiduciary obligation in the 'Uniform Prudent Investor Act,' which includes the prudent investor rule (Maatman and Huijzer 2019). The financial interests of beneficiaries, based on modern portfolio theory, are key elements of a trustee's objective function.

In the US, the prudent investor act in many states is interpreted quite narrowly. Pension fund fiduciaries are charged with maximizing financial performance in order to meet pension obligations. This focus explains why sustainability information receives little attention in the boards of many US pension funds. The US Department of Labor (DOL), the supervisor under the Employee Retirement Income Security Act of 1974 (ERISA), has demonstrated substantial ambivalence on this matter. In 2015, the DOL stated in one of its Interpretative Bulletins: 'Environmental, social, and governance issues may have a direct relationship to the economic value of the plan's investment. In these instances, such issues are not merely collateral considerations or tie-breakers, but rather are proper components of the fiduciary's primary analysis of the economic merits of competing investment choices' (US Department of Labor 2015: 65136).

A few years later, the DOL chose quite a different path: 'Rather, ERISA fiduciaries must always put first the economic interests of the plan in providing retirement benefits. A fiduciary's evaluation of the economics of an investment should be focused on financial factors that have a material effect on the return and risk of an investment based on appropriate investment horizons' (US Department of Labor 2018: 2). Beneficiaries' sustainable investment preferences are not part of the equation, and neither is beneficiaries' interest in building a livable world.

In 2020, the US Department of Labor adopted amendments to the 'investment duties' regulation under Title I of the Employee Retirement Income Security Act of 1974: 'The amendments require plan fiduciaries to select investments and investment courses of action based solely on financial considerations relevant to the risk-adjusted economic value of a particular investment or investment course of action' (US Department of Labor 2020: 72846). Remarkably, a few months later, the new administration announced that it will not enforce the former administration's rules and is reviewing whether a rewrite or other action is necessary (US Department of Labor 2021).

In the UK, inspired by the Kay Review (Kay 2012), the Law Commission No. 350 foresaw an important role for sustainability information in the investment process: 'Whilst it is clear that trustees may take into account environmental, social and governance factors in making investment decisions where they are financially material, we think the law goes further: trustees should take into account financially material factors' (Law Commission 2014: 113). Interestingly, the Law Commission also hinted indirectly at involving beneficiaries' preferences in decision-making: 'Our conclusion is that quality[sic] of life factors are a subordinate objective, and are therefore subject to the two tests we set out below. Trustees should have good reason to think that beneficiaries would welcome the lifestyle benefit and there should be no risk of significant financial detriment to the scheme' (Law Commission 2014: 116).

## Peer pressure and benchmarking

The level of peer pressure and benchmarking of pension funds' sustainable investments strategies also varies by region and nation, and as a result, it can determine the speed and breadth of activities in the sustainable investment domain. Every year, Dutch-based VBDO publishes the VBDO Benchmark Responsible Investment by Pension Funds in the Netherlands (VBDO 2020). This benchmarking of the 50 largest Dutch pension funds is discussed extensively, both formally and informally, around many pension board tables. International examples of benchmarking are the PRI that scores asset owners and asset managers on their sustainable investment policy, and the Global Pension Transparency Benchmark (GPTB), recently issued by CEM Benchmarking and Top1000funds.com, in which responsible investments are an important factor (CEM Benchmarking and Top1000funds.com 2021). GPTB targets the largest pension funds in a large number of countries. These benchmarking initiatives show that funds increasingly are being confronted with peer pressure, which includes peers' activities and advancements, when having a dialogue with pension beneficiaries.

## Fund-specific factors

Next, we identify a set of fund-specific factors that may differ between individual pension funds. First, larger pension funds may allow them to set up relatively large sustainable investment teams, providing the full scale of activities and necessary knowledge. By contrast, smaller funds must prioritize their activities or delegate them to external parties. Having internal investment teams also probably has a longer-lasting effect on the sustainability culture and knowledge within the pension fund, as long as it accepts the intended direction. Many European pension funds have gone through this exercise in recent years. For smaller funds, there is always the free-rider option, although EU legislation requiring European pension funds to report on their sustainable investment activities, or its absence thereof, may change this.

Independent of size, the board's investment perspectives may differ across pension plans. Beliefs about the long-term consequences of divestment, the added value of integrating sustainability into investment decisions at all levels (strategic asset allocation, timing, and security selection), and the effectiveness of active ownership strategies may differ between boards and even across board members. Moreover, board members having substantial experience and research expertise on sustainable investments may boost the execution of sustainable investment strategies.

The composition of the board may also have a significant effect on the sustainable investment agenda. Board composition varies considerably between public, industry-wide, and corporate pension plans, as well as between jurisdictions, as pension laws are often nationally or at most regionally targeted. Additionally, many pension fund boards include a mix of representatives from employers, employees, and retirees (the latter especially in the Netherlands); and in some cases, also state, political, and independent appointees. Board composition can have a substantial effect on the strategic investment decisions of pension funds in other domains. Examples of these in the US public pension context include the amount of risk deemed acceptable (Andonov et al. 2017) and the selection of private equity investments (Andonov et al. 2018). A recent study of Dutch pension funds showed that a higher gap between the average age of board members and the average age of participants lowered the strategic allocation to equity by seven percentage points, after controlling for the fund's characteristics, including the liability structure (Bauer et al. 2021). The same authors concluded that corporate pension funds, having a greater representation of employers on the board, allocated more to equities, which may create a classic principal–agent problem between employer trustees and beneficiaries.

These examples show that a pension board's composition affects strategic investment decisions, and it will likely also affect how pension funds shape their agenda regarding sustainable investments. For example, a US public pension fund whose board consists purely of state-appointed members may come to different conclusions than would a board comprised of a large number of public representatives (Andonov et al. 2017). Another example is a corporate pension fund that is tightly connected to a company with a high score on the sustainability scale, versus other companies in the same industry. Potentially, these pension funds will take a more positive stance on sustainability, as the board is composed of employer and employee representatives of the higher-scoring company.

The listed external and fund-specific factors influence the sustainable investment policy of pension funds, and are likely to explain much of the global heterogeneity in fund actions in this matter.

## Examples of Member Involvement

Against the backdrop of legal contexts just described, it is no surprise that the Netherlands has the most involved pension fund members. Dutch funds pledge to integrate members' views in their investment decisions in a formal agreement (IRBC 2018), and some regularly engage their members regarding their preferences on sustainable investments. For example, ABP (civil servants) uses surveys to explore beneficiaries' preferences in all important matters in the design of the pension deal, such as risk attitude. Recently, these surveys have also contained questions regarding beneficiaries' sustainability preferences. ABP (2020) reported that 59 percent of their participants were in favor of sustainable investments, as long as financial returns are not negatively affected.

Another example is the Philips corporate pension fund (PPF 2021). The firm conducted a large-scale survey in 2020 on sustainable investments among its participants, and found that PPF's beneficiaries overwhelmingly supported the idea of integrating sustainability into the pension fund's investments. Moreover, participants signaled that they expected this integration, as sustainability was also a cornerstone in the daily routines of the (publicly listed) companies for which they worked (i.e., Philips and Signify). Many other Dutch pension funds are in the process of preparing or executing similar interactions with their beneficiaries.

In the UK and US, there are few examples of pension funds eliciting participants' sustainability preferences. As UK pension law is flexible in relation to DC arrangements, the USS offers participants the opportunity to reflect their own ethical concerns in their DC plan, stating that:

> as long as a member has a clear understanding that the investment criteria may lead to a lower return, it is acceptable to permit members to select funds

reflecting their own ethical views. To provide our members with the ability to reflect their views, the USS Investment Builder offers a number of ethical fund options. The Ethical Lifestyle and Ethical self-select funds are based upon an ethical policy which draws upon best practice and the indications of USS member preferences identified in surveys of their views.

(USS 2018: 1–2)

NEST, another UK occupational DC pension scheme, recently surveyed its members on responsible investments. One of the survey's key findings was that: 'People need to understand the benefits of responsible investment for them personally, alongside any broader environmental or social benefits' (Nest Insight 2020: 5). However, NEST did not further specify how it planned to transfer these insights to its sustainable investment program.

In the US, direct engagement with beneficiaries on nonfinancial preferences is virtually non-existent.[4] There is some indirect evidence that funds align investment strategies with beneficiaries' preferences. US public pension plans with internally managed equity departments align their investment choices with the political leanings of their beneficiaries when deciding whether to incorporate CSR (Corporate Social Responsibility) in their equity allocations (Hoepner and Schopohl 2019).

These examples indicate that many funds use surveys to explore their participants' preferences. Yet the academic literature on surveys shows that eliciting true preferences requires consequential choices (Vossler et al. 2012) that satisfy a number of other criteria to ensure that the results are not biased (Carson and Groves 2007). Consequently, one must be very careful in setting up these surveys and interpreting their results.

## Case Study on Involving Beneficiaries: Pensioenfonds Detailhandel (PD)

Pensioenfonds Detailhandel (PD), the Dutch pension fund for the retail sector, is probably the first pension fund in the world to have granted its participants a real vote in shaping the direction of the fund's sustainable investment agenda. PD is an industry-wide defined-benefit pension fund with more than a million participants; it is a medium-sized fund with approximately US$35 billion in assets under management. The PD board consists of representatives of employers, employees, and retirees, and it is supported by a small management team (bestuursbureau) of around ten staff members. Jointly, the board and management prepare and execute the pension fund's main activities. Guided by realism and pragmatism, they run a relatively straightforward investment program (Pensioenfonds Detailhandel 2020).

## PD's investment beliefs

In the investment context, the board's energy is focused on making strategic decisions regarding asset liability management and strategic asset allocation. PD invests in broadly diversified passive portfolios of public assets in the global equity, fixed-income, and real estate domains. Just a small fraction of assets under management is invested in private assets, mainly in Dutch real estate. Furthermore, PD ensures that what it delegates to financial service providers is governed well. The fund spends considerable resources on communication with plan beneficiaries regarding pension and investment matters.

In its public statement of investment beliefs (Pensioenfonds Detailhandel 2020), PD signaled that it takes sustainable investments seriously. In 2017, the fund expressed a wish to involve its participants in its sustainable investment decisions, and the PD board then initiated a joint research project with Maastricht University, resulting in two large-scale field surveys of PD participants.

At the time, PD had a limited divestment policy enforced by Dutch law. Article 21a of the Market Abuse Decree of the Financial Supervision Act prohibits Dutch pension funds (and other financial institutions) from investing in companies that contribute to the production of cluster munition (Van der Zwan et al. 2019). Since PD invested the large majority of its public assets in passive or buy-and-hold mandates, it did not yet integrate sustainable information into its investment strategies. Instead, PD started voting by proxy to cover, where possible, its equity investments guided by internal voting guidelines. To ensure that it had direct control over the voting process, PD hired a professional and independent (from PD's asset manager) agency to execute and report on the proxy voting program. Moreover, the board instructed the agency to carry out a targeted shareholder engagement program with companies, based on criteria related to three prioritized Sustainable Development Goals (SDG).

## A real vote

In 2018, PD decided to directly involve participants in the strategic direction and prioritization of the voting and engagement programs. With Maastricht University researchers, it granted participants a real vote through a method similar to a referendum (Bauer et al. 2021). In a survey, PD first asked participants whether it should extend and intensify the current voting and engagement program by adding a fourth SDG, and by extending the number of engagements based on these SDGs. Second, the board *ex ante* committed to execute the majority's decision. A large majority of participants voted in favor of extending and intensifying the voting and engagement program and approved the proposed fourth SDG put forward by the board. One week after the survey, the board executed the participants' vote.

In the meantime, PD further developed its sustainable investment agenda. Inspired by the overwhelming participant support, the board decided to integrate the four SDGs (Decent Work and Economic Growth (8); Climate Action (13); Peace, Justice and Strong Institutions (16); and—newly added—Responsible Consumption and Production (12)) into the equity investment decision process. With FTSE Russell, the fund developed an SDG-aligned index with the objective of creating a simple, transparent way to align a broad (developed and emerging) market portfolio including specific aspects of the SDGs. This approach was based on a detailed mapping exercise of FTSE Russell's sustainable investment research and the SDG framework (FTSE Russell 2020). The final result was a blend of PD's strong investment beliefs in holding broadly diversified portfolios, as well as the goal of integrating participants' preferences in their portfolios. The developed market SDG-aligned index portfolio consisted of well over 1,000 different companies spread across all major industries.

## Continued support and COVID-19

In 2020, the PD board conducted another participant survey to explore whether the board's discretionary decision to create an SDG-aligned index in developed and emerging markets was supported. Moreover, the board was interested in finding out whether members were still in favor of extending and intensifying the voting and engagement program. Additionally, as COVID-19 emerged, the board wanted to know whether participants' sustainability preferences were affected by beliefs about the perceived long-term effects of the pandemic on retirement benefits. The results of this new survey showed that a large majority of participants still supported the extended voting and engagement program, and that they also agreed with the newly created SDG-aligned index. Moreover, the support for sustainable investments was not affected by the COVID-19 crisis, despite participants' lower expected retirement benefits (Bauer et al. 2021).

## Eliciting Beneficiaries' Preferences

To further describe the two field surveys in which PD granted participants a real vote on its sustainable investment policy, we next provide additional details on what was dubbed the 'Get Real' study (Bauer et al. 2021).

## The elicitation method

In the field surveys with PD participants, we used a method to elicit participant preferences truthfully and in a way that required relatively little effort. First, we conducted a field survey with n=1669 participants (Study 1). Pension benefits and monthly contributions of participants in the Dutch regulatory context depend on the financial health of the pension fund. If the coverage (asset/liability) ratio of the fund is poor, then pension benefits can be cut and monthly pension contributions can increase, a situation that is not new to Dutch pension participants. PD's participants have already had to pay higher pension contributions in recent years as a result of the Global Financial Crisis, continuously decreasing interest rates, and strict solvency supervision by regulatory authorities. In addition, PD has canceled indexation (as a correction for inflation) in eight out of the last ten years, similar to what participants of most other pension funds in the Netherlands experienced.

The academic literature on surveys has extensively addressed the so-called 'hypothetical gap,' or the gap between what people *say* they do and what they *actually* do (List and Gallet 2001). Therefore it is crucial to explore real behavior rather than hypothetical choices. As part of Study 1, therefore, the board gave its members a real vote on the fund's future sustainable investment policy. Because of the above-described features, participants' benefits were directly at stake, making the vote highly relevant to their future financial situations. We informed participants that implementing sustainable development goals meant that the financial returns were not the only factor to take into consideration. Making investments with these goals in mind meant that considering the effect of investing on the environment and wider society was also important.[5]

To elicit truthful preferences for sustainable investments, not only are consequential choices critical (Vossler et al. 2012), but four other criteria should also be satisfied if possible (Carson and Groves 2007). First, participants have to actually care about the outcome of the survey. Second, an authority can enforce payments by voters. Third, the elicitation method involves a yes or no vote on a single project. Fourth, the probability that the proposed project will be implemented is weakly and monotonically increasing with the proportion of yes votes.

PD's discrete-choice field survey satisfied all four criteria. Participants' pension savings were indeed credibly at stake, and the board guaranteed it would implement the voting outcome, which satisfied criteria one and two. Furthermore, participants were given a consequential vote with only two choices, whereby the probability that more sustainable investments would be implemented was weakly, monotonically increasing with the proportion of yes votes, which satisfied the third and fourth criteria.

## Empirical results

In Study 1, we found that 67.9 percent of participants favored increasing the pension fund's engagement to boost sustainability in investments. Only 10.8 percent were against the increase, while 21.2 percent had no opinion (see Figure 8.1). This voting outcome gave PD a clear mandate to increase and intensify its engagement program.

In addition to engagement, another frequently used investment strategy is screening portfolios based on sustainability criteria (EUROSIF 2018). In PD's case, portfolio screening meant that it invested more in companies that scored high on the four SDGs, and less in companies that scored low. The

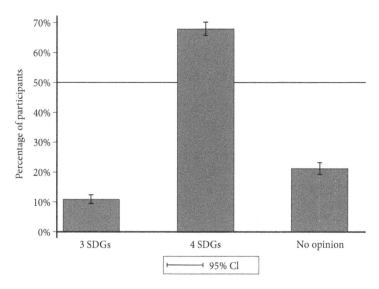

**Figure 8.1**  Preferences for sustainable investments (study 1)

*Note*: The graph presents the distribution of choices for the following question: 'Do you want Pensioenfonds Detailhandel to add the fourth sustainable development goal "Responsible consumption and production"? Yes, add; No, do not add; I have no opinion regarding this matter,' and takes on the corresponding three values: '3 SDGs,' '4 SDGs,' and 'I have no opinion regarding this matter.' 3SDGs refers to the sustainable development goals of 'Climate action,' 'Decent work and economic growth,' and 'Peace, justice, and strong institutions,' which the pension fund had already focused on prior to 2018. 4 SDGs refers to the three SDGs just mentioned plus the fourth SDG, 'Responsible consumption and production,' which participants are introduced to during the survey. The above-stated question refers to the default treatment where participants can add the fourth SDG. The default where participants can remove the fourth SDG is treated analogously, for brevity, without providing further explanation here. Choices are guaranteed to be implemented by the pension fund if more than 50% of respondents choose in favor of three (four) SDGs. Error bars represent 95% confidence intervals.
*Source*: Bauer et al. (2021).

results from a non-consequential question in Study 1 show that 74.4 percent of respondents also favored portfolio screening based on the four SDGs (see Figure 8.2).

We then explored three possibilities that could explain the support for sustainable investments (Bauer et al. 2021). First, participants might have a

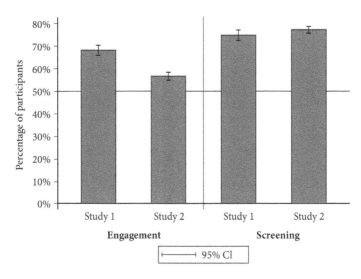

**Figure 8.2** Preferences for engagement and screening (studies 1 and 2)

*Note*: The graph presents the share of participants in favor of engagement and screening, respectively. Results for studies 1 and 2 are shown separately. The question on engagement in study 1 is, 'Do you want Pensioenfonds Detailhandel to add the fourth sustainable development goal "Responsible consumption and production"?' Answer options are 'Yes, add,' 'No, do not add,' and 'I have no opinion regarding this matter.' The fourth SDG refers to 'Responsible consumption and production,' which participants are introduced to during the survey and is in addition to the SDGs 'Climate action,' 'Decent work and economic growth,' and 'Peace, justice, and strong institutions,' which the pension fund had already focused on prior to 2018. For a full distribution of answers, see Figure 1. The question on screening in study 1 is, 'Do you prefer Pensioenfonds Detailhandel to invest more in companies that score high on environmental, social and governance factors and less in companies that score low?' Answer options are 'Yes,' 'No,' and 'I do not know.' For a full distribution of responses, see Figure A1, panel A. The question on engagement and screening in study 2 is, 'With which of the two parts of the sustainable investment strategy of Pensioenfonds Detailhandel do you agree?' Answer options are (1) 'More intensive dialogue with companies,' (2) 'Investing more in companies that score well on sustainability,' (3) 'Both,' (4) 'None,' and (5) 'I do not know.' For a full distribution of responses, see Figure A1, panel B. The fraction that supports engagement is the sum of participants who agree only to more engagement and those who agree to both engagement and screening. The fraction that supports screening is the sum of participants who agree only to more screening and those who agree to both screening and engagement. Error bars represent 95% confidence intervals.

*Source*: Bauer et al. (2021).

strong belief that sustainable investments financially outperform conventional investments. Second, participants could have strong social preferences in favor of sustainable investments in which case they may support sustainable investments even when these investments were financially costly. Third, subjects might not have taken their real choice seriously, or they could have simply been confused. We concluded that social preferences, rather than financial beliefs about sustainable investments or confusion, drove participants' choice in favor of more engagement. Moreover, a validated measure of social preferences (Falk et al. 2018a; Falk et al. 2018b) was positively related to the choice for more sustainable investments. Even among participants who expected lower returns, 58 percent chose an extension of the engagement program. Additionally, people who voted for a political party with a more sustainability-focused agenda were more likely to support the vote. Importantly, the choice for sustainable investments was not influenced by different defaults, confusion, or a lack of information.

One week after we presented the findings of our study (November 2018), the pension fund's board of trustees decided to start a voting and engagement program with a larger number of companies, by increasing the intensity of engagement interactions with these companies, and by voting more often at shareholder meetings to improve the sustainability of the companies in which it invested. Supported by a majority of 74.4 percent of PD's beneficiaries, the board began considering introducing portfolio screening as part of the sustainable investment strategy, even though the board had not *ex ante* committed to the question on portfolio screening. Several months later, PD launched the SDG-aligned index on developed equities markets.

In June 2020, a second field survey was conducted with n=3186 respondents (Study 2), seeking to investigate whether participants supported the actual implementation of sustainable investments by PD. Study 2 helped us understand whether the support for sustainable investments would last over time. It allowed us to test whether participants agreed with the actual implementation of the extended engagement program and also allowed us to separately address support for engagement and portfolio screening.

Figure 8.2 displays the results of Study 2, and results show that neither time, nor the actual implementation, nor the differentiation between engagement and portfolio screening, diminished the strong support for sustainable investments. A majority of participants (56.5 percent), albeit a bit smaller, still supported the intensified engagement program. The actual introduction of portfolio screening in the SDG-aligned index was supported by 77.1 percent. Participants still favored a further intensification of sustainable investments after finding out how PD implemented its previous commitment. Again, social preferences emerged as the key driver of the support.

Panel A of Figure 8.3 shows the distribution of participants' financial beliefs within our sample in Study 2. It documents greater heterogeneity in the beliefs about the financial consequences of more sustainable investments. Participants were slightly more positive about the financial effect of portfolio screening than about the influence of engagement for their retirement benefits. On average, return expectations were clearly not overly favorable toward sustainable investing. Panel B of Figure 8.3 shows that participants are generally in favor of engagement and portfolio screening, regardless of return expectations. There was a small group of individuals (under 10 percent) who expected engagement and screening would result in much lower pension benefits. The same held for individuals who were unsure about the effects of engagement on their retirement benefits.

These findings are fully consistent with the results of Study 1 and provide initial evidence supportive of the idea that sustainable investments are strong over time. The special circumstances during the time of the second study allowed us to go one step further. In June 2020, when the second study was run, the COVID-19 pandemic had caused a period of significant economic downturn that negatively affected Dutch pension funds' balance sheets. This environment gave us the opportunity to investigate how beliefs about an economic crisis affected the support for more sustainable investments.

## COVID-19

Panel A of Figure 8.4 shows that a substantial subset of participants expected the COVID-19 crisis would (slightly) lower their retirement benefits. Additionally, one-third of respondents felt the pandemic would eventually have no effect on their pension benefits, and 16.3 percent did not know. This belief distribution shows that, in June 2020, participants saw the economic effect of the COVID-19 pandemic as more than just a minor, temporary economic recession. Nonetheless, as shown in Panel B, the support for sustainable investments remained strong during the global pandemic.

Despite its strengths, this approach has two limitations. First, participants in Study 1 did not have a choice about whether sustainable investing should be introduced, but only had a choice on whether to increase the focus on sustainable investments. In essence, it was a conditional and restricted choice put forward by PD's board. Before the vote, the fund already engaged in sustainable investments by prioritizing three SDGs. Studying a case in which sustainable investments are introduced from scratch would give us an even richer research environment.

Second, the PD surveys had relatively low response rates of 6.7 percent and 6.3 percent, respectively. Response rates for similar surveys in the pension industry are similarly low since people rarely interact with their pension

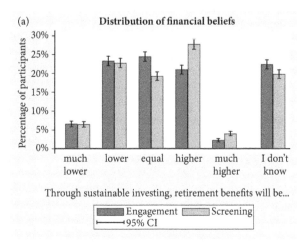

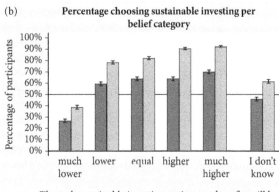

**Figure 8.3** Financial beliefs about sustainable investing (study 2)

*Note*: Panel A shows the distribution of financial beliefs. Return expectations for engagement are elicited by asking participants the following questions: 'How do you think that the dialogue that Pensioenfonds Detailhandel enters into with companies to enhance their sustainability will influence your retirement benefit once you retire?'; return expectations for screening through the question 'How do you think that the choice to invest more in companies that score well on sustainability and less in companies that score poor on sustainability will influence your retirement benefit once you retire?' Answer options in both cases are (1) 'lowers my retirement benefits a lot,' (2) 'lowers my retirement benefits a little,' (3) 'has no influence on my retirement benefits,' (4) 'increases my retirement benefits a little,' (5) 'increases my retirement benefits a lot,' and (6) 'I don't know.' Panel B presents the percentage of participants who agree to engagement or screening for each return expectation separately. The share of sustainable investing refers to the question, 'With which of the two parts of the sustainable investment strategy of Pensioenfonds Detailhandel do you agree?' Answer options are (1) 'More intensive dialogue with companies,' (2) 'Investing more in companies that score well on sustainability,' (3) 'Both,' (4) 'None,' and (5) 'I do not know.' For a full distribution of responses, see Figure A1, panel B. The fraction that supports engagement is the sum of participants who agreed only to more engagement and those who agree to both engagement and screening. The fraction that supports screening is the sum of participants who agree only to more screening and those who agree to both screening and engagement. Error bars represent 95% confidence intervals.
*Source*: Bauer et al. (2021).

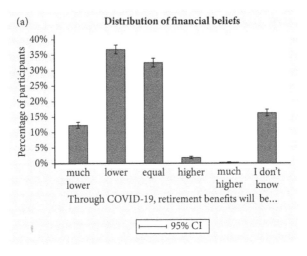

(a) **Distribution of financial beliefs**

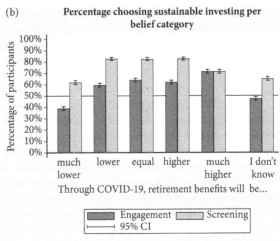

(b) **Percentage choosing sustainable investing per belief category**

**Figure 8.4** Beliefs about the influence of COVID-19 on retirement benefits (study 2)

*Note*: Figure 4, panel A, shows the distribution of financial beliefs about the impact of COVID-19 on retirement benefits. Beliefs about the impact of COVID-19 on retirement benefits are elicited by asking participants the following question: 'How do you think that the corona crisis will influence your retirement benefits once you retire?' Answer options are (1) 'it will lower my retirement benefits a lot,' (2) 'it will lower my retirement benefits a little,' (3) 'it eventually has no influence on my retirement benefits,' (4) 'it will increase my retirement benefits a little,' (5) 'it will increase my retirement benefits a lot,' and (6) 'I don't know.' Figure 4, panel B, presents the percentage of participants agreeing with engagement or screening for each COVID-19 belief category separately. The share of sustainable investing refers to the question, 'With which of the two parts of the sustainable investment strategy of Pensioenfonds Detailhandel do you agree?' Answer options are (1) 'More intensive dialogue with companies,' (2) 'Investing more in companies that score well on sustainability,' (3) 'Both,' (4) 'None,' and (5) 'I do not know.' For a full distribution of responses, see Figure A1, panel B. The fraction that supports engagement is the sum of participants who agree only to more engagement and those who agree to both engagement and screening. The fraction that supports screening is the sum of participants who agree only to more screening and those who agree to both screening and engagement. Error bars represent 95% confidence intervals.

*Source*: Bauer et al. (2021).

funds (Debets et al. 2018). For this reason it is important to establish the representativeness of the respondents. Since the political preferences of our sample proved to be similar to the outcome of the last Dutch national election, we believe we have little bias in our sample.

## Conclusion

We have explored whether beneficiaries of DB and DC pension plans have a voice in the fund's sustainable investment agenda, and we hypothesized that the answer to this question depends on a fund's legal and societal contexts, benchmarking pressure, and fund-specific factors such as the fund's size and the board's composition. We have found great heterogeneity in the degree to which beneficiaries are engaged with or involved in their pension fund decision-making. In many cases, investment policy remains purely a board matter, and at best, most DC participants can select a sustainability fund in the fund menu. Generally, however, the features of this option are solely determined by asset managers and the asset owners that hire them. Beneficiaries do not have a vote.

In some countries, mostly in Europe and the UK, pension fund boards are increasingly being pushed to emphasize engagement with participants on strategic matters, as well as on sustainable investments. Particularly in the Netherlands, a number of pension funds have started a dialogue with their participants, mainly using surveys. We also discussed a real-world example of a Dutch pension fund that gave its participants a vote in choosing the intensity and focus of the sustainable investment policy, while avoiding the pitfalls that come with hypothetical surveys on individuals' preferences.

We conclude that, irrespective of a fund's legal environment and the board's beliefs and preferences, it is valuable to understand how participants think about the topic of sustainable investments. Trust in the financial sector, including the pension fund sector, plummeted after the Global Financial Crisis. A better understanding of the beliefs and preferences of the clients of financial services is an important tool to bring back confidence in the financial sector. Beyond this argument, earlier research shows that the clients of financial services who strongly identify with their service provider are more likely to be loyal customers (Bauer and Smeets 2015). Since collective pension systems experience much pressure, paying attention to beneficiaries' preferences and beliefs may help the funds provide more sustainable plans in the old-fashioned sense.

Many young millennials across the globe are active in pressing decision makers on global challenges such as climate change, inequality, and human rights violations of many kinds. This cohort will demand a voice, and if it does not feel heard, pension systems may lose the intergenerational commitment needed to provide adequate and sustainable retirement solutions for all of us. Ultimately, trustworthiness is a pension fund's most valuable asset.

## Acknowledgments

The project leading to this application received funding from the European Union's Horizon 2020 research and innovation program under grant agreement No. 894345 (in LEVEL EEI Project). We also gratefully acknowledge research support from Netspar.

## Notes

1. More information can be found in Principles for Responsible Investment (PRI) (2021) and Climate Action 100+ (2021).
2. We use these terms interchangeably, which may be up for debate.
3. The term 'nonfinancial' may be a bit confusing as material sustainability information does provide insight into a company's risks and opportunities beyond the regular financial information. It complements the information set for any investment decision maker and at all levels of the investment process. It also shows that some nonfinancial information is not material for financial decisions, and some is.
4. We welcome information on other examples of beneficiary involvement in the US.
5. Several academic papers on sustainable investment behavior have been published (e.g., Riedl and Smeets 2017; Hartzmark and Sussman 2019) focusing mainly on retail clients in the mutual fund sector. To our knowledge, very few papers have focused on eliciting the preferences for pension fund investments from the beneficiaries.

## References

ABP (2018). *ABP stopt met beleggen in tabak en kernwapens.* The Netherlands: ABP. https://www.abp.nl/over-abp/actueel/nieuws/abp-stopt-met-beleggen-in-tabak-en-kernwapens.aspx.

ABP (2020). *Duurzaam en Verantwoord Beleggingsbeleid ABP vanaf 2020.* The Netherlands: ABP. https://www.abp.nl/images/dvb-beleid-abp.pdf.

Andonov, A., R. Bauer, and M. Cremers (2017). 'Pension Fund Asset Allocation and Liability Discount Rates,' *Review of Financial Studies,* 30(8): 2555–2595.

Andonov, A., Y. Hochberg, and J. Rauh (2018). 'Political Representation and Governance: Evidence from the Investment Decisions of Public Pension Funds,' *Journal of Finance,* 73(5): 2041–2086.

Azar, J., M. Duro, I. Kadach, and G. Ormazabal (2021). 'The Big Three and Corporate Carbon Emissions around the World,' *Journal of Financial Economics.* 142 (2): 674–696.

Bauer, R. and P. Smeets (2015). 'Social Identification and Investment Decisions,' *Journal of Economic Behavior & Organization*, 117: 121–134.

Bauer, R., T. Ruof, and P. Smeets (2021). 'Get Real! Individuals Prefer More Sustainable Investments,' *Review of Financial Studies*, 34(8): 3976–4043.

Bollen, N.P. (2007). 'Mutual Fund Attributes and Investor Behavior,' *Journal of Financial and Quantitative Analysis*, 42(3): 683–708.

Carson, R.T. and T. Groves (2007). 'Incentive and Informational Properties of Preference Questions,' *Environmental and Resource Economics*, 37(1): 181–210.

CEM Benchmarking and Top1000funds (2021). Global Pension Transparency Benchmark. Top1000funds. http://www.top1000funds.com/global-pension-transparency-benchmark/.

Climate Action 100+ (2021). *Global Investors Driving Business Transition*. Climate Action 100+. https://www.climateaction100.org.

Debets, S., H. Prast, M. Rossi, and A. Van Soest (2018). 'Pension Communication in the Netherlands and Other Countries,' Netspar Discussion Paper, 07/2018-036.

Dimson, E., O. Karakaş, and X. Li (2015). 'Active Ownership,' *Review of Financial Studies*, 28(12): 3225–3268.

Dimson, E., O. Karakaş, and X. Li (2021). 'Coordinated Engagements,' ECGI Finance Series, 721/2021.

Edmans, A. (2020). *Grow the Pie: How Great Companies Deliver both Purpose and Profit*. London: Cambridge University Press.

European Commission (2020a). *Consultation Document: Consultation on the Renewed Sustainable Finance Strategy*. Brussels: European Commission, Directorate-General for Financial Stability, Financial Services and Capital Markets Union. https://ec. europa.eu/info/consultations/finance-2020-sustainable-finance-strategy_en.

European Commission (2020b). *Summary Report of the Stakeholder Consultation on the Renewed Sustainable Finance Strategy*. Brussels: European Commission, Directorate-General for Financial Stability, Financial Services and Capital Markets Union. https://ec.europa.eu/info/consultations/finance-2020-sustainable-finance-strategy_en.

EUROSIF (2018). European SRI Study 2018. Brussels: EUROSIF. http://www. eurosif.org/wp-content/uploads/2018/11/European-SRI-2018-Study-LR.pdf.

Falk, A., A. Becker, T. Dohmen, B. Enke, D. Huffman, and U. Sunde (2018b). 'Global Evidence on Economic Preferences,' *The Quarterly Journal of Economics*, 133(4): 1645–1692.

Falk, A., A. Becker, T. Dohmen, D. Huffman, and U. Sunde (2018a). 'The Preference Survey Module: A Validated Instrument for Measuring Risk, Time, and Social Preferences,' Working Paper, Bonn University, Bonn.

Fossil Free Campaign UK (2020). Universities' Superannuation Scheme Divest from Fossil Fuels. London: Fossil Free Campaign UK. https://campaigns.gofossilfree. org/petitions/university-staff-for-fossil-fuel-divestment.

Frijns Report (2010). *Pensioen: 'Onzekere zekerheid,' Een Analyse van het Beleggingsbeleid en het Risicobeheer van de Nederlandse Pensioenfondsen*. The Hague: Tweede Kamer. www.tweedekamer.nl/kamerstukken/detail?id=2010Z01007&did=2010D02733.

FTSE Russell (2020). *Case Study: Pensioenfonds Detailhandel and FTSE Russell.* London: FTSE Russell. https://content.ftserussell.com/sites/default/files/case_study_-_pensioenfonds_detailhandel_as_written_v1_0.pdf?_ga=2.236125569.1891467829.1613833726-1540910117.1613833726.

Gibson, R., S. Glossner, P. Krueger, P. Matos, and T. Steffen (2020). 'Responsible Institutional Investing Around the World,' ECGI Finance Series, 712/2020.

The *Guardian* (2020). 'Half of UK Universities Have Committed to Divest from Fossil Fuel,' *The Guardian*, January 13. https://www.theguardian.com/environment/2020/jan/13/half-of-uk-universities-have-committed-to-divest-from-fossil-fuel.

Hartzmark, S.M. and A.B. Sussman (2019). 'Do Investors Value Sustainability? A Natural Experiment Examining Ranking and Fund Flows,' *The Journal of Finance*, 74(6): 2789–2837.

Hoepner, A. and L. Schopohl (2019). 'State Pension Funds and Corporate Social Responsibility: Do Beneficiaries' Political Values Influence Funds' Investment Decisions?' *Journal of Business Ethics*, 165: 489–516.

IRBC (2018). *Dutch Pension Funds' Agreement on Responsible Investment.* The Netherlands: IRBC. https://www.imvoconvenanten.nl/en/pension-funds.

Kay, J. (2012). *The Kay Review of UK Equity Markets and Long-Term Decision Making: Final Report.* London: UK Government.

Kölbel, J.F., F. Heeb, F. Paetzold, and T. Busch (2020). 'Can Sustainable Investing Save the World? Reviewing the Mechanisms of Investor Impact,' *Organization & Environment*, 33(4): 554–574.

Krueger, P., Z. Sautner, and L.T. Starks (2020). 'The Importance of Climate Risks for Institutional Investors,' *The Review of Financial Studies*, 33(3): 1067–1111.

Kuiper, S.H. and E. Lutjens (2011). 'Zorgen om en voor Pensioenbeleggingen,' *Tijdschrift voor Pensioenvraagstukken*, 3: 5–13.

Law Commission (2014). 'Fiduciary Duties of Investment Intermediaries,' Law Commission No. 350. Ordered by the House of Commons to be printed on June 30, 2014. London: UK Government.

List, J.A. and C.A. Gallet (2001). 'What Experimental Protocol Influence Disparities between Actual and Hypothetical Stated Values?' *Environmental and Resource Economics*, 20(3): 241–254.

Maatman, R. and E.M.T. Huijzer (2019). '15 Years of the Prudent Person Rule: Pension Funds, ESG Factors and Sustainable Investing.' In F.E.J. Beekhoven van den Boezem, Jansen, C.J.H. and B.A. Schuijling, eds., *Sustainability and Financial Markets*. Deventer, Netherlands: Wolters Kluwer, pp. 255–285.

Matos, P. (2020). *ESG and Responsible Institutional Investing around the World: A Critical Review.* Charlottesville, VA: CFA Research Foundation Literature Review.

Nest Insight (2020). *Responsible Investment as a Motivator of Pension Engagement.* London: Nest Corporation.

Pensioenfonds Detailhandel (2020). *Verklaring Beleggingsbeginselen.* Utrecht, The Netherlands: Pensioenfonds Detailhandel. https://www.pensioenfondsdetailhandel.nl/content/pdfs/1886310667-TPW-Beleidsstuk-PFDH_v5_Spreads-gecomprimeerd.pdf.

PGGM (2020). *Responsible Investment.* https://www.pggm.nl/en/our-services/responsible-investment. Zeist, Netherlands: PGGM.

Philips Pension Fund (2021). 'Veel Draagvlak voor Duurzaam Beleggen,' *Generaties Magazine*, Philips, Netherlands.

Principles for Responsible Investment (PRI) (2021). PRI Strategic Plan 2021–2024. London: PRI. https://www.unpri.org/download?ac=13269.

Riedl, A. and P. Smeets (2017). 'Why Do Investors Hold Socially Responsible Mutual Funds?' *The Journal of Finance*, 72(6): 2505–2550.

Tobacco Free Portfolios (2021). *The Pledge.* Tobacco Free Portfolios. https://tobaccofreeportfolios.org/the-pledge/.

US Department of Labor (2015). 'Interpretive Bulletin Relating to the Fiduciary Standard Under ERISA in Considering Economically Targeted Investments,' 29 CFR Part 2509, RIN 1210-AB73: 65135-65137. Washington, DC: US Department of Labor.

US Department of Labor (2018). Field Assistance Bulletin 2018-01. Washington, DC: US Department of Labor.

US Department of Labor (2020). 'Financial Factors in Selecting Plan Investments,' 29 CFR Parts 2509 and 2550, RIN 1210-AB95: 72846-72885. Washington, DC: US Department of Labor.

US Department of Labor (2021). 'Statement on Enforcement of its Final Rules on ESG Investments, Proxy Voting by Employee Benefit Plans,' News Release March. Washington, DC: US Department of Labor.

USS (2018). 'The Universities' Superannuation Scheme Statement on Responsible Investment,' USS Responsible Investment Statement June 2018. Universities Superannuation Scheme, Liverpool.

USS (2020). 'USS to Make First Divestments after Long-term Investment Review,' Universities Superannuation Scheme, Liverpool. https://www.uss.co.uk/news-and-views/latest-news/2020/06/06012020_uss-to-make-first-divestments-after-long-term-investment-review.

Van der Zwan, N., K. Anderson, and T. Wiss (2019). 'Pension Funds and Sustainable Investment Comparing Regulation in the Netherlands, Denmark, and Germany,' Netspar Discussion Paper, Tilburg, The Netherlands.

VBDO (2020). '*Benchmark on Responsible Investment by Pension Funds in the Netherlands 2020: From Boardroom Governance to Portfolio Implementation: Closing the Gap,*' Utrecht, The Netherlands: VBDO. https://www.vbdo.nl/wp-content/uploads/2020/10/VBDO-Benchmark-pensioenfondsen-2020-web.pdf.

Vossler, C.A., M. Doyon, and D. Rondeau (2012). 'Truth in Consequentiality: Theory and Field Evidence on Discrete Choice Experiments,' *American Economic Journal: Microeconomics*, 4(4): 145–171.

Waitzer, E.J. and D. Sarro (2014). 'Reconnecting the Financial Sector to the Real Economy: A Plan for Action,' *Rotman International Journal of Pension Management*, 7(2): 28–35.

Willis Towers Watson (2020). Global Pension Assets Study 2020. Arlington, VA: Willis Towers Watson. https://www.thinkingaheadinstitute.org/en/Library/Public/Research-and-Ideas/2020/01/Global-Pension-Asset-Study-2020.

# Chapter 9

# Private Retirement Systems
# and Sustainability

Insights from Australia, the UK, and the US

*Nathan Fabian, Mikael Homanen, Nikolaj Pedersen,*
*and Morgan Slebos*

Aligning the financial system with the real economy is necessary for society
to address urgent sustainability challenges, including the climate crisis and
economic inequality. Connecting the financial system and the real economy
requires the alignment of financial policy and regulation with sustainability
objectives and frameworks, along with the consideration of market structure. The aim of this study is to understand the policy frameworks and
important structural variables—fund concentration, number and types of
actors, and relative market power—specifically for private retirement systems in Australia, the UK and the US.[1] Private retirement systems are among
the largest pools of long-term capital globally, and the three selected countries are those with the most total assets. By reviewing policy and structure,
we sought to better understand the behavior of various actors, their key challenges, retirement systems functioning, and the ability of the system to align
with sustainability objectives (e.g., human rights or net-zero policy commitments). We therefore define retirement system sustainability as the ability of
plan boards and managers to be responsible investors, active stewards, and
allocators of capital to economic activities with desirable social and environmental outcomes. Systemic sustainability issues such as the climate crisis and
economic inequality hold the potential for environmental and economic
destruction, devastation of livelihoods, and political upheaval and conflict,
with clear negative implications for global financial markets. Pension fund
members face risk both of a financial nature and in relation to quality of
life in retirement. In order to tackle these issues, we need to redirect capital flows and ensure that assets are stewarded to align economic activities
with science-based thresholds and commitments. Pension systems should

Nathan Fabian et al., *Private Retirement Systems and Sustainability*. In: *Pension Funds and Sustainable Investment*.
Edited by P. Brett Hammond, Raimond Maurer, and Olivia S. Mitchell, Oxford University Press. © Nathan Fabian et al.,
(2023). DOI: 10.1093/oso/9780192889195.003.0009

be designed to fulfill a central part of this sustainability realignment in the interests of their members.

In recent years, there has been an upsurge in environmental, social, and governance (ESG), climate, and sustainable policies (PRI 2021) and related regulations (Eskander et al. 2021). These policies have not only grown in numbers, but they are also becoming increasingly detailed. For example, the European Union (EU) Sustainable Finance Disclosure Regulation (SFDR) has recently introduced requirements for financial service firms (at both entity and product level) to document, on a 'comply or explain' basis, how they consider sustainability risks in their investment decision-making and how their decisions influence sustainability factors. The SFDR (European Parliament and the Council of the European Union 2019) includes a reference to the EU Taxonomy Regulation, requiring financial institutions to document the extent to which they use the taxonomy to determine the sustainability of their products and the degree to which they are aligned. The taxonomy sets performance thresholds for specific economic activities to determine the extent to which they make a substantial contribution to environmental objectives within the EU while avoiding significant harm to other environmental objectives (PRI 2020a). Other major capital markets such as Canada, China, and the UK have already developed, or are in the process of developing, similar taxonomies. Such policy frameworks designed to deliver both sustainability objectives—such as net-zero emissions—and market stability by aiming to redirect capital to sustainable economic activities and promote active stewardship of asset owners (e.g., pension funds), although it is not clear whether and when retirement system designs serve as obstacles or accelerators of these policies.

Policy frameworks vary across the three jurisdictions examined. The design of conventional retirement and pension policy has implications for the sustainability of private retirement systems. Whether it is policymakers encouraging fund consolidation, tightening of solvency requirements, automatic enrollment legislation, or measures to protect consumers and savers from excessive costs, policy instruments influence asset pools, as well as governance and investment activities regarding sustainability. Currently, the US retirement system is generally subject to a more market-led approach, whereas Australian and UK policymakers have played a more active role. UK policymakers have been particularly proactive, recently introducing new requirements for consideration of ESG factors by retirement plans, including stewardship. Australian policymakers have been the most forceful in driving fund consolidation in the private retirement system. However, they have not put sustainability at the core of policymaking.

Our research gathers quantitative and qualitative data from various national pension and retirement authorities, consultants, think tanks, and investment industry organizations; reviews related literature, policy, and regulatory documents; and includes interviews with experts and practitioners across the three countries. We identify three key issues: (1) market fragmentation, which tends to undermine responsible investment support and activities among retirement plans; (2) the increasing importance of fund managers and investment consultants, along with their limited responsible investment incentives; and (3) the growth in personal pensions systems which have tended to lack emphasis on sustainability.

Our research shows, first, that public sector retirement plans generally benefit more from economies of scale. Larger plans with greater assets under management generally tend to have more market power (i.e., ability to influence services and products in the market), stronger governance, and, in some cases, internal investment expertise. As the degree of cross-sectional ownership of the economy—through diversified, global and long-term portfolios—is higher, large-asset owners have an increased interest in reducing market risk and externalities presented by sustainability challenges to improve financial performance overall. In its most developed form, this is commonly referred to as universal ownership. From a system perspective, if we use PRI membership[2] as a proxy, our findings suggest that when the number of asset owners with scale in the system is low, the system-wide consideration of sustainability challenges is also low. At the same time, we find that other segments of the retirement system with very high fragmentation in terms of assets, often showcase potential shortcomings such as weak governance, insufficient investment expertise and resources, investment chain complexity, and principal–agent issues. Overall, fragmented systems face the greatest challenges in developing sustainable investment practices.

Second, we show that the weight of capital and influence of actors in private retirement systems has shifted away from institutional asset owners undertaking investment strategy, asset allocation, and manager selection on behalf of beneficiaries, toward financial service providers, who have assigned responsibility to individuals to determine their own investment strategies. As a consequence, we find that most retirement plans rely heavily on the fund management and investment consulting industries in the formulation and execution of their investment strategies. Both industries are dominated by a relatively small number of firms with significant asset concentration. Accordingly, while their market power and resources could, in theory, imply that that they would be best situated to drive responsible investment and stewardship, in practice their lack of incentives results in limited execution.

Last, we examine personal pension savings, which currently total US$12 trillion, the fastest-growing segments of the three countries examined. Here we find that individual savers are faced with complex choices that they are generally ill-equipped to make, and therefore they must often rely on independent financial advisors where cost, a more comprehensible metric than value or quality, is often the focus. For this reason, sustainability is often not considered, despite increasing interest. We also find the data in personal pension markets to be insufficient to draw a complete picture in terms of market share and product uptake. While the general lack of transparency limits the insights we generate on firms and products, we conclude that the structural challenges and lack of market focus hinder sustainability in this large and growing market.

The remainder of the chapter is structured as follows. We first discuss our methodology and data collection process. Next, we report main findings, focusing on market fragmentation, the role of service providers, and principal–agent conflicts in personal pensions. A final section concludes.

## Prior Related Literature

Our research is broadly related to the emerging literature on sustainable finance. To date, prior work has documented a range of institutional investor specific responsible investment (RI) developments, including ESG investment allocation (Gibson et al. 2020; Gibson et al. 2021), proxy voting (Bolton et al. 2020; He et al. 2020), and engagement (Dimson et al. 2015; Dimson et al. 2020; Hoepner et al. 2021). In addition, there is a growing understanding that client interest in these issues is also on the upswing (Hartzmark and Sussman 2019; Riedl and Smeets 2017; Bauer et al. 2021). Nevertheless, we have identified very few studies that concentrate on pension system structures specifically and the institutional investors therein. While there are useful broader analyses (OECD 2017, 2020), we have not found related literature examining how jurisdictional characteristics influence the ESG integration practices of these institutional actors, or whether client interests are served differentially across these jurisdictions. This is most likely due to data limitations, as few datasets exist that enable analysis of client demand and jurisdictional characteristics by design. We therefore complement the literature by adopting a mixed-methods approach to examining these gaps and opportunities for research.

## Methodology and Data

The first phase of this research focused on obtaining and analyzing data on retirement plans, assets and members from various national pension and retirement authorities, pension and investment consultants, think tanks, pension trade press as well as investment industry organizations. Sources reviewed included the Australian Prudential Regulation Authority, the Productivity Commission, the Royal Commission, the Responsible

Investment Association Australasia, QMV and the Financial Services Council in Australia; The Pension Regulator, the Financial Conduct Authority, the Department of Work and Pensions, ShareAction and the Pension Protection Fund in the UK; Influence Map, the Employee Benefit Research Institute, the Employee Benefits Security Administration, the Investment Company Institute, the Milliman Corporate Pension Funding Study and Callan in the US; and global sources such as Willis Towers Watson's Global Pension Assets study and the 500 Largest Asset Managers study, the Melbourne Mercer Global Pension Index, and the PRI signatory database (see Appendix Table A1 for additional details on these sources).

We furthermore reviewed academic literature and policy and regulatory documents and conducted interviews with a range of experts and practitioners. To validate the research, we also sought input from selected pension experts and academics on each of the markets examined. These included leading thinkers with decades of experience in pension policy and practice from governments, academia, think tanks, and industry, across the three countries examined. Our findings reflect the feedback received and verify many of our generated insights.

## Main Findings

It is important to recognize the idiosyncratic characteristics of the retirement systems examined. Each system is a construction of different policies and various features—defined contributions (DC) and/or defined benefit (DB), single employer and/or multi-employer or industry, public and/or private sector, for-profit and/or not-for-profit—and while many of the building blocks are the same, the unique combination of these policies and features makes quantitative comparison challenging. We are aware of these analytical constraints and therefore complement the quantitative methods with qualitative assessment and comparative commentary.

### Market fragmentation

In this sub-section, we examine the role of market fragmentation for private retirement system sustainability. We collected and analyzed 2019 data from national retirement and pension agencies, regulators, and industry associations, and we found that there is significant variation in asset fragmentation levels, both across countries as well as within pension systems. In Table 9.1, we show that the scale in terms of assets (indicated through average plan size) of public and industry retirement plans such as not-for-profit superannuation funds in Australia (average size of US$12 billion), local government pension schemes (LGPS) in the UK (US$22.5 billion), and public DB plans in the US (US$35 billion) exhibit significantly more scale in terms of assets

TABLE 9.1 Asset concentration, growth trends, and PRI coverage within workplace retirement and personal pension systems

| | Assets US$bn | # plans | Average plan size ($bn) | 5-year CAGR | PRI signatory base |
|---|---|---|---|---|---|
| US independent retirement accounts | 11,025 | N/A | N/A | 8.6% | n/a |
| US public employees DB | 6,730 | 190 | 35.42 | 5.3% | 27% |
| US 401(k) | 6,200 | 56,000 | 0.01 | 7.1% | <1% |
| US private sector workplace DB | 3,380 | 46,500 | 0.07 | 2.4% | 0% |
| UK private sector workplace DB | 2,125 | 5,500 | 0.39 | 7.7% | 18%* |
| Australia not-for-profit super funds | 895 | 74 | 12.09 | 11.7% | 75% |
| UK personal pensions | 620 | N/A | N/A | N/A | n/a |
| Australia self-managed super funds | 515 | N/A | N/A | 5.1% | n/a |
| UK local government pension schemes | 450 | 20 | 22.50 | 9.8% | 66% |
| Australia retail super funds | 430 | 112 | 3.84 | 3.1% | 45% |
| UK workplace DC contract | 240 | 12** | 19.58 | N/A | N/A |
| UK workplace DC trust | 95 | 2,000 | 0.05 | 17.9%*** | 18%* |

* UK data does not allow the separation of DB and DC trust-based workplace assets.

** 12 private pension providers cover more than 2,000 company schemes.

*** Excludes micro schemes.

Note: Personal pensions—such as independent retirement accounts and self-managed super funds—exhibit relatively high 5-year compound annual growth rates and are highly fragmented. The public sector retirement assets are significantly more concentrated across the three countries than private sector retirement assets, with the exception of the UK workplace DC contract segment (this is due to a distinct feature of asset pooling of company schemes). Fragmented segments of retirement systems—that is, exhibiting lower average plan size in asset terms—are less engaged on responsible investment than segments with a concentration of assets using PRI membership as an indicator. Membership of the PRI entails a commitment to implement six principles, including ESG incorporation, active ownership, and the annual public disclosure of information to document progress; this also includes a requirement to meet certain minimum requirements related to governance and implementation. There are no institutional entities in the personal pension system eligible for PRI asset owner membership. Sources: APRA, UK LGPS, TPR, FCA, EBSA, Investment Company Institute. All data (rounded) are from 2019.

than other segments such as US 401(k) plans (US$0.01 billion), private sector DB plans in the US (US$.07 billion) and in the UK (US$0.39 billion), and workplace DC trust schemes in the UK (US$0.05 billion). Unsurprisingly, the private sector segments (both DB and DC), which are often single-employer plans, are quite fragmented parts of the systems in asset terms, meaning that these segments include a very high number of plans (e.g., there are 560,000 401(k) plans in the US), many of which are small. By using PRI membership as a proxy for support of responsible investment, we find that the most fragmented segments of each national retirement system have the lowest PRI coverage in asset terms: 401(k) plans (<1 percent) and private sector DB plans (0 percent) in the US, and private sector DB and DC plans in the UK (18 percent).[3] This suggests that fragmented segments have very low levels of support for responsible investment.

Over time, the weight of capital and influence of actors in private retirement systems has shifted away from institutional asset owners that undertake investment strategy, asset allocation, and manager selection, on behalf of beneficiaries. Increasingly, influence has shifted toward financial service providers, who have assigned responsibility to individuals to determine their own investment strategies. In the US, this is indicated by total asset size and five-year compound annual growth rate (CAGR) figures for Independent Retirement Accounts (IRAs) (total assets equal US$11 trillion and five-year CAGR is 8.6 percent), and 401(k) plans (US$6.2 trillion and 7.1 percent). The story in Australia is somewhat different, with not-for-profit superannuation funds being the dominating type of pension provision with US$895 billion in total assets and five-year CAGR at 11.7 percent. Nonetheless, self-managed superannuation funds, the personal pension vehicle in Australia, amount to more than 25 percent of total retirement system assets. In the UK, the picture is less clear, with LGPS only accounting for US$450 billion in total assets but a high five-year CAGR of 9.8 percent, private sector workplace DB plans are the largest segment accounting for more than US$2 trillion and five-year CAGR of 7.7 percent. Data are not available to calculate five-year CAGR for either workplace DC contract schemes or personal pensions.

In essence, we find significant asset fragmentation within the three retirement systems. This is most noticeable in private sector segments, as indicated by the average plan sizes above. Generally speaking, small plans tend to be less engaged with sustainable investment as indicated by PRI membership figures. In Table 9.2, we see the results at the national retirement system level. The UK and US systems, both of which include large, fragmented private sector, single-employer segments, have considerably lower PRI membership ratios than Australia. Additionally, if we include the personal pension assets in the equation, where IRAs in the US make up the largest share (36.7 percent of total US retirement assets), the contrast is even more

TABLE 9.2 Country-by-country overview of private retirement assets, PRI coverage and DB/DC shares

| | Total private retirement assets (US$bn) | Workplace retirement assets (US$bn) | Personal pension assets (US$bn) | Approximate total PRI signatory coverage | Approximate workplace PRI signatory coverage | DB as % of total workplace assets | DC as % of total workplace assets |
|---|---|---|---|---|---|---|---|
| **Australia** | 1,945 | 1,430 | 515 | 47.1% | 64% | 14% | 86% |
| **UK** | 3,650 | 3,030 | 620 | 19.5% | 23.5% | 70% | 30% |
| **US** | 27,570 | 17,860 | 9,720 | 8.1% | 12.5% | 53% | 47% |

Exchange rates used: US$1= A$1.45, US$1= £0.76

*Note*: The US private retirement system with a total of more than US$27trn in assets dwarfs those of Australia (US$1.95trn) and the UK (US$3.65trn). The PRI's signatory base covers nearly 50 percent of the assets in the Australian retirement system and over 60 percent of workplace retirement savings. In the UK, the figures are 19.5 percent and 23.5 percent respectively. In the US, PRI signatories hold only 8 percent of system assets and 13 percent of workplace retirement assets. Just over half of the total workplace assets across these three countries are held in DB plans. The general trend from DB to DC is all but complete in Australia, with only a handful of superannuation funds offering purely DB plans and is gathering pace in the UK and the US, where public sector workplace retirement provision remains primarily DB. The private retirement systems include retirement plans and pension schemes that are not part of the social security or other statutory pension program administered by the government. This can either be: (1) workplace plans which are linked to an employment or professional relationship between the plan member and the plan sponsor and are established by employers or groups thereof (e.g., industry associations) and labor or professional associations, jointly or separately; or (2) personal pensions which are established and administered directly by a pension fund or other financial institution without intervention by employers and where individuals independently purchase and select material aspects of the arrangements while employers may make contributions.

*Sources*: APRA, TPR, FCA, ICI, PRI signatory database. All data (rounded) are from 2019.

stark. This complements a previous finding that larger plans are generally more engaged with sustainable investment (PRI 2019).

As Table 9.2 shows, DB remains a large share of private retirement pools, accounting for US$17.4 trillion in assets across the three nations examined here. In the UK and US, many private sector DB plans are already closed to new members (88 percent and 25 percent in the UK and US, respectively), and more plans are now closed to new accruals (41 percent and 12 percent respectively) (PRI 2020b). With the notable exception of a small number of UK private sector workplace DB plans, there has been limited leadership on sustainability in the DB segment as indicated by the PRI membership ratios. We also find that with sponsors and trustees focused on liabilities and de-risking, sustainability has become even less of a priority. Therefore, in the absence of regulatory intervention or determined action by trustees and sponsors, private workplace DB plans are unlikely to be major providers of new sustainable capital going forward.

The governance set-up of private sector workplace DB plans also reveals some challenges. Sponsors in the UK and US routinely establish governing bodies that take on responsibility for managing and administering the plans. In the UK, the governing body is comprised of independent trustees required to act impartially and in members' best interests. In the US, the equivalent is a plan fiduciary, who is typically a corporate officer. The trustee/fiduciary is the ultimate steward of the assets and of beneficiaries' interests. The sponsor remains ultimately responsible for making up any shortfall in the plan's funding, so it has a continuing interest in the investment strategy. In the UK, trustees have the final say on investments, but in the US, given the dual role of fiduciaries and potential absence of impartiality, the lines are less clear. Figures 9.1 and 9.2 below illustrate the differences between the two models and reveal a complex structure of advisors (actuaries and consultants), administrators, and asset managers in both countries. Overall, the structure and governance set-up leave private sector DB plans with limited influence on the complex intermediation chain, that is, as Figures 9.1 and 9.2 illustrate, the investment chain has multiple entities involved in both investment strategy and execution.

The picture is similar for US 401(k) plans where there is also a relatively long chain of intermediaries—as shown in Figure 9.3—between the ultimate owner of the invested assets of a 401(k) plan—the employee—and the actual investment decision. Plan sponsors are ultimately responsible for the design and operation of the plan. They usually use third-party trustees and recordkeepers for day-to-day operations, relying on external advisors in choosing the provider and determining the investment line-up. As plan participants are increasingly enrolled into a default option, termed in the US a Qualified Default Investment Alternative (QDIA), the selection of the default asset manager—and, where the QDIA is a Target Date Fund or a

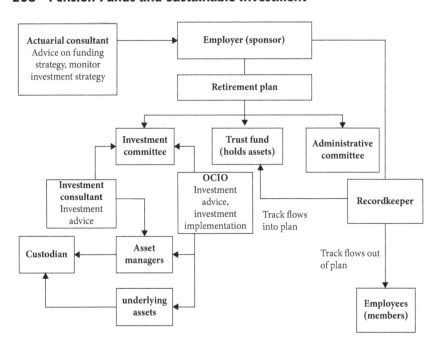

**Figure 9.1** US private DB plan governance and investment decision-making chain

*Note*: Sponsors of private DB plans in the US routinely establish governing bodies that take on responsibility for managing and administering the plans. The governing body is comprised of plan fiduciaries who typically are corporate officers. The fiduciaries are the ultimate stewards of the assets and of beneficiaries' interests. The sponsor remains ultimately responsible for making up any shortfall in the plan's funding, so it has a continuing interest in the investment strategy. This dual role of fiduciaries and potential absence of impartiality influences the governance model. The figure also reveals a complex structure of advisors (actuaries and consultants), administrators, and asset managers. The investment chain has multiple entities involved in both investment strategy and execution, and the structure and governance set-up leaves US private sector DB plans with limited influence on the complex intermediation chain. *Source*: PRI (2020b).

balanced fund, that manager's selection of underlying instruments—will be the primary determinant of how DC assets are invested.[4] As our interviews indicated, this complex intermediation chain increases the risk of beneficiary or plan preferences on sustainability not being expressed in investment decisions or proxy voting behavior. It is also important to note that the current language of the US Labor Department's Employee Benefits Security Administration's (EBSA) 2018 Field Assistance Bulletin leaves fiduciaries reluctant to deviate from peers to avoid litigation risk. Overall, regulatory signals, structural barriers, and governance challenges leave 401(k) plans with limited scope to address sustainability issues.

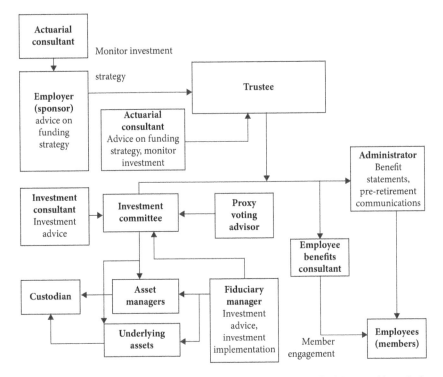

**Figure 9.2** UK private DB plan governance and investment decision-making chain

*Note*: Sponsors of private DB retirement plans in the UK routinely establish governing bodies that take on responsibility for managing and administering the plans. The governing body is comprised of independent trustees required to act impartially and in members' best interests. Trustees are the ultimate stewards of the assets and of beneficiaries' interests. The sponsor remains ultimately responsible for making up any shortfall in the plan's funding, so it has a continuing interest in the investment strategy. Trustees have the final say on investments. The investment chain has multiple entities involved in both investment strategy and execution, and the structure and governance set-up leave private sector DB plans in the UK with limited influence on the complex intermediation chain. *Source*: PRI (2020b).

## The role of service providers

To examine the role of service providers in private retirement system sustainability, we review data from P&I, The Largest Money Managers (US, May 2019), IPE (UK, August 2019), Australian Managed Funds Industry, FSC/Morningstar (July 2016), PRI signatory database (April 2020), and Willis Towers Watson, The World's Largest 500 Asset Managers (2019); see Appendix Table A1. We find that there is considerable asset concentration

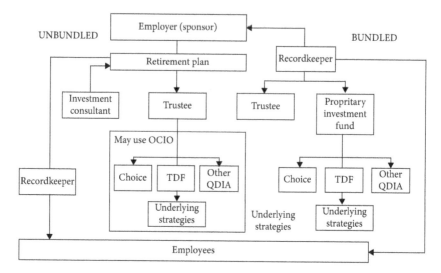

**Figure 9.3** US DC plan governance and investment decision-making chain

*Note*: The value chain of US 401(k) plans also includes a long chain of intermediaries between the ultimate owner of the invested assets of a 401(k) plan—the employee—and the actual investment decision. Plan sponsors are ultimately responsible for the design and operation of the plan. They usually use third-party trustees and recordkeepers for day-to-day operations, relying on external advisors in choosing the provider and determining the investment line-up. As plan participants are increasingly enrolled into a default option, termed in the US a QDIA, the selection of the default asset manager—and, where the QDIA is a Target Date Fund or a balanced fund, that manager's selection of underlying instruments—will be the primary determinant of how DC assets are invested. The complex intermediation chain increases the risk of beneficiary or plan preferences on sustainability not being expressed in investment decisions or proxy voting behaviour. *Source*: PRI (2020b).

among the largest asset managers in all three countries. Thus, Table 9.3 shows that the top 10 asset managers in Australia hold 50 percent of externally managed retirement assets. In the US, the top 10 asset managers for DB funds account for more than 20 percent of externally managed assets and more than 50 percent for DC assets. Lastly, in the UK, the top three asset managers hold more than 70 percent of externally managed retirement assets. This is important, since fragmented retirement systems leave more authority in the hands of service providers, including investment managers and consultants.

In situations where retirement plans use external managers to run segregated mandates on their behalf, plan sponsors can retain a high degree of control over both the shape of the portfolio and the opportunities for engagement associated with these investments. However, retirement plans that invest through pooled funds are usually unable to exercise

TABLE 9.3 Asset concentration of outsourced private retirement assets by top asset management firms per country

|  | Market concentration of externally managed retirement assets | Largest asset managers | |
|---|---|---|---|
| **Australia** | Top 10 asset managers >50% of assets | State Street Global Advisors AMP Group Commonwealth/Colonial Group Vanguard IFM Investors Macquarie Bank Group BlackRock Schroder Investment Management UBS Asset Management BT Investment Management | |
| **UK** | Top 3 asset managers >70% of assets | Legal and General Investment Management Insight Blackrock | |
| **US** | Top 10 asset managers for DB have >20% of assets | DB | PIMCO NISA Investment* BNY Mellon* Goldman Sachs Group Legg Mason* |
|  |  | Both | BlackRock State Street Global Advisors Prudential Financial JP Morgan AM Northern Trust |
|  | Top 10 asset managers for DC have >50% of assets | DC | Vanguard Fidelity Investment Nuveen T Rowe Price Capital Group |

* Not PRI signatories

*Note*: The asset management industry's assets under management have continued to rise steadily over the past ten years, with US firms leading the pack. US asset managers also have the largest market share across the three private retirement systems examined. In Australia, the ten largest asset managers hold more than 50 percent of outsourced retirement assets. The UK retirement asset management market is extremely concentrated, with the top three providers managing over 70 percent of total outsourced assets under management. In the US, the top 10 asset managers for DB plans are responsible for over 20 percent of outsourced DB assets and the top 10 managers for DC plans for nearly 50 percent of outsourced DC assets.

*Sources*: P&I The Largest Money Managers (2019), IPE (2019), Australian Managed Funds industry, FSC/Morningstar (2016), PRI signatory database (2020).

their ownership rights, and many of the bigger asset managers have poor track records on proxy voting and other aspects of stewardship. Recent research has found that the three biggest passive asset managers globally have stewardship budgets that are only 0.2 percent of the estimated fees they earn from managing equity assets, and that there is no real incentive for them to dedicate more resources to stewardship activities (Bebchuk and Hirst 2019). In addition to limited stewardship activities, there is also evidence on poor voting records on sustainability issues, and significant variation between the largest asset managers (InfluenceMap 2019; Share-Action 2019). In a private retirement system where the majority of savers increasingly invest through passive funds, this is becoming a major concern. Notably, Australian superannuation funds—which have more actively managed investments—are insourcing a growing proportion of their asset management, while at the same time, they are increasingly adopting sustainable investment activities and undertaking stewardship of their assets. A few larger plans in the UK and US—mainly public plans—with internal investment teams and sufficient resources, are also adopting this model. While this potentially addresses the sustainability shortcomings of service providers for sizable public plans, such an option may not be available to smaller retirement plans lacking internal investment expertise.

Australia, the UK, and the US represent more than half of the total private retirement assets globally. Given that all three markets rely heavily on the fund management industry, the practices of the largest firms are vital determinants of the sustainability practices of private retirement systems. The investment consultant market is similarly dominated by a small number of firms. For instance, in the US, the top ten consulting firms account for 80 percent of institutional, tax-exempt assets under advice (US$24 trillion) and the top 20 for over 90 percent. In the UK, two firms (Mercer and Aon/WTW)[5] have an estimated combined market share of 40 percent. In Australia, four consulting firms dominate the industry. In essence, a few international firms hold significant market shares and therefore they can exert influence on the extent to which retirement plans consider sustainability issues.

Moreover, investment consultants are instrumental in determining the degree of sustainability embedded in the investment strategies of the retirement plans they advise (PRI 2017a). They provide a range of advisory services ranging from funding, to asset allocation, manager selection, platform recommendations, fund options, and reporting processes. They frequently train sponsors and trustees on approaches to investment and emerging investment trends, and they are generally a recognized source of authority and knowledge. The influence of consultants is especially marked in the OCIO and fiduciary management markets, which are relatively small but are the fastest-growing areas for consulting services. Therefore, investment consultants are already key actors in facilitating the sustainability of private retirement systems, and their continued expansion in services will only further emphasize their importance.

We also note that the UK Competition and Market Authority found that, although retirement plans accounted for 90 percent of consultants' revenues, most trustees did not engage with them. In addition, consultants usually do not include new investment strategies in their watch lists until these have built a three-year track record, and we have learned that there are still relatively few sustainable investment funds that meet this threshold. This has been a particular barrier for the adoption of new Target Date Funds (TDFs) focusing on sustainability by US 401(k) plans. The investment consulting sector—despite pockets of excellence—has also generally failed to incorporate ESG considerations into standard advice templates (PRI 2017b). The market power, resources and influence of asset managers, investment consultants, and other service providers imply that they are often better placed than retirement plan sponsors to drive responsible investment and stewardship, yet to date there are few incentives to do so. Overall, their lack of incentives in practice—which are driven mainly by offering low-cost products and services in competitive markets—lead to limited execution. We find that legal and regulatory frameworks focused on reducing costs—for example, the UK charge cap and class action suits in the US—are important measures to protect savers from high costs and fees in fragmented retirement systems. Nevertheless, they are also very likely to contribute to the lack of incentives on sustainability. We find this to be a key structural challenge, which may undermine long-term system sustainability.

## Principal–agent conflicts in personal pensions

Next, we examine the role of principal–agent conflicts in personal pensions and how it contributes to private retirement system sustainability. To this end, we again examine the 2019 data from national retirement and pension agencies, regulators, and industry associations cited previously. Nevertheless, there are limited data available on service providers, market shares, and investment products, which makes it difficult to judge some aspects of the market. Personal pensions constitute a large and growing share of private retirement systems in all three countries. In Table 9.1, we showed that Independent Retirement Accounts (IRAs) in the US account for 36.7 percent of total US retirement system assets. In Australia, self-managed superannuation funds account for 25.5 percent, and personal pension assets in the UK account for 17 percent.

We conclude that individual savers in personal pensions tend not to have the same level of access to portfolio data as do institutional clients. Furthermore, many lack the time and resources to digest and analyze vast amounts of information, and large numbers will be insufficiently educated to make complex financial decisions. As a result, many rely on their independent financial advisers (IFAs), which is a fragmented market consisting of thousands of firms. In addition, current regulatory regimes raise concerns over levels of consumer protection. For example, most IFAs in the US are not fiduciaries and operate under a lesser 'suitability' standard. Personal pension savers are product-takers—to an even higher extent than 401(k) plans—with little leverage relative to service providers from the concentrated fund management industry. Consequently, participants are disengaged from the process of choosing their product, provider, and investments. Cost, which is often a more comprehensible metric than value or quality, is often the focus guiding peoples' decisions. For this reason, sustainability is often not considered an asset feature, so providers have limited commercial incentives to introduce and promote new sustainable products and services. As a result, more than US$12 trillion of personal pension savings are being managed across three countries with minimal stewardship and consideration of sustainability issues.

## Conclusions and Implications

The aim of this study was to understand the policy frameworks and important structural variables—fund concentration, number and types of actors, and relative market power—within the private retirement systems in Australia, the UK, and the US. By reviewing policy and structure, we sought to better understand the behavior of various actors, their key challenges, how retirement systems function, and their ability to align with sustainability objectives. We also identified key challenges for specific national retirement systems and analyzed comparative aspects in relation to policy and regulation, structure, governance, and the role of service providers. This, in turn, afforded us with new insights into how, or whether, specific system designs facilitate sustainable investments.

We identified three key issues: (1) the issue of market fragmentation, which tends to undermine the responsible investment support and activities among retirement plans; (2) the increasing importance of fund managers and investment consultants, along with their limited sustainable investment incentives; and (3) the growth and lack of a sustainability emphasis in personal pension systems.

While regulators in many parts of the world seek more sophisticated policies to align the financial system and economies with sustainability objectives, we conclude that one should not overlook the need to devote equal attention to retirement system structure, in ways to align these with sustainability policies. Furthermore, policymakers should consider fund consolidation in private sector retirement systems. The presence of well-governed, influential retirement plans with cross-sectoral ownership of the economy and a universal ownership outlook, and their relative weight in the financial system, is key to counter collective action problems and drive how systemic sustainability issues are addressed by other actors. Fund consolidation may be achieved, for example, by raising the professional standards of trustees and fiduciaries or through the introduction of new ESG-related obligations on pension funds (such as the Taskforce for Climate-related Financial Disclosure by UK pension funds). Given the right regulatory options, as we've seen with UK master trusts and the Australian superannuation structure, this forces smaller pension funds (often single employer), which do not comply with new standards, to consider letting assets be absorbed under available multi-employer alternatives. Fortunately, the emergence of environmental taxonomies will provide us with information about the extent to which various retirement plans perform relative to national goals. This has the potential to further our understanding on the relationship between structure, governance and sustainability performance and thereby better refine our policy recommendations in the future.

We also find room for concern, in that smaller retirement plans are less likely to consider responsible investment practices, while commercial service providers lack incentives to deviate from the 'norm.' Policymakers should therefore consider whether service-provider incentives should be aligned with sustainability incentives. Our findings also emphasize that it remains an open question as to whether beneficiary sustainability interests are truly being met and serviced. We therefore suggest that policymakers could do much to boost transparency in these markets, helping generate better-informed policies and provide beneficiaries with information relevant to their savings choices.

There remains much more to do to improve our understanding by analyzing how ESG is being integrated and adopted across the board. In the future, it would be useful to study the proxy voting behavior of various actors including retirement plans (public and private), providers of personal pension products, and third-party managers. In a similar spirit, analyzing 'sustainable' capital flows at the aggregate level would also be useful. Furthermore, we identified other future research opportunities in personal pension markets, including investigating asset concentration, market shares by various actors, and sustainable product uptake. Lastly, our study concentrated on identifying structural characteristics of three main jurisdictions. We suggest that additional major retirement systems in terms of assets be analyzed, including Canada, Denmark, Japan, the Netherlands, and Sweden, as they are likely to face different structural challenges. By analyzing these, we will better understand the common, comparable, and unique pension system challenges globally.

# Appendix

TABLE A1  Sources for country-by-country retirement system analysis

| | Sources |
| --- | --- |
| **Australia** | |
| • Australian Prudential Regulation Authority<br>• Productivity Commission<br>• Royal Commission into Misconduct in the Banking, Superannuation, and Financial Services Industry<br>• Responsible Investment Association Australasia<br>• Financial Services Council<br>• Financial Services Council/Morningstar | APRA—Annual Superannuation Bulletin (2019)<br>APRA—Annual Fund-Level Superannuation Statistics (2019)<br>APRA—Quarterly Superannuation Performance Statistics (September 2019)<br>APRA—Climate change: Awareness to action (2019)<br>PC—Superannuation: Assessing Efficiency and Competitiveness, Inquiry Report, No. 91 (2018)<br>RC—Background Paper 25: Legal framework governing aspects of the Australian Superannuation System (2018)<br>RIAA—Responsible Investment Benchmark Report (2019)<br>RIAA—Responsible Investment Super Study (2019)<br>FSC—State of the industry report (2019)<br>FSC/Morningstar—Australian Managed Funds Industry (2016) |
| **UK**<br>• The Pension Regulator<br>• Financial Conduct Authority<br>• Department of Work and Pensions<br>• ShareAction/UNISON<br>• ShareAction<br>• Competition and Market Authority<br>• Willis Towers Watson<br>• The Investment Association<br>• Pension Protection Fund<br>• IPE<br>• Local Government Pension Schemes | TPR—DC trust: scheme return data 2019 (2020)<br>TPR—Automatic enrollment—Commentary and analysis: April 2018 to March 2019 (2019)<br>FCA—Consultation on proposed amendment of COBS 21.3 permitted links rules (2018)<br>FCA—Independent Governance Committees: extension of remit. FCA Policy Statement PS19/30 (2019)<br>FCA—Effective competition in non-workplace pensions (2019)<br>FCA—Patient Capital and Authorised Funds, Discussion Paper DP18/10 (2018)<br>DWP—Investment Innovation and Future Consolidation: A Consultation on the Consideration of Illiquid Assets and the Development of Scale in Occupational Defined Contribution schemes (2019)<br>DWP—The Occupational Pension Schemes (Investment and Disclosure) (Amendment) Regulations (2019)<br>ShareAction/UNISON—Responsible Investment in LGPS—Research and review of the pension fund's investment strategy statements (England and Wales) (2019)<br>ShareAction—Is regulation enough? A review of UK master trusts' ESG policies (2019)<br>ShareAction—Voting Matters (2019) |

| | |
|---|---|
| | CMA—Investment Consultants Market Investigation (2018) |
| | WTW—FTSE 350 DC Pension Survey (2019) |
| | IA—Investment Association Annual Survey (2018) |
| | PPF—Purple Book (2019) |
| | IPE—The UK's biggest asset managers (2019) |
| | LGPS—Local government pension scheme (2020) |
| **US** | EBRI—Putting Numbers to the Shifting Retirement Landscape, Fast Facts (2020) |
| • Employee Benefit Research Institute | EBRI—EBRI Issue Brief no. 456: IRA Balances, Contributions, Rollovers, Withdrawals, and Asset Allocation, 2016 Update (2018) |
| • Employee Benefits Security Administration | |
| • Investment Company Institute | EBSA—Private Pension Plan Bulletin, Public Plans Database (2018) |
| • The BrightScope/Investment Company Institute | ICI—ICI Research Perspective, Vol. 25, No. 10 (December 2019) |
| • Milliman | ICI—ICI Quarterly Retirement Market Data (Second Quarter 2019) |
| • Callan | |
| • Influence Map | ICI—ICI Research Perspective, Vol. 24, No. 10 (December 2018) |
| • Pensions & Investments | The BrightScope/Investment Company Institute—Defined Contribution Plan Profile: A Close Look at 401(k) Plans (2016) |
| | Milliman—Corporate Pension Funding Study (2019) |
| | Callan—DC Trends Survey (2019) |
| | Influence Map—Asset Managers and Climate Change—How the sector performs on portfolios, engagement and resolutions (2019) |
| | P&I—The Largest Money Managers (2019) |
| **Global** | |
| • Willis Towers Watson | WTW—Global Pension Assets Study (2020) |
| • Mercer | WTW—The world's largest 500 fund managers (2019) |
| • PRI | Mercer—Melbourne Mercer Global Pension Index (2019) |
| | PRI—Signatory database—internal database of signatory organizations and their assets under management based on annually reported information |

## Notes

1. We use the OECD term 'private retirement system' which includes retirement plans and pension schemes that are not part of the social security or other statutory pension program administered by the government—private pension schemes and retirement plans may be administered directly by an employer acting as the plan sponsor, by a private sector pension provider or other financial institution.
2. PRI membership is a commitment to implement the six principles, including ESG incorporation, active ownership, and the annual public disclosure of information

to document progress; this also entails a requirement to meet certain minimum requirements related to governance and implementation.

3. Data from the UK pension authorities do not allow the separation of DB and DC trust-based workplace assets to determine PRI signatory coverage.

4. Most new members of private sector workplace DC plans are automatically enrolled into the default option, which is likely to be a Target Date Fund (TDF) or other balanced strategy; 21 percent of 401(k) assets are in TDFs, rising to 49 percent of the assets of recently hired participants in their 20s.

5. A planned merger between the two firms was announced in 2020.

# References

Bauer, R., T. Ruof, and P. Smeets (2021). 'Get Real! Individuals Prefer More Sustainable Investments,' *The Review of Financial Studies*, 34(8): 3976-4043.

Bebchuk, L.A. and S. Hirst (2019). 'Index Funds and the Future of Corporate Governance: Theory, Evidence, and Policy,' NBER Working Paper No. w26543, National Bureau of Economic Research, Cambridge, MA.

Bolton, P., T. Li, E. Ravina, and H. Rosenthal (2020). 'Investor Ideology,' *Journal of Financial Economics*, 137(2): 320–352.

Dimson, E., O. Karakaş, and X. Li (2015). 'Active Ownership,' *The Review of Financial Studies*, 28(12): 3225–3268.

Dimson, E., O. Karakaş, and X. Li (2020). 'Coordinated Engagements,' European Corporate Governance Institute, Finance Working Paper No. 721/2021. http://dx.doi.org/10.2139/ssrn.3209072.

Eskander, S., S. Fankhauser, and J. Setzer (2021). 'Global Lessons from Climate Change Legislation and Litigation.' In M. Kotchen, J.H. Stock and C. Wolfram, eds., *Environmental and Energy Policy and the Economy, Volume 2*. Chicago, IL: Chicago University Press, pp. 44–82.

European Parliament and the Council of the European Union (2019). Regulation (EU) 2019/2088 of the European Parliament and of the Council of 27 November 2019 on Sustainability-related Disclosures in the Financial Services Sector. Brussels: European Union. https://eur-lex.europa.eu/eli/reg/2019/2088/oj.

Gibson, R., S. Glossner, P. Krueger, P. Matos, and T. Steffen (2021). 'Do Responsible Investors Invest Responsibly?' Swiss Finance Institute Research Paper No. 20-13, European Corporate Governance Institute, Finance Working Paper 712/2020. http://dx.doi.org/10.2139/ssrn.3525530.

Gibson, R., P. Krueger, and S. Mitali (2020). 'The Sustainability Footprint of Institutional Investors: ESG Driven Price Pressure and Performance,' Swiss Finance Institute Research Paper No. 17-05, European Corporate Governance Institute (ECGI), Finance Working Paper No. 571/2018. http://dx.doi.org/10.2139/ssrn.2918926.

Hartzmark, S.M. and A.B. Sussman (2019). 'Do Investors Value Sustainability? A Natural Experiment Examining Ranking and Fund Flows,' *The Journal of Finance*, 74(6): 2789–2837.

He, Y., B. Kahraman, and M. Lowry (2020). 'ES Risks and Shareholder Voice,' European Corporate Governance Institute, Finance Working Paper No. 786/2021. http://dx.doi.org/10.2139/ssrn.3284683.

Hoepner, A.G., I. Oikonomou, Z. Sautner, L.T. Starks, and X. Zhou (2021). 'ESG Shareholder Engagement and Downside Risk,' AFA 2018 Paper, European Corporate Governance Institute Finance Working Paper No. 671/2020. https://ssrn.com/abstract=2874252.

InfluenceMap (2019). 'Asset Managers and Climate Change: How the Sector Performs on Portfolios, Engagement and Resolutions,' InfluenceMap (accessed November 29, 2019). https://influencemap.org/report/FinanceMap-Launch-Report-f80b653f6a631cec947a07e44ae4a4a7.

OECD (2017). *Investment Governance and the Integration of Environmental, Social and Governance Factors.* Paris: OECD.

OECD (2020). *OECD Business and Finance Outlook 2020: Sustainable and Resilient Finance.* Paris: OECD Publishing. https://doi.org/10.1787/eb61fd29-en.

PRI (2017a). *Working Towards a Sustainable Financial System: Investment Consultant Services Review.* London: PRI. https://www.unpri.org/sustainable-financial-system/investment-consultants-services-review/571.article.

PRI (2017b). *Investment Consultants and ESG: An Asset Owner Guide.* London: PRI. https://www.unpri.org/asset-owner-resources/investment-consultants-and-esg-an-asset-owner-guide/4577.article.

PRI (2019). *Consultation Response: DWP Consultation Paper on Investment Innovation and Future Consolidation.* London: PRI. https://d8g8t13e9vf2o.cloudfront.net/Uploads/q/a/k/investmentinnovationandfutureconsolidationconsultation priresponse_645347.pdf.

PRI (2020a). *Investor Briefing: EU Taxonomy.* London: PRI. https://www.unpri.org/Uploads/d/s/r/taxonomyinvestorbriefingpostdeal_612580.pdf.

PRI (2020b). *In Search of Sustainability: Private Retirement Systems in Australia, the United Kingdom, and the United States.* London: PRI. https://www.unpri.org/private-retirement-systems-and-sustainability/in-search-of-sustainability-private-retirement-systems-in-australia-the-uk-and-the-us/5993.article.

PRI (2021). *Responsible Investment Regulation Map.* London: PRI. https://www.unpri.org/policy/responsible-investment-regulation-map/208.article.

Riedl, A. and P. Smeets (2017). 'Why Do Investors Hold Socially Responsible Mutual Funds?' *The Journal of Finance,* 72(6): 2505–2550.

ShareAction (2019). 'Voting Matters: Are Asset Managers Using Their Proxy Votes for Climate Action?' London: ShareAction. https://shareaction.org/research-resources/voting-matters/.

Chapter 10

# How the Norwegian SWF Balances Ethics, ESG Risks, and Returns

*Anita Margrethe Halvorssen*

A decade and a half ago, Lord Nicholas Stern characterized climate change as 'the greatest market failure the world has ever seen' (Stern 2006: viii). We are slowly beginning to see the market address this failure, as a wide range of actors increasingly realizes that we need to internalize the greenhouse gas (GHG) externalities generated by burning fossil fuels. Many market actors now recognize what most scientists have known for decades: that the atmosphere does not have an infinite capacity to absorb GHGs without leading to catastrophic heating of the planet. Without actually reducing GHGs, we will not achieve the Paris Agreement's target of limiting global warming to below 2 degrees Celsius above pre-industrial levels (preferably, 1.5 degrees Celsius) (IPCC 2018), to avoid the worst of the climate change impacts (Paris Agreement 2015).

Stern's statement (2006: vi) that 'the benefits of strong and early action far outweigh the economic costs of not acting,' is becoming more persuasive as costly extreme weather events become increasingly common. The previous lack of renewable energy technology and its early high costs are no longer barriers to producing renewable energy, since the technology has been scaled up and its price has plummeted (IRENA 2021). Instead, it is more a question of *the will* to take climate action by politicians and other decision makers, including investors.

As the impacts of climate change become more visible, it is slowly but surely being recognized as constituting a financial risk (Reuters 2021a). At the ExxonMobil annual shareholder meeting on May 26, 2021, the company was forced to fill three board seats with pro-climate nominees (Krauss 2021). This was a strong manifestation that focusing on environmental, social, and governance (ESG) issues, and climate change risk management in particular, has become mainstream and that 'the market has now caught up' (Marsh and Kishan 2021). Furthermore, in their communique from the 2021 annual meeting of the G7, the member states expressed support for a move toward 'mandatory climate-related financial disclosures' (G7 2021).

Anita Margrethe Halvorssen, *How the Norwegian SWF Balances Ethics, ESG Risks, and Returns*. In: *Pension Funds and Sustainable Investment*. Edited by P. Brett Hammond, Raimond Maurer, and Olivia S. Mitchell, Oxford University Press.
© Anita Margrethe Halvorssen (2023). DOI: 10.1093/oso/9780192889195.003.0010

Sustainable development has become a legitimate concern for institutional investors, be they private- or state-owned funds. This chapter[1]
examines how the Norwegian sovereign wealth fund (SWF),[2] officially the
Government Pension Fund—Global (GPFG), has evolved into a responsible investor. It can serve as a model for other institutional investors if the
GPFG, while remaining profitable, continues to move toward sustainable
investment. In the context of climate change, this means the Fund has to
follow the pathway set out in the International Energy Agency's report,
*Net Zero by 2050* (IEA 2021), to make certain its investment portfolio supports the goal of limiting the global temperature rise to 1.5 degrees Celsius
(Flood 2021).

## Government Pension Fund—Global (GPFG)

In the last 50 years, Norway has transformed the revenue from its oil and gas
resources into financial assets, providing savings for present and future generations. Formally established in 1990, the GPFG has managed to balance
ethics and the high standards of ESG objectives with a steady investment
return. The GPFG (also referred to here as the Fund) is the largest pension
fund in Europe and the largest SWF in the world, now valued at over US$1.3
trillion (NBIM 2021a). The Fund is a universal investor, holding diversified
assets in the equity market with an average ownership participation of 1.5
percent of around 9,000 listed companies in 70 countries (NBIM 2019a).[3]
The GPFG also has investments in fixed income, real estate, and infrastructure for renewable energy (NBIM 2020a: 24). The Fund is not allowed to
invest in assets located in Norway (Ministry of Finance 2019, 2:1).[4]

The GPFG was created to reduce the effects of volatile oil prices on the
Norwegian economy, to support the long-term management of petroleum
revenues, and to facilitate the government savings necessary to finance rising public pension expenditures (Ethics Committee Report 2020).[5] The
name of the Fund was changed in 2006 from the Petroleum Fund to the
GPFG, to emphasize this focus. Unlike most pension funds, however, GPFG
has no explicit pension liabilities. The Fund is well known for being the
most transparent of its type (Caner and Grennes 2009).

The GPFG is owned by the Norwegian people (Government Pension
Fund Act 2005). The Norwegian Ministry of Finance establishes the overall
investment strategy for the Fund based on the framework set by the Norwegian Parliament ('Storting'), while operational management is delegated to
the Central Bank ('Norges Bank') (Government Pension Fund Act 2005).

The Fund is managed by Norges Bank Investment Management (NBIM),
the asset management unit of Norges Bank (Government Pension Fund
Act 2005).[6] The Ministry determines the Guidelines for Observation and

Exclusion from the Fund (also referred to as the Guidelines) that must be followed by an independent Council on Ethics when making recommendations to exclude individual companies from the Fund or place them under observation (Ministry of Finance 2022).

The goal of the GPFG is to invest the funds so as to achieve the highest possible return with an acceptable level of risk based on sound long-term management, contingent upon sustainable development (Government Pension Fund Act 2005). The long-term investment horizon is meant to ensure that this wealth can benefit all generations (present and future), that is, intergenerational equity or justice between generations (Brown Weiss 1989: 17–18). The GPFG's mandate specifically states that a 'good long-term return is considered to depend on sustainable economic, environmental and social development as well as on well-functioning, legitimate and efficient markets' (Norwegian Ministry of Finance 2019: 1–3).

Since receiving its first funds in 1996, the GPFG has gradually built the world's largest single-owner global portfolio of listed companies, focused on diversifying its risk. The starting point for the Fund's equity investments is the FTSE Global All Cap stock index, the benchmark index applied by the Ministry of Finance (NBIM 2020a: 39). In its first 21 years, GPFG saw an investment return averaging 1.1 percent per annum over the benchmark, with an excess return totaling 87 billion kroner (US$10 billion) (NBIM 2021b: 43).

Drawing on the Graver Committee's Report (Graver Committee 2003), the Storting approved a set of Guidelines for Observation and Exclusion from the Fund[7] in 2004, based on a broad international and national (Norwegian) consensus reflecting fundamental ethics norms (Ethics Committee Report 2020). Essentially, the GPFG has two primary ethics obligations, to attain 'a good return for future generations and, at the same time, to avoid being invested in companies that contribute to grossly unethical conditions' (Ethics Committee Report 2020: 2).

## Active Investor and ESG

Once the shares in companies are purchased by the GPFG, NBIM manages the Fund as an active and responsible investor: it seeks to reduce the long-term risks, recognizing the broader potential environmental and social consequences of company operations (NBIM 2020b: 67). As an active investor, NBIM uses several approaches to influence corporations. It exercises its ownership rights by setting standards, voting on shareholder proposals at the annual general meetings (AGMs), and engaging companies in dialogue (NBIM 2020b: 67). It also meets with regulatory authorities and collaborates with other investors. The NBIM may also divest from a company based on ESG risk assessments (NBIM 2020b: 85).

In 2007, NBIM began publishing some of the standards, specifically expectation documents, to inform companies how the Fund expects them to manage the environmental and social impacts of their company's operations, supply chains, and other activities. These investor expectations align closely with the UN Sustainable Development Goals (NBIM 2021a). Seven expectation documents are made public: Climate Change, Children's Rights, Human Rights, Water Management, Ocean Sustainability, Anti-corruption, and Tax and Transparency. These disclosure documents aim to promote positive changes on sustainability issues. The expectation document on climate change, for instance, requires companies to consider the possible transition and physical risks and opportunities that climate change represents, by integrating these elements into their corporate policy, strategy, risk management, and reporting (NBIM 2021c). This approach is in line with the recommendations of the Task Force on Climate-related Financial Disclosures (TCFD 2017: 22). In response to the expectation documents, companies are to self-report on their GHG emissions and the actions they take to address climate change (NBIM 2020c: 59).

As part of exercising its ownership rights, in the last year alone, NBIM attended nearly 3500 company meetings, voted at over 11,000 shareholder meetings (NBIM 2020b: 47), and now publicizes its intended vote five days before the meetings take place (NBIM 2020c).[8] It also gives an explanation in cases where it disagrees with a board's recommendation. NBIM has published voting guidelines and principles which are available on its website (NBIM 2021e). At Chevron's AGM, the Fund supported the shareholder proposal over the board's objection, calling for the company to reduce emissions from its products (both upstream and downstream) (NBIM 2021f). This action correlated with the expectation document NBIM has published on climate change (NBIM 2021c: 3).

The Fund engages in dialogue with both large companies and those that are weakest on disclosing ESG issues. Because of its relatively large ownership in any one company, the GPFG has much easier access to the board and management of a company compared to other small shareholders and, as such, it may influence company behavior.

## Environment-related investment mandates

As part of the GPFG's investments, the Ministry of Finance introduced environment-related mandates in 2009 (NBIM 2020b: 37). These are earmarked for eco-friendly assets or technology that is expected to yield indisputable environmental benefits, such as low-emission energy, clean energy, improving energy efficiency, carbon capture and storage, water technology, and the management of waste and pollution (NBIM 2020b: 36). The

Fund's environment-related equity mandates promote sustainable companies ahead of others in the investment universe, which could be interpreted as a form of positive screening. In 2020, the GPFG invested in 98.9 billion Norwegian kroner (US$11.8 billion) in environmental investments (NBIM 2020c), which generated a 34.3 percent return on this portion of the total equity portfolio.

Recently, the Fund added unlisted renewable energy infrastructure projects to the environmental mandate. With the new mandate in place, the Fund can now make investments that promote the use of renewable energy around the world. NBIM has published a guidance document for its investment partners and asset managers, outlining its approach to the responsible management of unlisted renewable energy infrastructure (NBIM 2021g). Last April, the Fund bought its first unlisted energy infrastructure, specifically 50 percent of the Offshore Wind farm (off the coast of the Netherlands), for around US$1.63 billion. The other half is owned by the Danish company Ørsted, which will continue as the operator (Frangoul 2021).

## ESG risk-based divestment

In order to reduce its exposure to unacceptable risk, the GPFG integrated environmental, social, and governance issues into its financial risk management (NBIM 2020c: 82). In addition, the Fund developed a strategy for risk-based divestments in 2010 (NBIM 2020b). As part of being a responsible investor, the GPFG may divest from companies where it sees elevated long-term risks, that is, companies that impose substantial costs on other companies and society as a whole and are not considered long-term sustainable (NBIM 2020b: 26). Hence, these are deemed financial risks, not ethics risks. Examples of activities that are unsustainable are business models that do not conform to prevailing technological, regulatory, or environmental trends (NBIM 2020b). The GPFG chooses not to invest in these companies. Risk-based divestment is one way to allocate capital to companies with more sustainable business models (NBIM 2020b).

This is a dynamic approach that is evolving over time. The Fund identifies relatively small companies in the portfolio whose business models are not sustainable given their high environmental (e.g., high carbon emissions) or social risks, and where other actions are not considered suitable (NBIM 2020b). By divesting from them, the GPFG has reduced its exposure to unacceptable risks (NBIM 2021h). It has carried out 282 risk-based divestments since it began this practice in 2012 (NBIM 2020a). For instance, GPFG has divested from coal (Carrington 2015), palm oil, and soy producers (operating in areas of tropical deforestation), as well as oil and gas producers (upstream only) (NBIM 2020b). The Fund is not required to explain its rationale for risk-based divestments, but it is transparent about the criteria it uses for these decisions (NBIM 2020b). The GPFG does not publish which companies it has divested from, however the list of companies in which it has invested, and its holdings in them, are publicly accessible (NBIM 2020b).

## Guidelines for Observation and Exclusion from the Fund

The GPFG is renowned for its Guidelines for Observation and Exclusion from the Fund.[9] Some nations hosting SWFs worried that the investment decisions by SWFs would be made for political or strategic reasons, rather than strictly financial or economic ones (Backer 2009). Hence, there were calls to have special regulations for SWFs. The international community responded by agreeing to the Generally Accepted Principles and Practices (GAPP), often referred to as Santiago Principles (GAPP 2008). These principles allow for considerations other than economic and financial ones, as long as they are clearly set out in the investment policy and made public (GAPP 2008: Princ.19.1).[10]

The GPFG is the world's largest investor that uses ethics assessments (Nystuen et al. 2011). The independent Council on Ethics recommends exclusion or observation of individual companies (not countries), for breach of fundamental ethics principles as stipulated in the Guidelines for Observation and Exclusion from the Fund (Ministry of Finance 2022). The Executive Board of Norges Bank makes the final decision on whether any given company should be excluded, placed under observation, or addressed using active ownership (e.g., dialogue).

The Guidelines are meant to ensure that the Fund avoids making investments which constitute an unacceptable risk of contributing to a violation of fundamental ethics principles. There is a high threshold for the use of exclusions, and a high probability of future violations is required (NBIM 2020b). The Fund is not meant to be a political tool. The product-based criteria of the Guidelines encompass production of tobacco, certain kinds of weapons (e.g., cluster bombs), or companies with operations based on coal (NBIM 2020b). This is considered negative screening. The conduct-based criteria (acts or omissions) encompass serious violations of human rights, individuals' rights in armed conflict, gross corruption, severe environmental damage, and unacceptable greenhouse gas emissions (on an aggregate company level) (Ministry of Finance 2022).

GPFG is the only institutional fund in the world whose Council on Ethics publishes thorough explanations for its recommendation to exclude companies or place them under observation (Council on Ethics 2020a). The recommendation is given to the Executive Board of Norges Bank which makes the final decision. These are specific to each individual company.

Since 2004, this negative screening has led to a total of 148 exclusions (NBIM 2020b).

Using the product-based coal criteria, the Executive Board of Norges Bank has also excluded thermal coal mining companies (or those with considerable coal-related operations) on its own initiative without a recommendation from the Council on Ethics (NBIM 2020b: 97). Since 2002, 73 coal companies were excluded from the Fund and 17 were placed under observation (NBIM 2020b: 25).

The Council on Ethics first applied the conduct-based climate exclusion (for unacceptable greenhouse gas emissions) in 2020. Four Canadian companies with a substantial output of oil from oil sand resources were excluded (Council on Ethics 2020b).

There is some overlap between the exclusions recommended by the Council on Ethics and responsible investment practices carried out by NBIM. By exercising its ownership rights (e.g., dialogue, voting), NBIM contributes to compliance with respect to the criteria in the Guidelines, against which the Council on Ethics assesses companies in the Fund's portfolio (Ministry of Finance 2022). This leads to a gradual decrease in the number of companies that warrant exclusion from the Fund (Ministry of Finance 2022). The complementary relationship between NBIM's responsible management activities, for example use of expectation documents, and the Council on Ethics' application of the Guidelines is particularly evident in the climate area, and it shows the importance of a holistic approach. The various measures addressing climate change can reinforce each other (NOU 2020: 7).

## Challenges

Some finance experts believe that the GPFG could be better managed if the overall strategy were overseen by an independent board rather than a team of bureaucrats at the Ministry of Finance. For instance, Kapoor (2017) claims that the current structure causes the Fund to lose greater money-making opportunities. Nevertheless, since the Fund is the 'savings account' owned by the Norwegian people, it must maintain political backing; accordingly, major changes to the GPFG's overall investment strategies must be made by the Ministry of Finance and presented to the Storting before being implemented by Norges Bank (Government Pension Fund Act 2005). All of this, of course, takes time.

This process played out in the case of approving investments in unlisted renewable energy infrastructure mentioned above. By the time the mandate was amended, the assets being considered had become too expensive (Taraldsen 2021).

In the context of climate change, the road has been a long one. As an example, in 2014, the ruling parties in the Storting agreed to study whether to exclude coal, oil, and gas from the Fund. By 2016, after first being turned down in Parliament, the GPFG was able to add certain coal producing companies to its list of product-based exclusions in the Guidelines for Observation and Exclusion from the Fund (Ministry of Finance 2022). In addition, it added climate change to the conduct-based criteria. Then, in 2018, the Fund excluded companies with substantial revenue from coal-fired power production from its investment universe. Furthermore, in 2019, the Fund did the same with companies which exclusively explored and produced oil and gas (NBIM 2020b).

With regard to investments, Nicolai Tangen, the CEO of NBIM, has said that the Fund will continue to track the reference index, but 'should be more selective when choosing stocks' (Reuters 2021b). He also said that 'NBIM can do more on negative selection, get rid of things which are bad' (Reuters 2021b). Accordingly, the GPFG will begin screening all new companies in which the Fund invests (about 500–600 per year), not just the large ones, even if they are included in the index. By running them through an automated data system (a 'washing machine' of sorts), the Fund will weed out the companies that are unsustainable (Langved 2021). This could be an improvement over the current approach.

In addition, the Storting has approved the Ministry of Finance's recommendation to reduce the number of companies in which the GPFG invests (especially the smaller ones), from around 9,000 companies down to 6600 (Milne 2021). This could save costs and likely make the Fund more manageable, increasing its ability to follow its investments more closely (Katz 2021). Since the smaller companies targeted for divestment amount to only 2 percent of the Fund's value, divesting from them would have little effect on the Fund's diversity (Katz 2021).

Critics have called for the Fund to change its mandate in order to utilize positive screening at the front end, being proactive by not investing in companies which overlook ESG issues (Rapp Nilsen et al. 2019). The 2020 report from the committee reviewing the Guidelines for Observation and Exclusion from the Fund stated that there were no suitable indices for a filtering or a rule-based delimitation of investments toward countries or industries (Ethics Committee Report 2020: 6). Furthermore, positive screening could worry some host nations as to whether the Fund, a SWF, was going beyond its stated financial objective and moving into politics (Backer 2009).

Another approach could be that the Fund continues being a universal investor yet uses its new method of weeding out 'bad' companies once they are bought, as mentioned above. Since the GPFG considers climate change and other ESG issues as financial risks, it is already strengthening its sustainable investments.

Several additional changes might be beneficial, such as increasing its staff at the Council on Ethics and allowing the Guidelines for Observation and Exclusion from the Fund to be implemented more forcefully to exclude more of the high GHG emitters from the investment universe, rather than focusing only on the worst ones. This would clearly demonstrate that such behavior is no longer acceptable in the transition to a green economy.

## IEA's report: net zero by 2050

On May 18, 2021, the IEA (2021) announced that the energy industry must put a stop to all new fossil fuel production projects beginning *this year* if global $CO_2$ emissions are to reach net zero by 2050, thereby limiting the rise in global temperature to 1.5 degrees Celsius. Furthermore, the agency set out clear milestones for what needs to happen, and when, to 'transform the global economy from one dominated by fossil fuels into one powered predominantly by renewable energy like solar and wind' (IEA 2021: 3). This report has major implications for all market actors. It also states that 'net zero means a huge decline in the use of fossil fuels,' reducing the amount from four-fifths to one-fifth of the total energy supply by 2050 (IEA 2021: 18).

As the world now starts to get more serious about transitioning to renewable energy, which will entail a sharp drop in fossil fuel demand, investors can avoid investing in companies with potentially 'stranded assets' by steering clear of energy companies that are not taking climate change into account. The GPFG has already taken steps in this direction, adding coal companies to its product-based exclusion criteria. It has also added unacceptable GHG emissions to the conduct-based exclusion criteria of its Guidelines and divested from companies that exclusively explore and produce fossil fuels—the upstream companies—to reduce the total oil price risk to the Norwegian economy (NBIM 2019b).

Another step the GPFG can take on the path to net zero is to exercise its ownership rights to 'urge' fossil fuel companies, both upstream *and* downstream, to speed up their transition to predominantly renewable energy production.

The financial climate risk management approach will also need to be aggressively used, engaging with companies that are not reporting on their climate change efforts in accordance with the NBIM's expectation document. If the companies then fail to take action on climate change, they will be divested, as they no longer have a sustainable business model. This may require a change in the management mandate to allow for greater flexibility to divest also from the larger companies.

Voting on shareholder proposals is also an important tool of active ownership, as seen in the case of the ExxonMobil shareholder meeting mentioned above. In line with its stated goal of maintaining transparency, the Fund could explain why it did not support the seating of three pro-climate change nominees on Exxon's board (Fixsen 2021; NBIM 2021i), especially as a majority of the shareholders supported this shareholder proposal, including other large funds such as BlackRock and the California Public Employee Retirement System (CalPERS). This heightened transparency would provide more insight into how the voting principles of the GPFG are implemented (NBIM 2021d). NBIM could then decide if the principles or their implementation need to be adjusted, to move farther away from business as usual and transition more quickly to the green economy.[11]

The environmental mandate, which has led to profitable investments, should be a sector targeted for much stronger growth, especially since this, together with the unlisted renewable energy infrastructure, is hugely important as a funding mechanism on the path toward a green economy with the goal of net zero by 2050.

## More diversification

Nicolai Tangen has also talked about diversifying the Fund's leadership group, increasing the number of women (NBIM 2020d). As the GPFG continues to develop as a responsible pension fund, so too must its expertise shift to include more experts on environmental (climate change, etc.) and social issues (human rights, etc.). If the Fund intends to act in support of the goal of net zero by 2050, then the sustainability focus must be expanded at NBIM so that every portfolio manager picking new investments and managing those already held, sees climate change risk as a red flag, as important as the financial health of a company.

## Conclusion

The Norwegian GPFG is considered a responsible investor, using its Guidelines for Observation and Exclusion from the Fund and its focus on ESG issues in the management of its investments, while remaining profitable. This chapter has examined the GPFG with its varied approaches to ethics and ESG issues. There is no doubt that the Fund has taken steps to support sustainable development, yet there is still more to be done. This system will become a good model for other institutional investors, if it continues evolving in the direction the IEA report sets out. With a successful transition, by 2050 the GPFG will be a major player in the effort to reach the goal of net zero emissions. This will be critical in limiting global warming to 1.5 degrees Celsius and avoiding the worst impacts of climate change.

## Notes

1. This chapter builds on Halvorssen (2011).
2. Sovereign wealth funds (SWFs) are special purpose investment funds or arrangements that are owned by the general government. See Santiago Principles (GAPP 2008: 3).
3. The Fund's shares in a listed company cannot surpass 10 percent (NBIM 2021b).
4. To avoid the 'Dutch Disease' that would occur if the economy were flooded with oil money.
5. The Fiscal Rule ('handlings regelen') was introduced to limit the amounts of funds transferred from the GPFG to the national budget to no more than 4 percent (3 percent after 2017) (NBIM 2019b).
6. The new CEO of NBIM is a Wharton alumnus—Nicolai Tangen (hired 2020), a Norwegian who was head of a London-based investment fund.
7. In 2017, the name of the Guidelines was changed from Ethical Guidelines to Guidelines for Observation and Exclusion from the Fund.
8. This is done in the interests of transparency for the companies and shareholders (NBIM 2020b).
9. Referred to as the 'Gold Standard' by the EU Commissioner (VG 2008).
10. Backer (2009: 108) argues that this disclosure could suggest that such deviation might open that fund to special regulation.
11. On another management recommendation to reject a shareholder proposal, the GPFG voted for the shareholder proposal entitled 'Report on Corporate Climate Lobbying Aligned with Paris Agreement' (NBIM 2021f). This was a positive move. For many years, fossil fuel companies have lobbied to block or delay governments' action on climate change. This proposal would counter such lobbying.

## References

Backer, L.C. (2009). 'Sovereign Wealth Funds as Regulatory Chameleons: The Norwegian Sovereign Wealth Funds and Public Global Governance Through Private Global Investment,' *Georgetown Journal of International Law*, 41(2): 114–192.

Brown Weiss, E. (1989). *In Fairness to Future Generations: International Law, Common Patrimony and Intergenerational Equity*. Ardsley, NY: Transnational Pub Inc.

Caner, M. and T. Grennes (2009). 'Performance and Transparency of the Norwegian Sovereign Wealth Fund,' *Perseé*, pp. 119–125. https://www.persee.fr/doc/ecofi_1767-4603_2009_hos_9_1_5498#:~:text=The%20Norwegian%20sovereign%20wealth%20fund%20(SWF)%20is%20widely%20acknowledged%20to,those%20of%20other%20institutional%20investors.

Carrington, D. (2015). 'Norway Confirms [US]$900bn Sovereign Wealth Fund's Major Coal Divestment,' The Guardian, June 5. https://www.theguardian.com/environment/2015/jun/05/norways-pension-fund-to-divest-8bn-from-coal-a-new-analysis-shows.

Council on Ethics (2020a). Council on Ethics for the Norwegian Government Pension Fund Global, Annual Report 2020. Oslo, Norway: Council on Ethics. https://files.nettsteder.regjeringen.no/wpuploads01/blogs.dir/275/files/

2021/04/Etikkradet_arsmelding_2020_engelsk_UU_V2-%E2%80%93-Kopi. pdf.

Council on Ethics (2020b). *Recommendation, Unacceptable Climate Gas Emissions*. Oslo, Norway: Council on Ethics. (accessed June 8, 2021) https://etikkradet.no/ recommendations/unacceptable-climate-gas-emissions/.

Ethics Committee Report (2020). Values and Responsibility: The Ethics Framework for the Norwegian Government Pension Fund Global. Report by the Committee appointed to review the Guidelines for Observation and Exclusion of Companies from the Norwegian Government Pension Fund Global, White Paper no. 7. https://www.regjeringen.no/contentassets/86dac65c 22384dda9584dc2b1a052a91/en-gb/pdfs/nou202020200007000engpdfs.pdf. Unofficial Translation of the report's Summary and Chapter One of 'Verdi og Ansvar,' pp. 6. https://www.regjeringen.no/no/dokumenter/nou-2020-7/ id2706536/.

Fixsen, R. (2021). 'Norway's SWF Stands Back from Looming Shareholder Battle for Exxon,' IPE Magazine, May 21. https://www.ipe.com/news/norways-swf-stands-back-from-looming-shareholder-battle-for-exxon/10052963.article.

Flood, C. (2021). 'Heavyweight Investors Demand More Disclosure of Environmental Risks,' Financial Times, June 21. https://www.ft.com/content/7d23ef7f-33ba-4466-b2f1-2a5dfeba1e33?desktop=true&segmentId=d8d3e364-5197-20eb-17cf-2437841d178a.

Frangoul, A. (2021). 'Norway's Huge Oil-backed Wealth Fund Invests in an Offshore Wind Farm,' CNBC, April 8. https://www.cnbc.com/2021/04/08/ norways-huge-oil-backed-wealth-fund-invests-in-an-offshore-wind-farm.html.

G7 (2021) *Carbis Bay G7 Summit Communiqué: Our Shared Agenda for Global Action to Build Back Better* (accessed June 22, 2021). https://www.g7uk.org/wp-content/ uploads/2021/06/Carbis-Bay-G7-Summit-Communique-PDF-430KB-25-pages-1-2.pdf.

Government Pension Fund Act (2005). *No. 123 of December 21, 2005, Act relating to the Government Pension Fund, Replaced the Act of the Government Petroleum Fund*, Act 1990–06-22, no. 36. English translation. https://www.regjeringen. no/contentassets/9d68c55c272c41e99f0bf45d24397d8c/government-pension-fund-act-01.01.2020.pdf (accessed May 5, 2021).

Graver Committee (2003). *The Report from the Graver Committee: The Petroleum Fund –Management for the Future: Proposed Ethical Guidelines for the Government Petroleum Fund*. Ministry of Finance (accessed June 15, 2021). https://www.regjeringen. no/en/dokumenter/Report-on-ethical-guidelines/id420232/.

Halvorssen, A.M. (2011). 'Addressing Climate Change Through the Norwegian Sovereign Wealth Fund (SWF) – Using Responsible Investments to Encourage Corporations to Take ESG Issues into Account in their Decision-making,' *International and Comparative Corporate Law Journal*, 8(2). University of Oslo Faculty of Law Legal Studies, Research Paper Series, No. 2010-06.

IEA (2021). Net Zero by 2050: A Roadmap for the Global Energy System. Paris: IEA. https://www.iea.org/reports/net-zero-by-2050.

IPCC (2018). Summary for Policymakers: Global Warming of 1.5 degrees Celsius. Geneva: IPCC. https://www.ipcc.ch/sr15/chapter/spm/.

IRENA (2021). Renewable Power Generation Costs in 2020. Abu Dhabi: International Renewable Energy Agency. https://www.irena.org/publications/2021/Jun/Renewable-Power-Costs-in-2020.

Kapoor, S. (2017). 'How Not to Run a Sovereign Wealth Fund,' Bloomberg (updated June 7, 2021). https://www.bloomberg.com/opinion/articles/2017-12-04/how-not-to-run-a-sovereign-wealth-fund?sref=BX5f2LOD.

Katz, M. (2021). 'Norway Pension Giant Asked to Shed 25% to 30% of Companies from Index,' Chief Investment Officer. April 14.

Krauss, C. (2021). 'Exxon Board to Get a Third Activist Pushing Cleaner Energy,' The New York Times, June 2. https://www.nytimes.com/2021/06/02/business/exxon-board-clean-energy.html#:~:text=The%20three%20directors%20nominated%20by,Malaysia's%20state%2Downed%20oil%20company.

Langved, Å. (2021). 'Sentralbanksjefen endret kontrakt med oljefondssjefen etter kritikk,' DN. May 3. https://www.dn.no/politikk/oljefondet/nicolai-tangen/norges-ank/sentralbanksjefen-endret-kontrakt-med-oljefondssjefen-etter-kritikk/2-1-1004358.

Marsh, A. and S. Kishan (2021). 'Engine No. 1's Exxon Win Provides Boost for ESG Advocates,' Bloomberg, May 27. https://www.bloomberg.com/news/articles/2021-05-27/engine-no-1-s-exxon-win-signals-turning-point-for-esg-investors.

Milne, R. (2021). 'Norway's $1.3tn oil fund broadens ESG screening to smaller companies,' Financial Times. https://www.ft.com/content/f6649a49-03cb-47ef-89ab-2181ae9b30c2.

Ministry of Finance (2019). Management Mandate for the Government Pension Fund Global. Oslo: Ministry of Finance. November 30: Section 1-3(3) and 4-2(3), Translation from Norwegian official Management Mandate (updated May 16, 2021). https://www.regjeringen.no/contentassets/9d68c55c272c41e99f0bf45d24397d8c/gpfg-management-mandate-30.11.2019.pdf.

Ministry of Finance (2020). *Verdier og Ansvar—Det Etiske Rammeverket for Statens Pensjonsfond Utland*. NOU 2020:7. Oslo: Ministry of Finance.

Ministry of Finance (2022). *Guidelines for Observation and Exclusion of Companies from the Norwegian Government Pension Fund Global (GPFG)*. Oslo: Ministry of Finance.

NBIM (Norges Bank Investment Management) (2019a). *The Fund's Market Value.* Oslo: NBIM. (updated June 8, 2021) https://www.nbim.no/en/.

NBIM (2019b). *About the Fund.* Oslo: NBIM. (updated June 8, 2021) https://www.nbim.no/en/the-fund/about-the-fund/.

NBIM (2020a). Investing With a Mandate—The Thirty Year History Oslo: NBIM. (updated June 8, 2021) pp.24, 39, 80, 81. https://www.nbim.no/contentassets/cd563b586fe34ce2bfea30df4c0a75db/investing-with-a-mandate_government-pension-fund-global_web.pdf.

NBIM (2020b). Investing Responsibly: The Twenty Year History. Oslo: NBIM. pp. 25, 36, 37, 67, 85. https://www.nbim.no/contentassets/aee68d3bc8e145c8bc5c5636c1bafe5b/investing-responsibly_government-pension-fund-global_web.pdf.

NBIM (2020c). Responsible Investments 2020—Government Pension Fund Global. Oslo: NBIM. pp.2, 59, 82, 97 (updated June 8, 2021) https://www.nbim.no/en/publications/reports/2020/responsible-investment-2020/.

NBIM (2020d). *Technology and Ownership Strengthened*. Oslo: NBIM. (updated June 5, 2021) https://www.nbim.no/en/the-fund/news-list/2020/technology-and-ownership-strengthened/.

NBIM (2021a). *Expectation Documents*. Oslo: NBIM. (updated June 8, 2021) https://www.nbim.no/en/publications/.

NBIM (2021b). Investing with Insight. Oslo: NBIM. (updated June 8, 2021) https://www.nbim.no/contentassets/aa58b0677fe54ab4accdd36ad48154b3/investing-with-company-insight_web.pdf,pp.43.

NBIM (2021c). Climate Change—Expectations of Companies. Oslo: NBIM.https://www.nbim.no/en/the-fund/responsible-investment/principles/expectations-to-companies/climate-change/.

NBIM (2021d). *Responsible Investment: Our Voting*. Oslo: NBIM. (updated June 8, 2021) https://www.nbim.no/en/the-fund/responsible-investment/our-voting-records/.

NBIM (2021e). *Global Voting Guidelines*. Oslo: NBIM. (updated June 8, 2021) https://www.nbim.no/contentassets/1059e60479784796bac26e0cee596613/global-voting-guidelines–2021.pdf.

NBIM (2021f). *Our Voting—Chevron Posted*. Oslo: NBIM. May 21 (updated June 8, 2021). https://www.nbim.no/en/the-fund/responsible-investment/our-voting-records/meeting/?m=1529161.

NBIM (2021g). *Responsible Management of Renewable Energy Infrastructure*. Oslo: NBIM. https://www.nbim.no/en/the-fund/responsible-investment/responsible-management-of-renewable.energy-infrastructure/.

NBIM (2021h). *Divestments*. Oslo: NBIM. https://www.nbim.no/en/the-fund/responsible-investment/divestments/.

NBIM (2021i). *Our Voting - Exxon Mobil Corporation*, May 21. Oslo: NBIM. https://www.nbim.no/en/the-fund/responsible-investment/our-voting-records/meeting/?m=1517600.

Nystuen, G., A. Follesdal, and O. Mestad (2011). *Human Rights, Corporate Complicity and Disinvestment*. Cambridge: Cambridge University Press.

Paris Agreement to the United Nations Framework Convention on Climate Change (2015). T.I.A.S. No. 16-1104, Article 2.1(a) (December 12, 2015). https://unfccc.int/process-and-meetings/the-paris-agreement/the-paris-agreement.

Rapp Nilsen, H., B. Sjåfjell, and B.J. Richardson (2019). 'The Norwegian Government Pension Fund Global: Risk Based versus Ethics Investments,' *Vierteljahrshefte zur Wirtschaftsforschung*, 88(1): 65–78 (updated June 19, 2021). https://www.econstor.eu/bitstream/10419/215469/1/10_3790_vjh_88_1_065.pdf.

*Reuters* (2021a). 'G7 Backs Making Climate Risk Disclosure Mandatory,' Reuters, June 5. https://www.reuters.com/business/environment/g7-backs-making-climate-risk-disclosure-mandatory-2021-06-05/.

*Reuters* (2021b). 'Norway's Wealth Fund to Get Rid of More Risky Stocks, Says CEO,' Reuters, April 22. https://www.reuters.com/world/europe/norways-wealth-fund-get-rid-more-risky-stocks-says-ceo-2021-04-22/.

Santiago Principles (GAPP) (2008). *Principle 19.1*. London: IFSWF. https://www.ifswf.org/santiago-principles-landing/santiago-principles.

Stern, N. (2006). *The Economics of Climate Change: The Stern Review.* Cambridge: Cambridge University Press. https://webarchive.nationalarchives.gov.uk/20100407172811/http://www.hm-treasury.gov.uk/stern_review_report.htm.

Taraldsen, L.E. (2021). 'Norway's [US]$1.3 Trillion Fund May Be Facing a Major ESG Handicap,' Bloomberg, February 22. (updated June 8, 2021) https://www.bloomberg.com/news/articles/2021-02-22/global-sovereign-wealth-fund-group-pinpoints-norway-s-weak-spot.

TCFD (2017). Final Report: Recommendations of the Task Force on Climate-related Financial Disclosures. Basel: TCFD. https://assets.bbhub.io/company/sites/60/2020/10/FINAL-2017-TCFD-Report-11052018.pdf.

*VG* (2008). Barroso Praises the Oil Fund,' Author's translation of 'Barroso Hyller Oljefondet,' *VG* (a Norwegian newspaper). https://www.vg.no/nyheter/innenriks/i/WQnlG/barroso-hyller-oljefondet.

## The Pension Research Council

The Pension Research Council is a research center at the Wharton School of the University of Pennsylvania, committed to generating knowledge and debate on key policy issues affecting pensions and other employee benefits. For over 60 years, the Council has sponsored high-level analysis of private and public retirement security and related benefit plans around the world. Research projects are motivated by the need to address the long-term issues that underlie contemporary concerns about retirement system structures and resiliency. Members seek to broaden understanding of the complex economic, financial, social, actuarial, and legal foundations for, and impacts of, privately and publicly provided benefits. The Pension Research Council is a non-profit organization, and contributions to it are tax deductible. For more information about the Pension Research Council please visit http://www.pensionresearchcouncil.org.

## The Boettner Center for Pensions and Retirement Research

Founded at the Wharton School to support scholarly research, teaching, and outreach on global aging, retirement, and public and private pensions, the Center is named after Joseph E. Boettner. Funding to the University of Pennsylvania was provided through the generosity of the Boettner family, whose intent was to spur financial well-being at older ages through work on how aging influences financial security and life satisfaction. The Center disseminates research and evaluation on challenges and opportunities associated with global aging and retirement, how to strengthen retirement income systems, saving and investment behavior of the young and the old, interactions between physical and mental health, and successful retirement. For more information see http://www.pensionresearchcouncil.org/boettner/.

### Executive Director

Olivia S. Mitchell, *International Foundation of Employee Benefit Plans Professor*, Professor of Business Economics/Public Policy and Insurance/Risk Management, The Wharton School, University of Pennsylvania.

### Advisory Board

Julie Agnew, Raymond A. Mason School of Business, William and Mary, Williamsburg, VA

Gary W. Anderson, Independent Consultant, Austin, TX

Robert L. Clark, Poole College of Management, North Carolina State University, Raleigh, NC

Peter Conti-Brown, Legal Studies and Business Ethics Department, The Wharton School, University of Pennsylvania, Philadelphia, PA

Julia Coronado, MacroPolicy Perspectives, New York, NY

## Members of the Pension Research Council

TIAA Institute
Willis Towers Watson
The Vanguard Group

## Recent Pension Research Council publications

*Remaking Retirement: Debt in an Aging Economy.* Olivia S. Mitchell and Annamaria Lusardi, eds. 2020. (ISBN 978-0-19-886752-4.)

*The Disruptive Impact of FinTech on Retirement Systems.* Julie Agnew and Olivia S. Mitchell, eds. 2019. (ISBN 978-0-19-884555-9.)

*How Persistent Low Returns Will Shape Saving and Retirement.* Olivia S. Mitchell, Robert Clark, and Raimond Maurer, eds. 2018. (ISBN 978-0-19-882744-3.)

*Financial Decision Making and Retirement Security in an Aging World.* Olivia S. Mitchell, P. Brett Hammond, and Stephen Utkus, eds. 2017. (ISBN 978-0-19-880803-9.)

*Retirement System Risk Management: Implications of the New Regulatory Order.* Olivia S. Mitchell, Raimond Maurer, and J. Michael Orszag, eds. 2016. (ISBN 978-0-19-878737-2.)

*Reimagining Pensions: The Next 40 Years.* Olivia S. Mitchell and Richard C. Shea, eds. 2016. (ISBN 978-0-19-875544-9.)

*Recreating Sustainable Retirement.* Olivia S. Mitchell, Raimond Maurer, and P. Brett Hammond, eds. 2014. (ISBN 0-19-871924-3.)

*The Market for Retirement Financial Advice.* Olivia S. Mitchell and Kent Smetters, eds. 2013. (ISBN 0-19-968377-2.)

*Reshaping Retirement Security: Lessons from the Global Financial Crisis.* Raimond Maurer, Olivia S. Mitchell, and Mark Warshawsky, eds. 2012. (ISBN 0-19-966069-7.)

*Financial Literacy.* Olivia S. Mitchell and Annamaria Lusardi, eds. 2011. (ISBN 0-19-969681-9.)

*Securing Lifelong Retirement Income.* Olivia S. Mitchell, John Piggott, and Noriyuki Takayama, eds. 2011. (ISBN 0-19-959484-9.)

*Reorienting Retirement Risk Management.* Robert L. Clark and Olivia S. Mitchell, eds. 2010. (ISBN 0-19-959260-9.)

*Fundamentals of Private Pensions.* Dan M. McGill, Kyle N. Brown, John J. Haley, Sylvester Schieber, and Mark J. Warshawsky. 9th Ed. 2010. (ISBN 0-19-954451-6.)

*The Future of Public Employees Retirement Systems.* Olivia S. Mitchell and Gary Anderson, eds. 2009. (ISBN 0-19-957334-9.)

*Recalibrating Retirement Spending and Saving.* John Ameriks and Olivia S. Mitchell, eds. 2008. (ISBN 0-19-954910-8.)

*Lessons from Pension Reform in the Americas.* Stephen J. Kay and Tapen Sinha, eds. 2008. (ISBN 0-19-922680-6.)

*Redefining Retirement: How Will Boomers Fare?* Brigitte Madrian, Olivia S. Mitchell, and Beth J. Soldo, eds. 2007. (ISBN 0-19-923077-3.)

*Restructuring Retirement Risks.* David Blitzstein, Olivia S. Mitchell, and Steven P. Utkus, eds. 2006. (ISBN 0-19-920465-9.)

*Reinventing the Retirement Paradigm.* Robert L. Clark and Olivia S. Mitchell, eds. 2005. (ISBN 0-19-928460-1.)

*Pension Design and Structure: New Lessons from Behavioral Finance.* Olivia S. Mitchell and Steven P. Utkus, eds. 2004. (ISBN 0-19-927339-1.)

*The Pension Challenge: Risk Transfers and Retirement Income Security.* Olivia S. Mitchell and Kent Smetters, eds. 2003. (ISBN 0-19-926691-3.)

*A History of Public Sector Pensions in the United States.* Robert L. Clark, Lee A. Craig, and Jack W. Wilson, eds. 2003. (ISBN 0-8122-3714-5.)

*Benefits for the Workplace of the Future.* Olivia S. Mitchell, David Blitzstein, Michael Gordon, and Judith Mazo, eds. 2003. (ISBN 0-8122-3708-0.)

*Innovations in Retirement Financing.* Olivia S. Mitchell, Zvi Bodie, P. Brett Hammond, and Stephen Zeldes, eds. 2002. (ISBN 0-8122-3641-6.)

*To Retire or Not: Retirement Policy and Practice in Higher Education.* Robert L. Clark and P. Brett Hammond, eds. 2001. (ISBN 0-8122-3572-X.)

*Pensions in the Public Sector.* Olivia S. Mitchell and Edwin Hustead, eds. 2001. (ISBN 0-8122-3578-9.)

Available from the Pension Research Council web site: http://www.pensionresearchcouncil.org/

# Index